The Presidency

DOCUMENTS IN AMERICAN GOVERNMENT

John P. Roche · Leonard W. Levy

BRANDEIS UNIVERSITY

THE
PRESIDENCY

HARCOURT, BRACE & WORLD, INC. NEW YORK · BURLINGAME

To JOANNA

CONTENTS

THE EMERGENCY POWERS

THE VETO POWER

THE REMOVAL POWER

MORAL AUTHORITY
OR NAKED POLITICAL POWER?

Part Two: THE EXECUTIVE BRANCH
AND FOREIGN POLICY

FOREIGN-POLICY INSTITUTIONS

The Presidency

INTRODUCTION

For obvious reasons of space, the authors of standard texts in the field of American government are unable to provide material in depth on the various areas and problems they examine. If they did, their works would begin to resemble the Corpus Juris Secundum, which, when last seen, was growing through the roofs of law libraries. Yet, with all due respect to the twin demons of time and space, there is a sense in which a course in American government taught without reference to the primary sources lying so close at hand is like a course in Hellenic archeology taught from slides at the University of Athens. Many instructors have, of course, introduced primary materials on their own, but often the best documents are unavailable in sufficient quantity for class use.

This series of paperbacks is designed to provide a solid body of source documentation in a number of areas of American government. This volume is concerned with the Presidency; others will deal with parties and pressure groups, Congress, the judiciary, and so forth. Every effort has been made in the course of editing to maintain the continuity and logic of a document even at the cost of brevity. The natural consequence of this policy is more limited coverage, but we are convinced that more can be gained by the use of fewer, longer selections than from the "seed catalogue" approach. A great deal depends upon the quality of the selections, and we hope that the materials presented here in adequate fullness meet the standards to which we have aspired.

In this volume we have gathered documents that illustrate the diverse powers, tasks, and roles of the President of the United States. The American President has been described as the most powerful democratic Chief Executive in the world. This statement is undoubtedly true in quantitative terms. It applies particularly to the sphere of foreign policy: when the American people are convinced that a national crisis exists, the President's decision-making power is virtually unlimited. For example, at the time of the Cuban crisis in October 1962, President Kennedy by his own decision took the nation to the edge of the abyss. All over the world, American military forces were mobilized; troops were gathered in Florida for a possible invasion of Cuba; the huge bombers of the Strategic Air Command went on twenty-four-hour alert; and the Navy instituted a blockade of Cuba. There were few objections to this policy: the American people were overwhelmingly agreed that the offensive missiles slipped into Cuba by the Soviet Union had to be eliminated, even at the risk of war. The Cuban confrontation cost over $100 million, yet Congress later passed an emergency appropriation to cover the expense without a murmur.

But the political realities that provide the background of Presidential power also supply limitations that are often not apparent to the superficial observer. The President's ability to take action on issues where consensus does not exist, chiefly on domestic issues, is sharply limited—usually by Congress. The same President who had successfully flexed his executive muscles to meet an international crisis could not even get his educational proposals before Congress for a vote! Between 1961 and 1963, the Rules Committee of the House of Representatives—a fifteen-man body with a theoretical Democratic majority—silently strangled more than twenty of President Kennedy's legislative policies by simply refusing to act, that is, by refusing to pass a "rule" to allow bills to reach the House floor for a vote. And when former Major-General Edwin Walker was absolved by a federal grand jury in Mississippi for his part in the segregation riot over the entrance of James Meredith to the University of Mississippi in 1962, the Chief Executive was powerless to initiate further action.

In short, "Presidential power" is not a coherent, across-the-board proposition. The wording of Article II of the Constitution emphasized the structural aspects of the Presidency but provided only the vaguest guidelines on the jurisdiction of the President. As will be seen in the selections on the subject, this has touched off a long-standing argument (which began in Washington's Administration) on whether the President is endowed with independent power ("prerogative") or whether he is essentially an agent of Congress whose main function is to "take Care that the Laws be faithfully executed." In practice, the President's powers vary enormously from time to time and from situation to situation, and to a very considerable degree precedent is of little value. The fact that a strong President exercised certain authority is no guarantee that a weak successor will be able to imitate him. The Constitution built into the American system an equilibrium between the Chief Executive and the legislature (with the judiciary hovering in the background), and a "strong" President attains this status largely by his power to convince, cajole, or intimidate (by political techniques) a Congressional majority to endorse his policies. Franklin D. Roosevelt could inform Congress in the midst of World War II that unless it instituted price controls, he would utilize his war powers to achieve the necessary goal. (See Document 10.) Congress did act, but only because it was convinced that the President in this matter was reflecting national sentiment and focusing public hostility upon the reluctant legislators. But a decade later President Harry Truman could not convince a corporal's guard, even though the Korean War was raging, that his seizure of the steel mills was necessary to the national interest. Put in non-judicial language, the nub of the Supreme Court's decision that Truman's steel seizure was unconstitutional (see Document 11) was that the President had employed emergency powers in a non-emergency.

The civil-rights issues that reached a climax in the summer of 1963 illustrate beautifully the complexities of Presidential power. From its inception in 1961, the Kennedy Administration attempted to work out a modus vivendi with the Southern Democrats by avoiding any requests for strong civil-rights bills and trying by persuasion and administrative techniques to break down segregation in the South (and in the North where, usually contrary to public policy, discrimination against Negroes is pervasive). In cold political terms, the President has to live with a Congress where a coalition of Southern Democrats and Republicans (the so-called conservative coalition) can, if they coalesce, destroy his program. Moving by seniority to key committee chairmanships in the House and Senate, Southern Democrats exercise enormous power in the legislature. The Kennedy Administration apparently felt that if it went after strong civil-rights bills, it would not only not get them but would jeopardize the rest of its legislative program as well.

Because of the nature of the American federal system the President was put in a difficult position when he confronted resistance to federal law by state governments such as Mississippi in 1962 and Alabama in 1963. In current military terminology, he lacked "conventional weapons"; when resistance continued in defiance of federal court orders, he was forced to employ his ultimate weapon: the Army. (There is no national police force—the FBI is an investigatory body only—and a handful of United States marshals could hardly defeat the Alabama national guard.) There is an absurdity about using battle-trained paratroops to escort Negro children to school in Little Rock or to protect a solitary Negro college student in Oxford, Mississippi, but a President has no alternatives once the local authorities have committed themselves to de facto rebellion against national authority.

President Kennedy, in short, had the power to declare martial law in Alabama, but he had no effective mechanism for taking action that could make the declaration of martial law unnecessary. The President must see to it that the laws of the United States are "faithfully executed," but he has no instrument for dealing with rebellious state governments, short of sending in the troops after the fact.

In the summer of 1963, faced by a rising tide of national indignation and Negro unrest (Negroes have strong voting power in the great industrial states), the Kennedy Administration went to Congress with a body of vigorous civil-rights laws. In doing so, President Kennedy crossed a Rubicon of sorts: from that point on, he could count on increased sabotage of his liberal legislative program by the

Southern Democratic magnates in Congress. It is not easy to be President of the United States, but nobody who does not want the job ever applies for it—or in Harry Truman's pungent words, "If you don't like heat, stay out of the kitchen."

The powers of the President, then, have to be understood and interpreted against the background of the American political system. And whatever the context, the task is tremendous. As Edward S. Corwin and Clinton Rossiter, among others, have pointed out, there are six or seven jobs combined in the one office. The President must as the ceremonial head of state greet visiting potentates—a time-consuming task that the British leave to the numerous members of the royal family. As Chief Executive, he must enforce the laws. In his role as party leader, he must try to keep his inevitably discordant supporters from "wandering off the reservation." As chief administrator, his task is to coordinate the work of the great federal bureaucracy —including a number of independent regulatory agencies who tend to view him as a troublesome snoop. As Commander-in-Chief of the Armed Forces, he has the ultimate responsibility under modern conditions for the maintenance of peace or the engagement in war, and he is the sole constitutional organ for the conduct of a foreign policy that will, hopefully, keep the peace. And finally, in an epoch of instantaneous communication dominated by radio and television, he is both a catalyst and an executor of public opinion—the moral spokesman for the nation in domestic and international crises.

He must, in other words, "run" the world's greatest free society, which is also the world's most complex industrial giant. And he must do so in the full glare of publicity and criticism, with Everyman as his kibitzer and with a national legislature that considers him its natural enemy. It is a position that does not lend itself to easy description or understanding, but we hope that these documents will provide a perspective on what is by all logical criteria an "impossible task."

Brandeis University   JOHN P. ROCHE
August 1963   LEONARD W. LEVY

part one

THE OFFICE
OF THE PRESIDENT

CONCEPTIONS
OF THE OFFICE

FROM WASHINGTON
TO LINCOLN

Between the Declaration of Independence and the adoption of the Constitution, American opinion underwent a considerable change in attitude toward executive power. Initially, in strong revulsion against the authority of the King and the royal governors, the new states severely limited the prerogatives of their governors or presidents. Indeed, only in Massachusetts did the governor have the veto power as we know it, and state governments were generally firmly committed to the principle of legislative supremacy. The Articles of Confederation, which in 1781 set up a loose framework of state cooperation, did not provide for an executive branch: what are normally considered executive functions (for example, the conduct of foreign relations or financial administration) were handled by committees of the Congress. Later, when this proved unwieldy, officials were appointed to key jobs but were responsible directly to the legislature.

The framers of the Constitution were convinced that a separate executive department was necessary, but they were seriously divided on whether it should be chosen by the people or by the Congress, whether it should be single or plural, and what the scope of its jurisdiction should be. Since they were in the happy position of knowing that George Washington would be the first President under any system, they simply established the office, improvised an electoral college that begged the problem of selection, and left future generations, and future Presidents, the tasks of explicit definition.

In short, the Constitution established a structurally distinct Presidency but left the question of executive jurisdiction to be worked out. And since that time Presidents and Congresses (with occasional intervention by the courts) have been engaged in these crucial problems of definition. The powers of the Presidency have thus evolved on an ad hoc basis, with a strong President gaining ground at the expense of Congress and a weak President retreating before the legislature.

George Washington initially conceived of the Presidency as a non-

political office; for example, he would only veto measures he considered unconstitutional. But the office shortly became the focus of American national politics and its occupant an unmistakably political figure: Thomas Jefferson saw himself not only as the head of the government but as the national leader of his party as well; Andrew Jackson vetoed any measure he opposed on political grounds. Abraham Lincoln used his position as Commander-in-Chief during the Civil War to justify an unusually broad range of political actions largely legislative in nature. This selection examines the early interpretations of executive jurisdiction up through Lincoln's Presidency.

The nature and limitations of Executive power have been a matter of controversy from the very beginning of our Nation. It is advisable to quote what appear to be two differing attitudes toward the Presidential power held by former Presidents. It is also useful to bear in mind that both viewpoints have been reconciled in practice in our history by a larger interpretation of the office of President which recognizes that the people have given certain powers to the Federal Government and prescribed a mechanism for functioning according to the basic blueprint of the Constitution. Under this blueprint the authority vested in the President is not untrammeled or unlimited.

President Theodore Roosevelt stated his views of the Presidential office as follows:

. . . I declined to adopt the view that what was imperatively necessary for the Nation could not be done by the President unless he could find some specific authorization to do it. My belief was that it was not only his right but his duty to do anything that the needs of the Nation demanded unless such action was forbidden by the Constitution or by the law. Under this interpretation of Executive power I did and caused to be done many things not previously done by the President and the heads of the Departments. I did not usurp powers, but I did greatly broaden the use of Executive power. . . .

In contrast, President William H. Taft expressed his views on the Presidential office in these words:

. . . that a President can exercise no power which cannot fairly and reasonably be traced to some specific grant of power, or justly implied and included within such grant of power and necessary to its exercise. Such specific grants must be either in the Federal Constitution, or in any act of Congress

FROM *Executive Orders and Proclamations: A Study of a Use of Presidential Powers*, House Committee on Government Operations, Eighty-Fifth Congress, first session (Washington, D.C., Government Printing Office, 1957), pp. 14–26, 34.

CONCEPTIONS OF THE OFFICE

passed in pursuance thereof. There is no undefined residuum of power which he can exercise because it seems to him to be in the public interest.

These assessments of the Executive power are in a sense later echoes of sentiments expressed in the early days of this Nation's history. One of the outstanding incidents involving a controversy over the nature of the Executive power occurred in connection with President George Washington's so-called Proclamation of Neutrality in 1793.

THE 1793 CONTROVERSY OVER WASHINGTON'S PROCLAMATION OF NEUTRALITY

When France declared war against Great Britain (and Holland) in February 1793, her action precipitated a crisis of substantial proportions within the Government of the United States and among the populace of the young Nation. Anti-British feeling ran high, as did pro-French sympathies.

President Washington had two viewpoints represented strongly in his own Cabinet. Secretary of State Thomas Jefferson was anti-British and pro-French while Alexander Hamilton was pro-British. President Washington was firmly determined to keep the United States neutral. So were Jefferson and Hamilton although each strongly favored a different side in the war. A fierce struggle ensued in Washington's Cabinet over whether he should issue a proclamation ". . . for the purpose of preventing interferences of the citizens of the United States in the war between France and Great Britain . . ." and whether the proclamation should contain a declaration of neutrality.

Jefferson opposed the issuance of a proclamation of neutrality on two grounds—one political and the other constitutional. As a political ground he urged holding back a proclamation as a device for bargaining with the belligerents. On constitutional grounds Jefferson argued that such a declaration was a declaration of no war and in his view it was not for the Executive to decide the question of war on the negative or the affirmative side. Jefferson was supported in this view by Madison, Monroe, and others. Hamilton was of the opposing view.

President Washington did issue a proclamation on April 22, 1793. His proclamation enjoined the citizens of the United States to ". . . avoid all acts and proceedings whatsoever, which may in any manner tend to contravene such disposition . . ." of ". . . a conduct friendly and impartial toward the belligerent powers. . . ." The President's proclamation also stated that he had ". . . given instructions to those officers, to whom it belongs, to cause prosecutions to be instituted against all persons, who shall, within the cognizance of the courts of the United States, violate the law of nations, with respect to the powers at war, or any of them."

The word "neutral" or "neutrality" was not used in the President's proclamation. But everyone recognized it as such a declaration and the Cabinet had another argument over the use of the term "neutrality" in drafting the President's speech to the Congress the next November. Washington closed the debate by stating that he never had any idea he could bind the Congress and that his proclamation could not look beyond the first day of their meeting. Moreover his speech to the Congress spoke of the proclamation merely as a declaration of the existing legal state of things.

The struggle within the Cabinet and around President Washington found its reflection in a series of articles printed under the name of Pacificus (Hamilton) who supported Washington's actions in issuing the proclamation, and under the name of Helvidius (Madison) who opposed Washington's actions as unconstitutional. In a sense the arguments in these two series of letters, as they were called, have remained the lines of argument down through the years as will be seen in the discussion [see Document 11] of the steel seizure case, the opinion in which was handed down by the Supreme Court in June 1952.

Basically, Hamilton's argument was that the Executive-power clause in article II was a grant of power in itself and authorized President Washington's action. Madison's opposing position was that the Executive-power clause was not a grant of power in itself since ours is not a government involving royal prerogatives. Hamilton also advanced other sources of authority for the President in the Constitution.

The second article of the constitution of the United States, section first, establishes this general proposition, that "the EXECUTIVE POWER shall be vested in a president of the United States of America."

The same article, in a succeeding section, proceeds to delineate particular cases of executive power. It declares, among other things, that the president shall be commander in chief of the army and navy of the United States, and of the militia of the several states, when called into the actual service of the United States; that he shall have power, by and with the advice and consent of the senate, to make treaties; that it shall be his duty to receive ambassadors and other public ministers, *and to take care that the laws be faithfully executed.*

It would not consist with the rules of sound construction, to consider this enumeration of particular authorities, as derogating from the more comprehensive grant in the general clause, further than as it may be coupled with express restrictions or limitations; as in regard to the co-operation of the senate in the appointment of officers, and the making of treaties; which are plainly qualifications of the general executive powers of appointing officers and making treaties. The difficulty of a complete enumeration of all the cases of executive authority, would naturally dictate the use of general terms, and would render it improbable, that a specification of certain particulars was designed as a substitute for those terms, when antecedently used. The different mode of expression employed in the constitution, in regard to the two powers, the legislative and the executive, serves to confirm this inference. In the article which gives the legislative powers of the government, the expressions are, "all legislative powers herein granted shall be vested in a congress of the United States." In that which grants the executive power, the expressions are, "the *executive power* shall be vested in a president of the United States."

The enumeration ought therefore to be considered, as intended merely to specify the principal articles implied in the definition of executive power; leaving the rest to flow from the general grant of that power, interpreted in conformity with other parts of the constitution and with the principles of free government.

The general doctrine of our constitution then is, that the *executive power* of the nation is vested in the president; subject only to the *exceptions* and *qualifications,* which are expressed in the instrument.

Two of these have been already noticed: the participation of the Senate in the appointment of officers, and in the making of treaties. A third remains to be mentioned: the right of the legislature "to declare war," and "grant letters of marque and reprisal."

With these exceptions, the *executive power* of the United States is completely lodged in the president. This mode of construing the constitution, has indeed been recognized by Congress in formal acts, upon full consideration and debate: of which the power of removal from office, is an important instance. It will follow, that if a proclamation of neutrality is merely an executive act, as it is believed has been shown, the step which has been taken by the president is liable to no just exception on the score of authority. . . .

Madison stated in part his opposing views as follows:

The basis of the reasoning is, we perceive, the extraordinary doctrine, that the powers of making war and treaties, are in their nature executive; and therefore comprehended in the general grant of executive power, where not specially and strictly excepted out of the grant. . . .

****

If we consult, for a moment, the nature and operation of the two powers to declare war and to make treaties it will be impossible not to see that they can never fall within a proper definition of executive powers. The natural province of the executive magistrate is to execute laws, as that of the legislature is to make laws. All his acts, therefore, properly executive, must pre-suppose the existence of the laws to be executed. A treaty is not an execution of laws; it does not pre-suppose the existence of laws. It is, on the contrary, to have itself the force of a *law,* and to be carried into *execution,* like all *other laws,* by the *executive magistrate.* To say then that the power of making treaties which are confessedly laws, belongs naturally to the department which is to execute laws, is to say, that the executive department naturally includes a legislative power. In theory, this is an absurdity . . . in practice a tyranny.

The power to declare war is subject to similar reasoning. A declaration that there shall be war, is not an execution of laws; It does not suppose pre-existing laws to be executed; it is not, in any respect, an act merely executive. It is, on the contrary, one of the most deliberative acts that can be performed; and when performed, has the effect of *repealing* all the *laws* operating in a state of peace, so far as they are inconsistent with a state of war; and of *enacting* as a *rule for the executive,* a *new code* adapted to the relation between the society and its foreign enemy. In like manner, a conclusion of peace *annuls* all the *laws* peculiar to a state of war, and *revives* the general *laws* incident to a state of peace.

These remarks will be strengthened by adding, that treaties, particularly treaties of peace, have sometimes the effect of changing not only the external laws of the society, but operate also on the internal code, which is purely municipal, and to which the legislative authority of the country is of itself competent and complete.

From this view of the subject it must be evident, that, although the executive may be a convenient organ of preliminary communications with foreign governments, on the subjects of treaty or war, and the proper agent for carrying into execution the final determinations of the competent authority, yet it can have no pretensions from the nature of the powers in question compared with the nature of the executive trust, to that essential agency which gives validity to such determinations.

It must be further evident that, if these powers be not in their nature purely legislative, they partake so much more of that, than of any other quality, that under a constitution leaving them to [revert] to their most natural department, the legislature would be without a rival in its claim.

Another important inference to be noted is, that the powers of making war and treaty being substantially of a legislative, not an executive nature, the rule of interpreting exceptions strictly, must narrow instead of enlarging executive pretensions on those subjects. . . .

❉❉❉❉

Whence then can the writer [Hamilton] have borrowed it?

There is but one answer to this question.

The power of making treaties and the power of declaring war, are *royal prerogatives* in the *British government,* and are accordingly treated as *executive prerogatives* by *British commentators.*

THE PRESIDENT AND THE SUPREME COURT IN THE ANDREW JACKSON NULLIFICATION CONTROVERSY AND BANK CHARTER VETO

President Andrew Jackson's term of office is sometimes referred to in connection with appraisals of Executive power under the Constitution, particularly as concerns the relationship of the powers of the

President to those of the Supreme Court. The impression is often created that President Jackson and Chief Justice John Marshall had a head-on collision in the form of a specific case or cases and that President Jackson defied the Court. This appears to be such a widely held misconception that it is worth while briefly to summarize the facts in order to clarify the record in considering the use of Executive powers.

The overlapping and coincidence of two events appear to have combined to obscure President Jackson's attitude toward the Supreme Court and its powers. One was the series of actions by the State of Georgia to assert its sovereignty over the Cherokee Nation within its borders and to deny the right of the Supreme Court to review its actions. The other was the struggle over the renewal of the charter of the Bank of the United States which took place from January to June 1832.

On March 3, 1832, Chief Justice John Marshall rendered the opinion of the Supreme Court holding a Georgia statute unconstitutional on the ground that the jurisdiction of the Federal Government over the Cherokees was exclusive, and that the State had no power to pass laws affecting them or their territory. The judgment of the Georgia Superior Court convicting [two missionaries who had defied the State law] was reversed and a special mandate ordered to issue to that Court, March 5, ordering their release.

It was in connection with the uproar which followed the Court's decision that President Jackson has been quoted as saying: "Well, John Marshall has made his decision, now let him enforce it." The source of this alleged quotation is a book by Horace Greeley in which Greeley quotes an alleged remark by a Member of Congress who is supposed to have heard President Jackson make the comment. There appears to be no substantiation for the quotation so often attributed to Jackson except that it was given an aura of likelihood by Jackson's veto message on the bill extending the charter of the Bank of the United States in July 1832, only a few months later. It is true that the State of Georgia resisted the effort of the Supreme Court to assert its jurisdiction but there is little to uphold the contention that Jackson would do anything to undermine the authority of the Federal judiciary. Jackson's interest in the Union and in national authority was demonstrated forcefully in November and December of 1832, when, after South Carolina passed its Nullification Ordinance, Jackson took forthright action and recommended enactment by the Congress of "vigorous and radical" legislation giving the Federal courts and officials authority to deal with the situation.

President Jackson's attitude toward the Supreme Court should not be misconstrued as an argument for unlimited executive power particularly in view of his veto message on the bill to renew the charter of the Bank of the United States. In that message, however, Jackson merely emphasized his right to use the veto power given to him by the Constitution irrespective of anyone else's views on pending legislation. Jackson never asserted any right to refuse to execute any law enacted according to constitutional processes. Jackson said in response to the argument by advocates of the bill to the effect that the Supreme Court had upheld the constitutionality of the Bank's charter that such a decision—

ought not to control the coordinate authorities of this Government. It is as much the duty of the House of Representatives, of the Senate, and of the President, to decide upon the constitutionality of any bill or resolution which may be presented to them for passage or approval, as it is of the Supreme Judges when it may be brought before them for judicial decision. The opinion of the Judges has no more authority over Congress than the opinion of Congress has over the Judges; and on that point the President is independent of both. The authority of the Supreme Court must not, therefore, be permitted to control the Congress, or the Executive, when acting in their legislative capacities, but to have only such influence as the force of their reasoning may deserve.

The eminent historian of constitutional law, Charles Warren, summarizes Jackson's viewpoint thus:

Jackson never asserted a right to decline to carry out a Court decision, when acting in his Executive capacity. It was when exercising his part of the law-making function of the Nation, and when deciding upon signature or veto of a bill presented to him, that he claimed the privilege of determining for himself the constitutionality of the proposed measure.

LINCOLN: THE COMMANDER-IN-CHIEF, AND THE USE OF MILITARY POWER

An extraordinarily vigorous use of executive power characterized President Abraham Lincoln's tenure of office and the Civil War period. Some interesting aspects of Presidential power came to the fore as Lincoln waged his battle to preserve the Union. Primary among these was the President's use of his position as Commander in Chief, a constitutional power which received increased significance immediately upon the outbreak of hostilities within the very borders of our Nation.

The President's position as Commander in Chief gains importance in periods of war or armed conflict affecting the United States.

The Supreme Court has stated that even with a declaration of war by the Congress the Commander in Chief powers are restricted to military affairs. The words of the Court are these:

. . . nor does the law declaring the war imply an authority to the President to enlarge the limits of the United States by subjugating the enemy's country. The United States, it is true, may extend its boundaries by conquest or treaty, and may demand the cession of territory as the condition of peace, in order to indemnify its citizens for the injuries they have suffered, or to reimburse the Government for the expenses of the war. But this can be done only by the treaty-making power or the legislative authority, and is not a part of the power conferred upon the President by the declaration of war. His duty and his power are purely military. As commander-in-chief, he is authorized to direct the movements of the naval and military forces placed by law at his command, and to employ them in the manner he may deem most effectual to harass and conquer and subdue the enemy. He may invade the hostile country, and subject it to the sovereignty and authority of the United States. But his conquests do not enlarge the boundaries of this Union, nor extend the operation of our institutions and laws beyond the limits before assigned to them by the legislative power. . . .

In practice President Lincoln and other Presidents have used this military office bestowed upon them by the Constitution to enlarge the powers of the presidency, although with good faith and with noble motives, with greater impact upon the civilian population and our constitutional system than upon the military forces. One writer [S. P. Huntington] has summed up the situation in this manner:

. . . Problems arise, however, from the nature of the grant of presidential power. This clause is unique in the Constitution in granting authority in the form of an *office* rather than in the form of a *function*. The President is not given the function "to command the Army and Navy"; he is given the office of "Commander in Chief." This difference in form is of considerable importance, for it left undefined the specific powers and functions. This eased the approval of the Constitution in the ratifying conventions, but it gave subsequent generations something to argue about.

The powers of the Commander in Chief might range from the extremely broad power to conduct war to a narrowly restricted power of military command. They certainly exclude all powers specifically assigned to Congress or the states, and they probably include all purely military powers not so assigned. But does the office possess nonmilitary powers as well? The Framers themselves seemed to hold conflicting opinions on this point. The Supreme Court in 1850, however, declared that the duty and power of the President as Commander in Chief were "purely military," and denied the similarity between the presidential authority and the royal prerogative. So long as the Commander in Chief power was interpreted as purely military, it remained, in Professor Corwin's phrase, "the forgotten clause" of the Constitution. In the Civil War and in World War II, however, Lincoln and Roosevelt used the clause to justify an extraordinarily broad range of nonmilitary presidential actions largely legislative in nature. The justification of these actions by the Commander in Chief clause was persuasive, however, only because John Rutledge defined that power as an office rather than a function. It could be argued that the office of Commander in Chief possesses authority to seize a strike-bound war plant. It would be harder to argue that the function of commanding the Army and Navy implied such authority. The Commander in Chief clause, in other words, has been of relatively little direct use in securing civilian control over the military. Indeed, in one respect it has been directly detrimental to such control. But because it was phrased as an office rather than a function, it has been of great use to the President in expanding his power at the expense of Congress. This, in turn, has broadened the area of conflict between these two institutions and, consequently, if indirectly, has further impeded civilian control by increasing the likelihood that military leaders will be drawn into political controversy. . . .

No sooner had the first shots been fired at Fort Sumter than President Lincoln was confronted with the most serious crisis in the Nation's history since the founding of the Republic.

On April 25, 1861, fearful for the safety of the Nation's Capital in view of pro-Confederate activities in Maryland, Lincoln addressed a letter of instructions to General Scott telling him to watch the activities of the Maryland State Legislature and to act to suppress insurrection including ". . . in the extremest necessity, the suspension of the writ of habeas corpus."

On May 25, 1861, one John Merryman was arrested by Federal soldiers and confined in Fort McHenry under the command of General Cadwalader. Merryman was alleged to be an officer of a company having arms and intending armed hostility against the United States. On May 26, 1861 a petition for habeas corpus was presented to Chief Justice Taney who thereupon ordered that the writ of habeas corpus issue and be returnable before the Chief Justice in the United States Circuit Court room in Baltimore on the following day, May 27, 1861. On May 27, 1861, General Cadwalader had the writ returned by a Colonel Lee. In the return to the writ General Cadwalader explained that Merryman was being held because of a charge of various acts of treason and that he, General Cadwalader, had been duly authorized by the President, in such cases, to suspend the writ of habeas corpus for the public safety. General Cadwalader asked the Chief Justice to postpone further action until the general could receive further instructions from the President.

The Chief Justice forthwith ordered a writ of attachment to issue against General Cadwalader for contempt in refusing to produce the body of John Merryman, the writ to be returned on the following day, May 28, 1861. On the following day the marshal made the following return to the writ of attachment:

. . . I hereby certify to the Honorable Roger B. Taney, Chief Justice of the supreme Court of the United States, that by virtue of the within writ of attachment, to me directed, on the 27th day of May 1861, I proceeded, on this 28th day of May 1861, to Fort McHenry, for the purpose of serving the said writ. I sent in my name at the outer gate; the messenger returned with

　　　　　　　　　　　　　CONCEPTIONS OF THE OFFICE

the reply, "that there was no answer to my card," and therefore, could not serve the writ, as I was commanded. I was not permitted to enter the gate. So answers

WASHINGTON BONIFANT,
United States Marshal for the District of Maryland.

The Chief Justice rendered his opinion after stating:

. . . that the marshal had the power to summon the *posse comitatus* to aid him in seizing and bringing before the court, the party named in the attachment, who would, when so brought in, be liable to punishment by fine and imprisonment; but where, as in this case, the power refusing obedience was so notoriously superior to any the marshal could command, he held that officer excused from doing anything more than he had done.

In his opinion Taney concluded that the power to suspend the writ of habeas corpus is exclusively a legislative power and that the President cannot suspend the privilege nor authorize a military officer to do it. Taney based his argument on legal and constitutional history and the fact that the power to suspend the writ is contained in the first or legislative article of the Constitution.

Taney went on to state that the civil courts and processes were functioning and that Merryman should have been charged and tried according to those processes.

Although Taney's position was later vindicated by the Supreme Court he had to content himself with addressing a plea to President Lincoln in the instant case. There is no evidence that the plea was heeded.

Lincoln himself was not unaware of the legal problems involved and he specifically referred the matter to the Congress in his message to the extraordinary session of Congress convened on July 4, 1861. Lincoln left the matter of legislation to the Congress and defended his action in suspending the writ of habeas corpus by asking:

Are all the laws but one to go unexecuted, and the Government itself go to pieces lest that one be violated? Even in such a case, would not the official oath [of the President] be broken if the Government should be overthrown when it was believed that disregarding the single law would tend to preserve it?

Lincoln himself underscored the fact in this message that ". . . nothing has been done beyond the constitutional competency of Congress."

It was almost 2 years before the Congress passed legislation dealing with the matter of habeas corpus. The Habeas Corpus Act of March 3, 1863, authorized the President to suspend the writ when ". . . in his judgment, the public safety may require it. . . ." The act went on, however, to provide that reports of persons so detained be furnished to the circuit and district courts of the United States (persons who are

". . . citizens of states in which the administration of the laws has continued unimpaired in the said Federal courts . . ." and who are held ". . . as state or political prisoners, or otherwise than as prisoners of war . . ."). The act provided that when a list had been furnished to the court and when a grand jury had terminated its session ". . . without finding an indictment or presentment, or other proceeding against any such person, it shall be the duty of the judge of said court forthwith to make an order that any such prisoner desiring a discharge from said imprisonment be brought before him to be discharged." The act made it a crime punishable by fine and imprisonment for any officer of the United States having custody of such persons to delay or refuse to execute the court's order.

Thus without saying so in specific language, the Congress legalized Lincoln's actions. In addition, however, the Congress asserted its jurisdiction over the matter of habeas corpus suspension.

It appears therefore, that in the face of most extreme emergency there may be a lag in statutory law as summarized above. As Professor Hart has pointed out ". . . in a really critical situation . . . President Lincoln could preserve the Union only by taking action of doubtful legality without waiting for legislative authorization."

When the lag in legislative action is overcome by action of Congress, except for criminal penalties, the Congress may ratify the actions of the President, thereby curing defects which may have existed. In *The Prize Cases* (2 Black 635; 1862) the Supreme Court dealt with the challenge to the President's right to proclaim a blockade which resulted in the capture of prizes by the public ships of the United States. President Lincoln had declared a blockade on the 27th and 30th of April 1861. The question was whether a state of war existed which authorized the use of blockade under the laws of nations.

The Supreme Court pointed out that by acts of Congress of February 28, 1795, and March 3, 1807, the President was authorized to call out the militia and use the military and naval forces of the United States in case of invasion by foreign nations, ". . . and to suppress insurrection against the government of a State or of the United States."

The Court stated:

. . . If it were necessary to the technical existence of a war, that it should have a legislative sanction, we find it in almost every act passed at the extraordinary session of the Legislature of 1861, which was wholly employed in enacting laws to enable the Government to prosecute the war with vigor and efficiency. And finally, in 1861, we find Congress *"ex majore cautela"* and in anticipation of such astute objections, passing an act "approving, legalizing, and making valid all the acts, proclamations, and orders of the President, etc., as if they had been *issued and done under the previous express authority* and direction of the Congress of the United States."

Without admitting that such an act was necessary under the circumstances,

CONCEPTIONS OF THE OFFICE

it is plain that if the President had in any manner assumed powers which it was necessary should have the authority or sanction of Congress, that on the well-known principle of law, *"omnis ratihabitio retrotrahitur et mandato equiparatur,"* this ratification has operated to perfectly cure the defect. In the case of *Brown* v. *United States,* (8 Cr. 131, 132, 133), Mr. Justice Story treats of this subject and cites numerous authorities to which we may refer to prove this position, and concludes, "I am perfectly satisfied that no subject can commence hostilities or capture property of an enemy, when the sovereign has prohibited it. But suppose he did, I would ask if the sovereign may not ratify his proceedings, and thus by a retroactive operation give validity to them?"

Although Mr. Justice Story dissented from the majority of the Court on the whole case, the doctrine stated by him on this point is correct and fully substantiated by authority.

The objection made to this act of ratification, that it is *ex post facto,* and therefore unconstitutional and void, might possibly have some weight on the trial of an indictment in a criminal Court. But precedents from source cannot be received as authoritative in a tribunal administering public and international law.

On this first question therefore we are of the opinion that the President had a right, *jure belli,* to institute a blockade of ports in possession of the States in rebellion, which neutrals are bound to regard. . . .

The circumstances of emergency periling the very existence of the Nation may also give rise to a lag in the application of the law by the courts in the area of Presidential action. This is illustrated by the contrast of the actions of the Supreme Court in the cases of Ex parte Vallandigham and Ex parte Milligan, the first decided during the Civil War and the second decided after hostilities had ceased.

Vallandigham, a civilian, was tried and convicted by a military commission appointed pursuant to an order of General Burnside, commanding the military department of Ohio. Vallandigham was arrested on May 6, 1863, for having spoken in public against the Union cause on May 1, 1863. His sentence was originally fixed at confinement for the remainder of the war, but Lincoln commuted the sentence and had Vallandigham put out beyond the Union lines in Tennessee.

Vallandigham petitioned the Supreme Court for certiorari and the Court held it had no jurisdiction to issue the writ. It stated its authority to issue the writ must come from the Constitution and the statutes and concluded that in neither place had the Court been given appellate jurisdiction over military commissions. These, the Court stated, were not "courts" within the meaning of the 14th section of the Judiciary Act of 1789.

❧❧❧❧

Thus, the Supreme Court on procedural grounds refused to inject itself into the controversy presented to it in 1863–64 over the actions of military commissions. In 1866, the war over, the Supreme Court met the substantive issues presented in the Vallandigham case head on in the case of Ex parte Milligan.

****

Milligan, a civilian, had been sentenced to be executed after a trial by a military commission in October 1864 on charges of insurrectionary activity. The sentence was approved by the President. Milligan petitioned the circuit court to be discharged from custody under the terms of the Habeas Corpus Act of 1863, supra, since a grand jury had met and been discharged since his confinement and had not returned any indictment against him. The Supreme Court held that Milligan was entitled to be discharged from custody under the terms of the act and that the military commission had no jurisdiction legally to try and to sentence Milligan.

In a sweeping opinion the majority refused to accept the contention that martial law could justify the proceedings of the military commission. The majority stated that martial law could not be justified in Indiana since there was no actual invasion and the courts and civil administration were functioning. The majority stated that the basic safeguards for the individual written into the Constitution could not be disturbed by either the President, the Congress, or the judiciary save for the provision for the suspension of the writ of habeas corpus.

****

History shows that the Presidency is an extremely powerful office, if only by virtue of the powers and resources that are necessarily placed at the President's disposal through legislation and appropriations by the Congress. The legality of some Presidential actions may be doubtful but the fact is that the President's position may impel and enable him to act while at the same time the greater legal authority under the Constitution may reside in the Congress.

Where Congress by inaction leaves a vacuum, the natural tendency may be for the President to fill that vacuum by executive action. The Congress may thus be required to legislate to prevent action by the executive in areas where Congress has the constitutional authority to act.

DOCUMENT 2   THE "STRONG" EXECUTIVE

Given the elusive definitions of executive power in the Constitution, a vigorous, dynamic President has plenty of room for maneuver. He

CONCEPTIONS OF THE OFFICE

can push just as hard as he likes, though the exercise of this pressure, of course, brings the Congress out fighting, and the legislature is well equipped with weapons of its own. It was Theodore Roosevelt who played the greatest practical joke on Congress that any President has ever essayed: he desperately wanted to send the U.S. fleet around the world to "show the flag" and generate international prestige, but an economy-minded Congress refused an adequate appropriation. Undaunted, T. R. sent the fleet off and then, when the battlewagons were roughly half-way around the globe, mildly asked Congress if it would like to provide funds to bring the Navy home. Since the presumable alternative was to sell the ships for scrap iron in Bombay, the infuriated solons put up the money. The President's roars of laughter (T. R. had a laugh that could break glassware) were allegedly heard as far out of Washington as Alexandria, Virginia.

It is, in fact, very difficult for a student of the Presidency to define a "strong" Presidency except in circular terms, that is, as a President who exercises strength. In historical terms, strong Presidents have been those endowed with vigorous views of their proper role and with political finesse sufficient to permit them to implement their notions. President Abraham Lincoln, for example, suspended the writ of habeas corpus, blockaded the South, called men to the colors without Congressional authorization, issued the Emancipation Proclamation, and generally rewrote Article II to fit the exigencies of the time! He was a "strong" President—that is, he got away with it.

This brief excerpt from a letter of President Theodore Roosevelt to the distinguished British historian George Otto Trevelyan provides an insight into the mood of a strong President. "Strong" presidents, it has been argued, are born and not made. And one characteristic they have all shared is a creative ebullience—they loved the job! It was T. R. who described the office as a "bully pulpit," a judgment that his cousin Franklin surely shared.

. . . I regard the memories of Washington and Lincoln as priceless heritages for our people, just because they are the memories of strong men, of men who cannot be accused of weakness or timidity, of men who I believe were quite as strong for instance as Cromwell or Bismarck, and very much stronger than the Louis Napoleon type, who, nevertheless, led careers marked by disinterestedness just as much as by strength; who, like Timoleon and Hampden, in very deed, and not as

FROM Letter by President Theodore Roosevelt to George Otto Trevelyan, June 19, 1908. Reprinted by permission of the publishers from *The Letters of Theodore Roosevelt*, Volume VI, edited by Elting E. Morison, Cambridge, Mass.: Harvard University Press. Copyright, 1952, by The President and Fellows of Harvard College.

a mere matter of oratory or fine writing, put the public good, the good of the people as a whole, as the first of all considerations.

Now, my ambition is that, in however small a way, the work I do shall be along the Washington and Lincoln lines. While President I have *been* President, emphatically; I have used every ounce of power there was in the office and I have not cared a rap for the criticisms of those who spoke of my "usurpation of power"; for I knew that the talk was all nonsense and that there was no usurpation. I believe that the efficiency of this Government depends upon its possessing a strong central executive, and wherever I could establish a precedent for strength in the executive, as I did for instance as regards external affairs in the case of sending the fleet around the world, taking Panama, settling affairs of Santo Domingo and Cuba; or as I did in internal affairs in settling the anthracite coal strike, in keeping order in Nevada this year when the Federation of Miners threatened anarchy, or as I have done in bringing the big corporations to book—why, in all these cases I have felt not merely that my action was right in itself, but that in showing the strength of, or in giving strength to, the executive, I was establishing a precedent of value. I believe in a strong executive; I believe in power; but I believe that responsibility should go with power, and that it is not well that the strong executive should be a perpetual executive. Above all and beyond all I believe as I have said before that the salvation of this country depends upon Washington and Lincoln representing the type of leader to which we are true. I hope that in my acts I have been a good President, a President who has deserved well of the Republic; but most of all, I believe that whatever value my service may have comes even more from what I *am* than from what I *do*. I may be mistaken, but it is my belief that the bulk of my countrymen, the men whom Abraham Lincoln called "the plain people"—the farmers, mechanics, small tradesmen, hard-working professional men—feel that I am in a peculiar sense their President, that I represent the democracy in somewhat the fashion that Lincoln did, that is, not in any demagogic way but with the sincere effort to stand for a government by the people and for the people.

❖❖❖❖

DOCUMENT 3　A STRICT CONSTITUTIONALIST'S VIEW

William Howard Taft, a man of great intelligence and ability, had the historical misfortune of being closely associated with Theodore

　　　　　　　　　CONCEPTIONS OF THE OFFICE

Roosevelt. T. R., who liked Taft, gave him high office and then designated the three-hundred-pound Ohioan as his heir to the Presidency. Obviously looking on Taft as an extension of his own ego, "Teddy" rushed off to Africa to shoot lions, secure in the faith that "his" man would continue his policies. It apparently never occurred to Roosevelt that Taft might have other views—in fact it is doubtful that he had ever considered that Taft had any views.

But William Howard Taft did have opinions of his own—and his strong-minded wife had a good many more, including a few on Roosevelt. And no sooner was Taft installed in the White House than it became apparent that trouble was brewing: the Roosevelt tong in the Administration began to murmur about weakness and to suggest that Taft had sold out to the "malefactors of great wealth." Now it is clear not only that Taft was less than enthusiastic about being President (the job he wanted, which he later received from President Harding, was Chief Justice of the United States), but that his lack of vigor was purposeful as well as characterological. He simply did not accept the definition of his constitutional role that T. R. had created for him. Thus between 1909 and 1912 there was a very different atmosphere about the Presidency from that of the preceding period, one that enraged T. R. and brought him back into politics as the Progressive candidate for President in 1912—where his intervention defeated Taft and elected Woodrow Wilson.

Taft's book, from which this selection is taken, is in a sense his revenge on Roosevelt. But it also contains a very thoughtful analysis of the powers of the Presidency from the traditionalist "Whig" viewpoint, the position that argues that the President is essentially chairman of the board of directors (Congress) rather than an autonomous institutional force.

✳✳✳✳

The true view of the Executive functions is, as I conceive it, that the President can exercise no power which cannot be fairly and reasonably traced to some specific grant of power or justly implied and included within such express grant as proper and necessary to its exercise. Such specific grant must be either in the Federal Constitution or in an act of Congress passed in pursuance thereof. There is no undefined residuum of power which he can exercise because it seems to him to be in the public interest and there is nothing in the Neagle case and its definition of a law of the United States, or in other precedents, warranting such an inference. The grants of Executive power are necessarily in general terms in order not to embarrass the Executive within the field of action plainly marked for him, but his jurisdiction

FROM Ex-President William Howard Taft, *Our Chief Magistrate and His Powers* (New York, Columbia University Press, 1916), pp. 138–48, 156–57.

A STRICT CONSTITUTIONALIST'S VIEW

23

must be justified and vindicated by affirmative constitutional or statutory provision, or it does not exist. There have not been wanting, however, eminent men in high public office holding a different view and who have insisted upon the necessity for an undefined residuum of Executive power in the public interest. They have not been confined to the present generation. . . . Men who are not . . . strict constructionists of the Constitution . . . may well feel real concern if such views are to receive the general acquiescence.

❖❖❖❖

The answer which at once suggests itself to one familiar with the structure of our government, in which all power is delegated, and is defined by law, constitutional or statutory, is, that to one or both of these sources we must resort in every instance. We have no officers in this government, from the President down to the most subordinate agent, who does not hold office under the law, with prescribed duties and limited authority. And while some of these, as the President, the Legislature, and the Judiciary, exercise powers in some sense left to the more general definitions necessarily incident to fundamental law found in the Constitution, the larger portion of them are the creation of statutory law, with duties and powers prescribed and limited by that law.

In the light of this view of the Supreme Court it is interesting to compare the language of Mr. Roosevelt in his "Notes for a Possible Autobiography" on the subject of "Executive Powers," in which he says:

The most important factor in getting the right spirit in my Administration, next to insistence upon courage, honesty, and a genuine democracy of desire to serve the plain people, was my insistence upon the theory that the executive power was limited only by specific restrictions and prohibitions appearing in the Constitution or imposed by Congress under its constitutional powers. My view was that every Executive officer and above all every Executive officer in high position was a steward of the people bound actively and affirmatively to do all he could for the people and not to content himself with the negative merit of keeping his talents undamaged in a napkin. I declined to adopt this view that what was imperatively necessary for the Nation could not be done by the President, unless he could find some specific authorization to do it. My belief was that it was not only his right but his duty to do anything that the needs of the Nation demanded unless such action was forbidden by the Constitution or by the laws. Under this interpretation of executive power I did and caused to be done many things not previously done by the President and the heads of the departments. I did not usurp power but I did greatly broaden the use of executive power. In other words, I acted for the common well being of all our people whenever and in whatever measure was necessary, unless prevented by direct constitutional or legislative prohibition.

I may add that Mr. Roosevelt, by way of illustrating his meaning as to the differing usefulness of Presidents, divides the Presidents into two classes, and designates them as "Lincoln Presidents" and "Buchanan Presidents." In order more fully to illustrate his division of Presidents on their merits, he places himself in the Lincoln class of Presidents, and me in the Buchanan class. The identification of Mr. Roosevelt with Mr. Lincoln might otherwise have escaped notice, because there are many differences between the two, presumably superficial, which would give the impartial student of history a different impression. It suggests a story which a friend of mine told of his little daughter Mary. As he came walking home after a business day, she ran out from the house to greet him, all aglow with the importance of what she wished to tell him. She said, "Papa, I am the best scholar in the class." The father's heart throbbed with pleasure as he inquired, "Why, Mary, you surprise me. When did the teacher tell you? This afternoon?" "Oh, no," Mary's reply was, "the teacher didn't tell me—I just noticed it myself."

My judgment is that the view of . . . Mr. Roosevelt, ascribing an undefined residuum of power to the President is an unsafe doctrine and that it might lead under emergencies to results of an arbitrary character, doing irremediable injustice to private right. The mainspring of such a view is that the Executive is charged with responsibility for the welfare of all the people in a general way, that he is to play the part of a Universal Providence and set all things right, and that anything that in his judgment will help the people he ought to do, unless he is expressly forbidden not to do it. The wide field of action that this would give to the Executive one can hardly limit. It is enough to say that Mr. Roosevelt has expressly stated how far he thought this principle would justify him in going in respect to the coal famine and the Pennsylvania anthracite strike which he did so much useful work in settling. What was actually done was the result of his activity, his power to influence public opinion and the effect of the prestige of his great office in bringing the parties to the controversy, the mine owners and the strikers, to a legal settlement by arbitration. No one has a higher admiration for the value of what he did there than I have. But if he had failed in this, he says he intended to take action on his theory of the extent of the executive power already stated. I quote from the same book from which his other words are taken. Mr. Roosevelt says:

In my own mind, I was already planning effective action, but it was of a very drastic character, and I did not wish to take it until the failure of all other expedients had rendered it necessary. . . . I had definitely determined that somehow or other, act I would, that somehow or other the coal famine should be broken. To accomplish this end it was necessary that the mines should be run, and if I could get no voluntary agreement between the contending sides, that an arbitration commission should be appointed which would command such public confidence as to enable me without too much difficulty, to enforce its terms on the parties. . . .

❋❋❋❋

Meanwhile the Governor of Pennsylvania had all the Pennsylvania militia in the anthracite region although without any effect upon the resumption of mining. The method of action upon which I had determined was to get the Governor of Pennsylvania to ask me to keep order. Then I would put in the army under the command of some first rate general. I would instruct this general to keep absolute order, taking any steps whatever that were necessary to prevent interference by the strikers or their sympathizers with men who wanted to work. I would also instruct him to dispossess the operators and run the mines as a receiver until such time as the commission might make its report, and until I as President might issue further orders in view of this report.

Now it is perfectly evident that Mr. Roosevelt thinks he was charged with the duty, not only to suppress disorder in Pennsylvania, but to furnish coal to avoid the coal famine in New York and New England, and therefore he proposed to use the army of the United States to mine the coal which should prevent or relieve the famine. It was his avowed intention to take the coal mines out of the hands of their lawful owners and to mine the coal which belonged to them and sell it in the eastern market, against their objection, without any court proceeding of any kind and without any legal obligation on their part to work the mines at all. It was an advocacy of the higher law and his obligation to execute it which is a little startling in a constitutional republic. It is perfectly evident from his statement that it was not the maintenance of law and order in Pennsylvania and the suppression of insurrection, the *only ground* upon which he could intervene at all, that actuated him in what he proposed to do. He used the expression that he would "get" the Governor of Pennsylvania to call for troops from him, and then having secured a formal authority for the use of the army to suppress disorder, he proposed to use it for the seizure of private property and its appropriation for the benefit of the people of other states. The benevolence of his purpose no one can deny, but no one who looks at it from the standpoint of a government of law could regard it as anything but lawless. I venture to think, however, that Mr. Roosevelt is mistaken in what he thinks he would have done. Mr. Roosevelt in office was properly amenable to the earnest advice of those whom he trusted, and there were men about him who would probably have dissuaded him from such a course.

I am aware that there are many who believe in government ownership of the sources of public comfort in the interest of the community at large; but it is certainly only the extremes of that school that favor the use of the army under the President to seize the needed mines

26   CONCEPTIONS OF THE OFFICE

without constitutional amendment or legislative and judicial action and without compensation. Mr. Roosevelt in his subsequent remarks seems to find a justification for his general view of the limitations of Executive power in what Mr. Lincoln did during the Civil War. That Mr. Lincoln with the stress of the greatest civil war in modern times felt called upon to do things, the constitutionality of which was seriously questioned, is undoubtedly true. But Mr. Lincoln always pointed out the source of the authority which in his opinion justified his acts, and there was always a strong ground for maintaining the view which he took. His claim of right to suspend the writ of habeas corpus I venture to think was well founded. Congress subsequently expressly gave him this right and the Supreme Court sustained his exercise of it under the act of Congress. His Emancipation Proclamation was attacked as an unconstitutional exercise of authority, but he defended it as an act of the Commander-in-Chief justified by military necessity to weaken the enemies of the Nation and suppress their rebellion. Certainly the arguments that he and those who supported his action brought to sustain it have great weight. But Mr. Lincoln never claimed that whatever authority in government was not expressly denied to him he could exercise.

✠✠✠✠

I have now concluded a review of the Executive power, and hope that I have shown that it is limited, so far as it is possible to limit such a power consistent with that discretion and promptness of action that are essential to preserve the interests of the public in times of emergency, or legislative neglect or inaction.

There is little danger to the public weal from the tyranny or reckless character of a President who is not sustained by the people. The absence of popular support will certainly in the course of two years withdraw from him the sympathetic action of at least one House of Congress, and by the control that that House has over appropriations, the Executive arm can be paralyzed, unless he resorts to a coup d'état, which means impeachment, conviction and deposition. The only danger in the action of the Executive under the present limitations and lack of limitation of his powers is when his popularity is such that he can be sure of the support of the electorate and therefore of Congress, and when the majority in the legislative halls respond with alacrity and sycophancy to his will. This condition cannot probably be long continued. We have had Presidents who felt the public pulse with accuracy, who played their parts upon the political stage with histrionic genius and commanded the people almost as if they were an army and the President their Commander-in-Chief. Yet in all these cases, the good sense of the people has ultimately prevailed and no danger has been done to our political structure and the reign of law has continued. In such times when the Executive power seems to be all prevailing, there have always been men in this free and intelligent people of ours, who apparently courting political humiliation and disaster have registered protest against this undue Executive domination and this use of the Executive power and popular support to perpetuate itself.

The cry of Executive domination is often entirely unjustified, as when the President's commanding influence only grows out of a proper cohesion of a party and its recognition of the necessity for political leadership; but the fact that Executive domination is regarded as a useful ground for attack upon a successful administration, even when there is no ground for it, is itself proof of the dependence we may properly place upon the sanity and clear perceptions of the people in avoiding its baneful effects when there is real danger. Even if a vicious precedent is set by the Executive, and injustice done, it does not have the same bad effect that an improper precedent of a court may have, for one President does not consider himself bound by the policies or constitutional views of his predecessors.

The Constitution does give the President wide discretion and great power, and it ought to do so. It calls from him activity and energy to see that within his proper sphere he does what his great responsibilities and opportunities require. He is no figurehead, and it is entirely proper that an energetic and active clearsighted people, who, when they have work to do, wish it done well, should be willing to rely upon their judgment in selecting their Chief Agent, and having selected him, should entrust to him all the power needed to carry out their governmental purpose, great as it may be.

DOCUMENT 4 THE "GREATEST OFFICE"

Between the short, unhappy tenure of William Howard Taft and the ebullient reign of Harry S. Truman, the White House was occupied by a number of figures who reflected radically different conceptions of the Presidency. Woodrow Wilson, with his historian's eye focused on the era of Thomas Jefferson, attempted to build his authority by controlling Congress—almost on the model of a British prime minister. Warren Harding and Calvin Coolidge took their directions from the legislature and relaxed: Coolidge took a long nap every afternoon, avoided controversy, and saved much of his salary. Herbert Hoover, a man of great talent, took his task to be largely that of chief administrator; in a different era he might have established a high reputation, but he was destroyed by the hurricane that hit in 1929, the depression.

Into the Presidency—in a wheel chair, though no one ever thought of him as a cripple—came Franklin D. Roosevelt, and suddenly things began to hum. Characteristically F. D. R. was far too busy being President ever to write about the job. Indeed, given his temperament, his genius for vital improvisation, and his profound suspicion of ideology, it is virtually impossible to conceive of Roosevelt ever enouncing a "Philosophy of the Presidency." Professors of political science, with nothing better to do with their time and energy, could handle that chore. Yet it is quite clear in retrospect that F. D. R. "invented" the modern American Presidency. This was partly a consequence of his personality; it was also partly an outgrowth of communications technology, notably the arrival of the radio as a standard feature in the American home. (In 1928 there were about 8.5 million radios in the United States; in 1932, 18 million; in 1936, 33 million!) Roosevelt converted the Presidency from a staid, somewhat remote office to the general headquarters of American society. Against the background of international crisis and the transformation of American life from rural-agrarian to urban-industrial patterns, the Chief Executive assumed a position in American politics far beyond the dreams of an Abraham Lincoln, a Theodore Roosevelt, or a Woodrow Wilson.

When Harry S. Truman succeeded Roosevelt, he entered office with an eye toward history. This selection sets out his premise that it is the skillful use of the unwritten *powers of the President, not explicitly stated in the Constitution, that makes great Presidents. Truman notes that these powers "go only to him who can take and use them," and he patterned his Administration on this credo. He justifies vigorous Presidential action by arguing that only the President—"the only lobbyist the whole people had in Washington"—can represent and be responsible to the whole people. In this selection, Roosevelt's successor provides his assessment of the role of the Presidency in midcentury.*

. . . The papers of Presidents of the United States are important because of the unique character and importance of the Presidential office. It is the greatest office in the history of the world. . . .

When the founding fathers outlined the Presidency in Article II of the Constitution, they left a great many details out and vague. I think they relied on the experience of the nation to fill in the outlines. The office of chief executive has grown with the progress of this great

FROM Speech at Truman Birthday Dinner by Ex-President Harry S. Truman, May 8, 1954, New York *Times*, May 9, 1954. Copyright by The New York Times. Reprinted by permission.

republic. It has responded to the many demands that our complex society has made upon the Government. It has given our nation a means of meeting our greatest emergencies. Today, it is one of the most important factors in our leadership of the free world.

Many diverse elements entered into the creation of the office, springing, as it did, from the parent idea of the separation of powers.

There was the firm conviction of such powerful and shrewd minds as that of John Adams that the greatest protection against unlimited power lay in an executive secured against the encroachment of the national assembly. Then there were the fears of those who suspected a plot to establish a monarchy on these shores. Others believed that the experience under the Confederation showed above all the need of stability through a strong central administration. Finally, there was the need for compromise among these and many other views.

The result was a compromise—a compromise which that shrewd observer, Alexis de Tocqueville, over 120 years ago, believed would not work. He thought that the Presidential office was too weak. The President, he thought, was at the mercy of Congress. The President could recommend, to be sure, he thought, but the President had no power and the Congress had the power. The Congress could disregard his recommendations, overrule his vetoes, reject his nominations. De Tocqueville thought that no man of parts, worthy of leadership, would accept so feeble a role.

This was not a foolish view and there was much in our early history which tended to bear it out. But there is a power in the course of events which plays its own part. In this case again, Justice Holmes' epigram proved true. He said a page of history is worth a volume of logic. And as the pages of history were written they unfolded powers in the Presidency not explicitly found in Article II of the Constitution.

In the first place, the President became the leader of a political party. The party under his leadership had to be dominant enough to put him in office. This political party leadership was the last thing the Constitution contemplated. The President's election was not intended to be mixed up in the hurly-burly of partisan politics. . . . The people were to choose wise and respected men who would meet in calm seclusion and choose a President and the runner-up would be Vice President.

All of this went by the board—though most of the original language remains in the Constitution. Out of the struggle and tumult of the political arena a new and different President emerged—the man who led a political party to victory and retained in his hands the power of party leadership. That is, he retained it like the sword Excalibur, if he could wrest it from the scabbard and wield it.

Another development was connected with the first. As the President came to be elected by the whole people, he became responsible to the whole people. I used to say the only lobbyist the whole people had in

CONCEPTIONS OF THE OFFICE

Washington was the President of the United States. Our whole people looked to him for leadership, and not confined within the limits of a written document. Every hope and every fear of his fellow citizens, almost every aspect of their welfare and activity, falls within the scope of his concern—indeed, it falls within the scope of his duty. Only one who has held that office can really appreciate that. It is the President's responsibility to look at all questions from the point of view of the whole people. His written and spoken word commands national and often international attention.

These powers which are not explicitly written into the Constitution are powers which no President can pass on to his successor. They go only to him who can take and use them. However, it is these powers, quite as much as those enumerated in Article II of the Constitution which make the Presidential system unique and which give the papers of Presidents their peculiar and revealing importance.

For it is through the use of these great powers that leadership arises, events are molded and administrations take on their character. Their use can make a Jefferson or a Lincoln Administration; their non-use can make a Buchanan or a Grant Administration.

Moreover, a study of these aspects of our governmental and political history will save us from self-righteousness—from taking a holier than thou attitude toward other nations. For brilliant and enduring as were the minds of the architects of our Constitution, they did not devise a foolproof system to protect us against the disaster of a weak government—that is, government unable to face and resolve—one way or another—pressing national problems. Indeed, in some respects, the separation of powers requires stronger executive leadership than does the parliamentary and cabinet system.

As Justice Brandeis used to say, the separation of powers was not devised to promote efficiency in government. In fact, it was devised to prevent one form of deficiency—absolutism or dictatorship. By making the Congress separate and independent in the exercise of its powers, and the executive separate and independent in the exercise of its powers, a certain amount of political conflict was built into the Constitution. For the price of independence is eternal vigilance and a good deal of struggle. And this is not a bad thing—on the contrary, it is a good thing for the preservation of the liberty of the people—if it does not become conflict just for its own sake.

I've always said that the President who didn't have a fight with the Congress wasn't any good anyhow. And that is no reflection on the Congress. They are always looking after their rights. You needn't doubt that.

Having been in these two branches of government, legislative and executive, I think I am expressing a considered and impartial opinion in saying that the powers of the President are much more difficult to exercise and to preserve from encroachment than those of the Congress. In part, this comes from the difficulty of the problems of our time, and from the fact that upon the President falls the responsibility of obtaining action, timely and adequate to meet the nation's needs. Whatever the Constitution says, he is held responsible for any disaster which may come.

And so a successful administration is one of strong Presidential leadership. Weak leadership—or no leadership—produces failure and often disaster.

This does not come from the inherent incapacity of the people of the nation. It is inherent in legislative government where there is no executive strong and stable enough to rally the people to a sustained effort of will and prepared to use its power of party control to the fullest extent.

Today, also, one of the great responsibilities and opportunities of the President is to lead and inspire public opinion. The words of a President carry great weight. His acts carry even more weight.

All of us remember the words of Franklin D. Roosevelt in his first inaugural address which did so much to rally the spirit of a nation struggling through the depths of a depression. He said "the only thing we have to fear is fear itself." These words, however, would have had little effect if President Roosevelt had not backed them up by action. Following that speech, President Roosevelt plunged into a vigorous course, striking at the depression on all fronts. He backed his words by his action, and words and action restored the faith of the nation in its government and in its form of government, too.

Today, there is the same need for a similar combination of words and action concerning the hysteria about communism. Our country has acted firmly and resolutely to hold Communist imperialism in check. Nevertheless, that concern has created fear and fear has been played upon by persons who see in it an easy way to influence votes. There is no dispute any more that this unreasonable fear exists. The leaders of both political parties have acknowledged it. I do not wish to go into this subject at length tonight. I have talked a good deal about it of late, and most recently at Westminster College in Missouri where Winston Churchill made his famous Iron Curtain speech. We all know the corrosive effect of this hysteria and the dangers it holds.

But, as I have said, the office of the Presidency is the one office of our Government to which all the people turn when they are beset by fears like these. It is to the President that they look to say a firm "No" to those who wish to destroy others through fear and innuendo. It is his duty to defend the unjustly accused and demonstrate in the executive branch of the Government that the ancient principles of fair play and decency prevail all the time. By such deeds and acts the Presidency can reassure the nation and stem the growth of hysteria.

Again, we see today history repeating itself as the legislative branch of the Government, under the overshadowing fear of communism, expands its functions and activities into the very center of the power of the executive branch.

The President is responsible for the administration of his office. And that means for the administration of the entire executive branch. It is not the business of Congress to run the agencies of government for the President.

Unless this principle is observed, it is impossible to have orderly government. The legislative power will ooze into the executive offices. It will influence and corrupt the decisions of the executive branch. It will affect promotions and transfers. It will warp and twist policies.

Not only does the President cease to be master in his own house, but the whole house of government becomes one which has no master. The power of decision then rests only in the legislative branch, and the legislative branch by its very nature is not equipped to perform these executive functions.

To this kind of encroachment it is the duty of the President to say firmly and flatly "No, you can't do it." The investigative power of Congress is not limitless. It extends only so far as to permit the Congress to acquire the information that it honestly needs to exercise its legislative functions. Exercised beyond those limits, it becomes a manifestation of unconstitutional power. It raises the threat of legislative dictatorship and that's the worst dictatorship in the world.

Our nation was once almost torn apart by such an expansion of Congressional power. That was in the age of President Johnson, when the Radical Republicans of that time tried to take over the functions of the President. But we cannot afford such an attack on the Presidency by today's version of the Radical Republicans.

Today the perils and problems which threaten us and our allies make all the difficulties of the Reconstruction period—that tragic era—seem rather pale. Today the tasks of leadership falling upon the President spring not only from our national problems but from those of the whole world. Today that leadership will determine whether our Government will function effectively, and upon its functioning depends the survival of each of us and also on that depends the survival of the free world, if I may be so bold as to say that.

And today our Government cannot function properly unless it follows the provisions of the Constitution. Our Government cannot function properly unless the President is master in his own house and unless the executive departments and agencies of the Government, including the armed forces, are responsible to the President. . . .

DOCUMENT 5 A PRESIDENTIAL CANDIDATE'S VIEWS

In the 1952 Presidential election, the American people voted over-whelmingly for an end to crisis living. For twenty years, it seemed, the bugles had never ceased: first there was the depression, then World War II, and finally, when according to hopeful prophecies the world would turn once and for all from its wicked ways, the Cold War and the Korean War. The Republican candidate in 1952, General Dwight Eisenhower, offered solace—an end to "corruption, communism, and Korea"; the Democratic candidate, Adlai Stevenson, predicted more trouble and called for continuing sacrifice. The voters, weary of the trumpet calls, trusted "Ike."

Although President Eisenhower basically accepted the Taft conception of the Presidency, he had important reservations. In domestic affairs he was generally prepared to follow the leadership of the Congress. In fact, he had a quite remarkable relationship with the Democratic Congressional leaders who dominated Congress through six of his eight years in office—the "Texas Regency" of Speaker Sam Rayburn and Senate Majority Leader Lyndon Johnson. However, in the field of foreign affairs the President seemed to feel that the Chief Executive had a responsibility as a national leader along much the same lines as those established by Roosevelt and Truman. His Secretary of State, John Foster Dulles, conducted American foreign policy with an autonomy and an immunity from criticism reminiscent of seventeenth-century statecraft.

As the 1960 Presidential campaign opened (with Eisenhower constitutionally barred from a third term), Democratic aspirant John F. Kennedy launched a series of attacks on what might be described as the "mood" of the Presidency between 1952 and 1960—he carefully avoided attacking Eisenhower himself—and in this selection gave his own impression of what the office demands.

The modern Presidential campaign covers every issue in and out of the platform from cranberries to creation. But the public is rarely alerted to a candidate's views about the central issue on which all the rest turn. That central issue—and the point of my comments this noon

FROM Speech to the National Press Club by Senator John F. Kennedy, January 14, 1960, New York *Times,* January 15, 1960. Copyright by The New York Times. Reprinted by permission.

—is not the farm problem or defense or India. It is the Presidency itself. Of course a candidate's views on specific policies are important —but Theodore Roosevelt and William Howard Taft shared policy views with entirely different results in the White House. Of course it is important to elect a good man with good intentions—but Woodrow Wilson and Warren G. Harding were both good men of good intentions—so were Lincoln and Buchanan—but there is a Lincoln Room in the White House, and no Buchanan Room.

The history of this nation—its brightest and its bleakest pages—has been written largely in terms of the different views our Presidents have had of the Presidency itself. This history ought to tell us that the American people in 1960 have an imperative right to know what any man bidding for the Presidency thinks about the place he is bidding for—whether he is aware of and willing to use the powerful resources of that office—whether his model will be Taft—or Roosevelt—Wilson —or Harding.

Not since the days of Woodrow Wilson has any candidate spoken on the Presidency itself before the votes have been irrevocably cast. Let us hope that the 1960 campaign, in addition to discussing the familiar issues where our positions too often blur, will also talk about the Presidency itself—as an instrument for dealing with those issues— as an office with varying roles, powers and limitations.

CRITICIZES EISENHOWER

During the past eight years, we have seen one concept of the Presidency at work. Our needs and hopes have been eloquently stated— but the initiative and follow-through have too often been left to others. And too often his own objectives have been lost by the President's failure to override objections from within his own party, in the Congress or even in his Cabinet.

The American people in 1952 and 1956 may well have preferred this detached, limited concept of the Presidency after twenty years of fast-moving, creative Presidential rule. Perhaps historians will regard this as necessarily one of those frequent periods of consolidation, a time to draw breath, to recoup our national energy. To quote the State of the Union Message: "No Congress . . . on surveying the state of the nation, has met with a more pleasing prospect than that which appears at the present time." Unfortunately this is not Mr. Eisenhower's last message to the Congress, but Calvin Coolidge's. He followed to the White House Mr. Harding, whose "sponsor" declared very frankly that the times did not demand a first-rate President. If true, the times and the man met.

But the question is what do the times—and the people—demand for the next four years in the White House?

They demand a vigorous proponent of the national interest—not a passive broker for conflicting private interests. They demand a man capable of acting as the commander-in-chief of the grand alliance, not merely a bookkeeper who feels that his work is done when the numbers on the balance sheet come out even. They demand that he be the head of a responsible party, not rise so far above politics as to be invisible—a man who will formulate and fight for legislative policies, not be a casual bystander to the legislative process.

Today a restricted concept of the Presidency is not enough. For beneath today's surface gloss of peace and prosperity are increasingly dangerous, unsolved, long-postponed problems—problems that will inevitably explode to the surface during the next four years of the next Administration—the growing missile gap, the rise of Communist China, the despair of the under-developed nations, the explosive situations in Berlin and in the Formosa Straits, the deterioration of NATO, the lack of an arms control agreement, and all the domestic problems of our farms, cities and schools.

This Administration has not faced up to these and other problems. Much has been said—but I am reminded of the old Chinese proverb: "There is a great deal of noise on the stairs but nobody comes into the room." The President's State of the Union Message reminded me of the exhortation from "King Lear" that goes: "I will do such things— what they are I know not . . . but they shall be the wonders of the earth."

In the decade that lies ahead—in the challenging, revolutionary Sixties—the American Presidency will demand more than ringing manifestoes issued from the rear of the battle. It will demand that the President place himself in the very thick of the fight, that he care passionately about the fate of the people he leads, that he be willing to serve them at the risk of incurring their momentary displeasure.

AS CHIEF EXECUTIVE

Whatever the political affiliation of our next President, whatever his views may be on all the issues and problems that rush in upon us, he must above all be the Chief Executive in every sense of the word. He must be prepared to exercise the fullest powers of his office—all that are specified and some that are not. He must master complex problems as well as receive one-page memoranda. He must originate action as well as study groups. He must reopen the channels of communication between the world of thought and the seat of power.

Ulysses Grant considered the President "a purely administrative officer." If he administered the Government departments efficiently, delegated his functions smoothly, and performed his ceremonies of state with decorum and grace, no more was to be expected of him. But that is not the place the Presidency was meant to have in American life. The President is alone, at the top—the loneliest job there is, as Harry Truman has said. If there is destructive dissension among the services, he alone can step in and straighten it out—instead of waiting for unanimity. If administrative agencies are not carrying out their mandate—if a brushfire threatens some part of the globe—he alone can act, without waiting for the Congress. If his farm program fails, he alone deserves the blame, not his Secretary of Agriculture.

"The President is at liberty, both in law and conscience, to be as big a man as he can." So wrote Professor Woodrow Wilson. But President Woodrow Wilson discovered that to be a big man in the White House inevitably brings cries of dictatorship. So did Lincoln and Jackson and the two Roosevelts. And so may the next occupant of that office, if he is the man the times demand. But how much better it would be, in the turbulent Sixties, to have a Roosevelt or a Wilson than to have another James Buchanan, cringing in the White House, afraid to move.

Nor can we afford a Chief Executive who is praised primarily for what he did not do, the disasters he prevented, the bills he vetoed—a President wishing his subordinates would produce more missiles or build more schools. We will need instead what the Constitution envisioned: a Chief Executive who is the vital center of action in our whole scheme of Government.

AS LEGISLATIVE LEADER

This includes the legislative process as well. The President cannot afford—for the sake of the office as well as the nation—to be another Warren G. Harding, described by one backer as a man who "would, when elected, sign whatever bill the Senate sent him—and not send bills for the Senate to pass." Rather he must know when to lead the Congress, when to consult it and when he should act alone. Having served fourteen years in the Legislative Branch, I would not look with favor upon its domination by the Executive. Under our Government of "power as the rival of power," to use Hamilton's phrase, Congress must not surrender its responsibilities. But neither should it dominate. However large its share in the formulation of domestic programs, it is the President alone who must make the major decisions of our foreign policy.

That is what the Constitution wisely commands. And even domestically, the President must initiate policies and devise laws to meet the needs of the nation. And he must be prepared to use all the resources of his office to insure the enactment of that legislation—even when conflict is the result. By the end of his term Theodore Roosevelt was not popular in the Congress—particularly when he criticized an amendment to the Treasury appropriation which forbade the use of Secret Service men to investigate Congressmen! And the feeling was mutual, Roosevelt saying: "I do not much admire the Senate, because it is such a helpless body when efficient work is to be done." And Woodrow Wilson was even more bitter after his frustrating quarrels—asked if he might run for the Senate in 1920, he replied: "Outside of the United States, the Senate does not amount to a damn. And inside the United States, the Senate is mostly despised. They haven't had a thought down there in fifty years."

But, however bitter their farewells, the facts of the matter are that Roosevelt and Wilson did get things done—not only through their Executive powers but through the Congress as well. Calvin Coolidge, on the other hand, departed from Washington with cheers of Congress still ringing in his ears. But when his World Court bill was under fire on Capitol Hill he sent no messages, gave no encouragement to the bill's leaders and paid little or no attention to the whole proceeding— and the cause of world justice was set back. To be sure, Coolidge had held the usual White House breakfasts with Congressional leaders— but they were aimed, as he himself said, at "good fellowship," not a discussion of "public business." And at his press conferences, according to press historians, where he preferred to talk about the local flower show and its exhibits, reporters who finally extracted from him a single sentence—"I am against that bill"—would rush to file tongue-in-cheek dispatches, proclaiming that: "President Coolidge, in a fighting mood, today served notice on Congress that he intended to combat, with all the resources at his command, the pending bill. . . ."

But in the coming years, we will need a real fighting mood in the White House—a man who will not retreat in the face of pressure from his Congressional leaders—who will not let down those supporting his views on the floor. Divided Government over the past six years has only been further confused by this lack of legislative leadership. To restore it next year will help restore purpose to both the Presidency and the Congress.

AS PARTY LEADER

The facts of the matter are that legislative leadership is not possible without party leadership, in the most political sense—and Mr. Eisenhower prefers to stay above politics (although a weekly news magazine last fall reported the startling news, and I quote, that "President Eisenhower is emerging as a major political figure"). When asked, early in his first term, how he liked the "game of politics," he replied with a frown that his questioner was using a derogatory phrase. "Being President," he said, "is a very great experience . . . but the word 'politics' . . . I have no great liking for that." But no President, it seems to me, can escape politics. He has not only been chosen by the nation—he has been chosen by his party. And if he insists that he is "President of all the people" and should, therefore, offend none of them—if he blurs the issues and differences between the parties—if he neglects the party machinery and avoids his party's leadership—then he has not only weakened the political party as an instrument of the democratic process—he has dealt a blow to the democratic process itself. I prefer the example of Abe Lincoln, who loved politics with the passion of a born practitioner. For example, he waited up all night in 1863 to get the crucial returns on the Ohio governorship. When the Unionist candidate was elected, Lincoln wired: "Glory to God in the highest! Ohio has saved the nation!"

AS A MORAL LEADER

But the White House is not only the center of political leadership. It must be the center of moral leadership—a "bully pulpit," as Theodore Roosevelt described it. For only the President represents the national interest. And upon him alone converge all the needs and aspirations of all parts of the country, all departments of the Government, all nations of the world. It is not enough merely to represent prevailing sentiment—to follow McKinley's practice, as described by Joe Cannon, of "keeping his ear so close to the ground he got it full of grasshoppers." We will need in the Sixties a President who is willing and able to summon his national constituency to its finest hour—to alert the people to our dangers and our opportunities—to demand of them the sacrifices that will be necessary. Despite the increasing evidence of a lost national purpose and a soft national will, F. D. R.'s words in his first inaugural still ring true: "In every dark hour of our national life, a leadership of frankness and vigor has met with that understanding and support of the people themselves which is essential to victory."

Roosevelt fulfilled the role of moral leadership. So did Wilson and Lincoln, Truman and Jackson and Teddy Roosevelt. They led the people as well as the Government—they fought for great ideals as well as bills. And the time has come to demand that kind of leadership again. And so, as this vital campaign begins, let us discuss the issues the next President will face—but let us also discuss the powers and tools with which he must face them. For he must endow that office with extraordinary strength and vision. He must act in the image of Abraham Lincoln summoning his war time cabinet to a meeting on the Emancipation Proclamation. That Cabinet had been carefully chosen to please and reflect many elements in the country. But "I have gathered you together," Lincoln said, "to hear what I have written down. I do not wish your advice about the main matter—that I have determined for myself." And later when he went to sign it after several hours of exhausting handshaking that had left his arm weak, he said to those present: "If my name goes down in history, it will be for this act. My whole soul is in it. If my hand trembles when I sign this proclamation, all who examine the document hereafter will say: 'He hesitated.' " But Lincoln's hand did not tremble. He did not hesitate. He did not equivocate. For he was the President of the United States. It is in this spirit that we must go forth in the coming months and years.

THE EXECUTIVE
OFFICE

DOCUMENT 6 TABLE
OF ORGANIZATION
AND PERSONNEL

Though Congress and the political hustings regularly resound with demands that the "swollen federal bureaucracy" be cut down, there has been little variation in the size of the Executive Office since the end of World War II. The minute the ax is sharpened and it appears that abstract denunciations of "waste" and "padded payrolls" are to be converted into actual dismissals, an appropriate victim cannot be found. The Department of Defense, the Veterans' Administration, and the Post Office—which account for about two-thirds of the total manpower—are well protected against any cuts because they have massive constituencies in and out of Congress that will fight for their prerogatives. For example, Congress has constantly been forced to authorize more mail-carriers to cope with the postal problems created by an expanding population; a Congressman who may not get ten letters protesting his stand on foreign aid will get five hundred if his district has poor mail service. The State Department, without benefit of a constituency, is, of course, a prime target for suggested cuts. (A foreign policy is an expensive nuisance.) But, as this document shows, the State Department could hardly be cut very much—it has a smaller staff than the Federal Aviation Agency. Consequently the "economy bloc" in Congress lives in eternal frustration: the legislature invariably agrees with its rhetoric and then in the course of legislation—for example, by authorizing the "Moon Race" and billions for NASA to hold up the American end of "competitive coexistence" with the Soviets—it adds to the federal payroll.

ORGANIZATION AND PERSONNEL SUMMARY, JAN. 1, 1947–JAN. 1, 1962

Organization	Jan. 1—				
	1947	1952	1957	1961	1962
Executive Office of the President	1,027	1,252	1,217	2,753	1,609
Executive departments	1,790,264	2,124,156	2,075,807	1,992,886	2,050,529
Department of State	22,704	30,194	33,595	38,332	39,718
Department of Defense:					
Office of the Secretary of Defense		2,157	1,690	1,809	3,146
Department of the Army	629,194	530,883	430,212	380,674	397,499
Department of the Navy	377,284	462,835	393,332	342,979	352,927
Department of the Air Force		281,052	350,681	306,571	305,488
Department of the Treasury	102,447	89,409	78,424	76,736	80,191
Department of Justice	24,280	31,306	30,520	30,542	30,861
Post Office Department	458,988	511,609	523,416	573,160	586,235
Department of the Interior	49,693	54,964	48,578	50,973	53,946
Department of Agriculture	80,325	66,162	82,421	87,870	91,644
Department of Commerce	37,600	55,747	47,065	31,155	28,334
Department of Labor	7,749	7,638	5,927	6,938	7,669
Department of Health, Education, and Welfare			49,946	64,847	72,871
Independent agencies	471,334	359,004	299,489	348,771	366,726
Advisory Commission on Intergovernmental Relations				19	36
American Battle Monuments Commission	87	466	628	455	424
Atomic Energy Commission		5,790	6,673	6,824	6,784
Civil Aeronautics Board	502	570	603	755	776

Agency					
U.S. Civil Service Commission	3,440	4,053	4,450	3,605	3,833
Commission on Civil Rights				78	65
Commission of Fine Arts	2	2	4	6	6
District of Columbia Redevelopment Land Agency					
Economic Stabilization Agency					103
Export-Import Bank of Washington	118	16,063	38	96	
Farm Credit Administration		133	188	237	258
Federal Aviation Agency			570	241	239
Federal Civil Defense Administration		813	1,115	39,835	43,315
Federal Coal Mine Safety Board of Review			8	7	7
Federal Communications Commission	1,393	1,148	1,147	1,360	1,361
Federal Deposit Insurance Corporation	1,181	1,002	1,139	1,234	1,275
Federal Home Loan Bank Board			698	1,052	1,139
Federal Maritime Commission					142
Federal Mediation and Conciliation Service		357	341	341	361
Federal Power Commission	790	715	707	853	900
Federal Security Agency	31,516	36,661			
Federal Trade Commission	554	753	717	801	984
Federal Works Agency	24,420				
Foreign Claims Settlement Commission			114	49	61
General Services Administration		28,152	27,100	29,191	30,598
Housing and Home Finance Agency		12,318	9,935	11,244	12,261
Indian Claims Commission		11	14	14	20
Interstate Commerce Commission	2,286	1,863	2,098	2,380	2,400
Mutual Security Agency		4,226			
National Advisory Committee for Aeronautics	5,650	7,521	7,698	16,120	19,104
National Aeronautics and Space Administration					
National Capital Housing Authority	280	337	253	338	420
National Capital Planning Commission	24	19	34	45	56
National Housing Agency	18,960				
National Labor Relations Board	788	1,179	1,115	1,774	1,848

ORGANIZATION AND PERSONNEL SUMMARY, JAN. 1, 1947–JAN. 1, 1962 (Continued)

Organization	Jan. 1—				
	1947	1952	1957	1961	1962
National Mediation Board	91	95	104	115	139
National Science Foundation		57	485	941	1,154
Panama Canal Company	27,418	18,981	14,425	14,361	14,409
Railroad Retirement Board	2,559	2,125	2,251	2,177	2,115
Reconstruction Finance Corporation	9,522	2,710			
Renegotiation Board		51	442	129	249
Saint Lawrence Seaway Development Corporation			42	163	161
Securities and Exchange Commission	1,209	904	788	1,030	1,179
Selective Service Commission	7,906	8,551	7,243	6,710	7,044
Small Business Administration			950	2,325	2,876
Smithsonian Institution	822	864	1,094	1,446	1,463
Subversive Activities Control Board		22	33	27	27
Tariff Commission, United States	227	199	206	269	267
Tax Court of the United States	122	127	144	150	149
Tennessee Valley Authority	13,431	20,593	14,887	14,855	18,545
U.S. Information Agency			11,496	10,773	10,957
Veterans' Administration	226,896	178,317	177,378	173,475	176,458
Veterans' Education Appeals Board			5		
Virgin Islands Corporation		20		547	531
War Assets Administration	56,575				
Temporary commissions and agencies	32,565	1,236	129	324	227
Total	2,262,625	2,484,412	2,376,513	2,344,410	2,418,864

FROM *Organization of Federal Executive Departments and Agencies*, Senate Committee on Government Operations, Eighty-Seventh Congress, second session (Washington, D.C., Government Printing Office, 1962), pp. 70–71.

THE POWER
TO RECOMMEND
LEGISLATION

DOCUMENT 7 THE NEW FRONTIER'S PROGRAM

As one might suspect, the transformation of the Presidency discussed in connection with prior documents has had great impact on executive-legislative relationships. When Thomas Jefferson decided that a Presidential address to Congress was a remnant of monarchy—resembling the Royal Speech from the Throne that opens a session of the British Parliament—he simply sent written communications from time to time to the legislature. This custom continued until Woodrow Wilson entered office in 1913, and reestablished the practice of addressing Congress in person. And until 1921, each executive department separately presented its budgetary requests to Congress, and the legislature compiled the annual budget! Indeed, until Franklin Roosevelt moved into the White House, most major pieces of legislation were drafted in Congress, though often in response to a Presidential request.

Congress still has enormous authority over the process of legislation; it can and does rewrite proposals to meet its view of events. But it is clear that today a President has the power of legislative initiative if he chooses to exercise it. All bills submitted by government agencies to Congress, for example, have to be approved by the Bureau of the Budget, which is in the Executive Office of the President; a comprehensive budget is then prepared by the Bureau of the Budget and submitted in toto to Congress. In addition, the President can conduct a vigorous direct and indirect campaign on behalf of his proposals. He can ask Congress directly for his measures as President Kennedy did in the following message; he can exert pressure on their behalf indirectly by talking to influential Congressmen, by making statements at press conferences, and, of course, by appealing via radio and television to the populace. Moreover, his legislative liaison staff spends most of its time on the Hill conveying the President's sentiments to *recalcitrant Congressmen (President Kennedy's group was dubbed the "Irish Mafia").*

This document not only illustrates a direct Presidential campaign for legislation but provides a vivid example of the scope of Presidential interests: the range of topics gives a sharp insight into President Kennedy's conception of his function.

Mr. Vice President—my old colleague from Massachusetts and your new Speaker, John McCormack—Members of the 87th Congress —Ladies and Gentlemen:

This week we begin anew our joint and separate efforts to build the American future. But, sadly, we build without a man who linked a long past with the present and looked strongly to the future. "Mister Sam" Rayburn is gone. Neither this House nor this Nation is the same without him.

The Constitution makes us not rivals for power but partners for progress. We are all trustees for the American people, custodians of the American heritage. It is my task to *report* the State of the Union —to *improve* it is the task of us all.

In the past year, I have travelled not only across our own land but to other lands—to the North and to the South, and across the seas. And I have found, as I am sure you have in your travels, that people everywhere, in spite of occasional disappointments, look to us—not to our wealth or power, but to the splendor of our ideals. For our nation is commissioned by history to be either an observer of freedom's failure or the cause of its success. Our overriding obligation in the months ahead is to fulfill the world's hope by fulfilling our own faith.

I. STRENGTHENING THE ECONOMY

That task must begin at home. For if we cannot fulfill our own ideals here, we cannot expect others to accept them. And when the youngest child alive today has grown to the cares of manhood, our position in the world will be determined first of all by what provisions we make today—for his education, his health, his opportunities for a good home and a good job and a good life.

At home, we began the year in the valley of recession—we completed it on the high road of recovery and growth. With the help of new Congressionally approved or Administratively increased stimulants

FROM State of the Union Address by President John F. Kennedy, January 11, 1962, *Congressional Record,* Eighty-Seventh Congress, second session (Washington, D.C., Government Printing Office, 1962), Vol. 108, pp. 49–54.

to our economy, the number of major surplus labor areas has declined from 101 to 60; non-agricultural employment has increased by more than a million jobs; and the average factory work-week has risen to well over 40 hours. At the year's end the economy which Mr. Khrushchev once called a "stumbling horse" was racing to new records in consumer spending, labor income and industrial production.

We are gratified—but we are not satisfied. Too many unemployed are still looking for the blessings of our prosperity. As those who leave our schools and farms demand new jobs, automation takes old jobs away. To expand our growth and job opportunities, I urge on the Congress three measures:

First, the *Manpower Training and Development Act,* to stop the waste of able-bodied men and women who want to work, but whose only skill has been replaced by a machine, or moved with a mill, or shut down with a mine;

Second, the *Youth Employment Opportunities Act,* to help train and place not only the one million young Americans who are both out of school and out of work, but the twenty-six million young Americans entering the labor market in this decade; and

Third, the *8% tax credit for investment in machinery and equipment,* which, combined with planned revisions of depreciation allowances, will spur our modernization, our growth and our ability to compete abroad.

Moreover—pleasant as it may be to bask in the warmth of recovery —let us not forget that we have suffered three recessions in the last seven years. The time to repair the roof is when the sun is shining— by filling three basic gaps in our anti-recession protection. We need:

1. *First,* Presidential stand-by authority, subject to Congressional veto, *to adjust personal income tax rates downward within a specified range and time,* to slow down an economic decline before it has dragged us all down;

2. *Second,* Presidential stand-by authority, upon a given rise in the rate of unemployment, *to accelerate federal and federally-aided capital improvement programs;* and

3. *Third, a permanent strengthening of our unemployment compensation system*—to maintain for our fellow citizens searching for a job who cannot find it, their purchasing power and their living standards without constant resort as we have seen in recent years by the Congress and the Administration to temporary supplement.

If we enact this six-part program, we can show the whole world that a free economy need not be an unstable economy—that a free system need not leave men unemployed—and that a free society is not only the most productive but the most stable form of organization yet fashioned by man.

II. FIGHTING INFLATION

But recession is only one enemy of a free economy—inflation is another. Last year, despite rising production and demand, consumer prices held almost steady—and wholesale prices declined. This is the best record of overall price stability of any comparable period of recovery since the end of World War II.

Inflation too often follows in the shadow of growth—while price stability is made easy by stagnation, or controls. But we mean to maintain both stability and growth in a climate of freedom.

Our first line of defense against inflation is the good sense and public spirit of business and labor—keeping their total increases in wages and profits in step with productivity. There is no single statistical test to guide each company, and each union. But I strongly urge them, for the country's interest and for their own, to apply the test of public interest to these transactions.

Within this same framework of growth and wage-price stability:

This Administration has helped keep our economy competitive by widening the access of small business to credit and government contracts, and by stepping up the drive against monopoly, price-fixing and racketeering;

We will submit a *Federal Pay Reform* bill aimed at giving our classified, postal and other employees new pay scales more comparable to those of private industry;

We are holding the fiscal 1962 budget deficit far below the level incurred after the last recession in 1958; and, finally,

I am submitting for fiscal 1963 a balanced Federal Budget.

This is a joint responsibility, requiring Congressional cooperation on appropriations, and on three sources of income in particular:

First, an increase in *postal rates,* to end the postal deficit.

Second, passage of the *tax reforms* previously urged, to remove unwarranted tax preferences, and to apply to dividends and interest the same withholding requirement we have long applied to wages; and

Third, extension of the *present excise and corporation tax rates,* except for changes which will be recommended in a message affecting transportation.

III. GETTING AMERICA MOVING

But a stronger nation and economy require more than a balanced Budget. They require progress in those programs that spur our growth and fortify our strength.

THE POWER TO RECOMMEND LEGISLATION

CITIES

A strong America depends on its cities—America's glory, and some-times America's shame. To substitute sunlight for congestion and progress for decay, we have stepped up existing urban renewal and housing programs, and launched new ones—redoubled the attack on water pollution—speeded aid to airports, hospitals, highways and our declining mass transit system—and secured new weapons to combat organized crime, racketeering and youth delinquency, assisted by the coordinated and hard-hitting efforts of our investigative services: The FBI, the Internal Revenue, the Bureau of Narcotics and many others. We shall need further *anti-crime, mass transit* and *transportation* legislation—and new tools to fight *air pollution*. And with all this effort underway, both equity and common sense require that our nation's urban areas—containing three-fourths of our population—sit as equals at the Cabinet table. I urge a new *Department of Urban Affairs and Housing*.

AGRICULTURE AND RESOURCES

A strong America also depends on its farms and natural resources. American farmers took heart in 1961—from a billion dollar rise in farm income—and from a hopeful start on reducing farm surpluses. But we are still operating under a patchwork accumulation of old laws, which cost us $1 billion a year in CCC carrying charges alone, yet fail to halt rural poverty or boost farm earnings.

Our task is to master and turn to fully fruitful ends the magnificent productivity of our farms and farmers. The revolution on our own countryside stands in the sharpest contrast to the repeated farm failures of the Communist nations, and is a source of pride to us all. Since 1950 our agricultural output per man hour has actually doubled! Without new, realistic measures, it will someday swamp our farmers and our taxpayers in a national scandal or a farm depression.

I will, therefore, submit to the Congress a *new comprehensive farm program*—tailored to fit the use of our land and the supplies of each crop to the long-range needs of the Sixties—and designed to prevent chaos in the Sixties with a program of common sense.

We also need for the Sixties—if we are to bequeath our full national estate to our heirs—a *new long-range conservation and recreation program*—expansion of our superb *National Parks and Forests*—preservation of our authentic *wilderness areas*—new starts on *water and power projects* as our population steadily increases—and expanded *REA* generation and transmission loans.

But America stands for progress in human rights as well as economic affairs, and a strong America requires the assurance of full and equal rights to all its citizens, of any race or of any color. This Administration has shown as never before how much could be done through the full use of executive powers—through the enforcement of laws already passed by the Congress—through persuasion, negotiation and litigation, to secure the constitutional rights of all: the right to vote, the right to travel without hindrance across state lines, and the right to free public education.

I issued last March a comprehensive order to guarantee the right to equal employment opportunity in all federal agencies and contractors. The Vice President's Committee thus created has done much, including the voluntary "Plans for Progress" which, in all sections of the country, are achieving a quiet but striking success in opening up to all races new professional, supervisory and other job opportunities.

But there is much more to be done—by the Executive, by the courts, and by the Congress. Among the bills now pending before you, on which the Executive Departments will comment in detail, are appropriate methods of strengthening these basic rights which have our full support. The right to vote, for example, should no longer be denied through such arbitrary devices on a local level, sometimes abused, as literacy tests and poll taxes. As we approach the 100th anniversary next January of the Emancipation Proclamation, let the acts of every branch of the Government—and every citizen—portray that "righteousness that exalteth a nation."

HEALTH AND WELFARE

Finally, a strong America cannot neglect the aspirations of its citizens —the welfare of the needy, the health care of the elderly, the education of the young. For we are not developing the nation's wealth for its own sake. Wealth is the means—and people are the end. All our material riches will avail us little if we do not use them to expand the opportunities of our people.

Last year, we improved the diet of needy people—provided more hot lunches and fresh milk to school children—built more college dormitories—and, for the elderly, expanded private housing, and nursing homes, and health services and Social Security. But we have just begun.

To help those least fortunate of all, I am recommending a *new public welfare program*, stressing services instead of support, rehabilitation instead of relief, and training for useful work instead of prolonged dependency.

To relieve the critical shortage of doctors and dentists, and this is a matter which should concern us all, and expand research, I urge action to *aid medical and dental colleges and scholarships* and *establish new National Institutes of Health.*

To take advantage of modern vaccination achievements, I am proposing a *mass immunization program,* aimed at the virtual elimination of such ancient enemies of our children as polio, diphtheria, whooping cough and tetanus.

To protect our consumers from the careless and the unscrupulous, I shall recommend *improvements in the Food and Drug laws*—strengthening inspection and standards, halting unsafe and worthless products, preventing misleading labels, and cracking down on the illicit sale of habit-forming drugs.

But in matters of health, no piece of unfinished business is more important or more urgent than the enactment under the Social Security system of health insurance for the aged.

For our older citizens have longer and more frequent illnesses, higher hospital and medical bills and too little income to pay them. Private health insurance helps some—but its cost is high and its coverage limited. Public welfare cannot help those too proud to seek relief but hard-pressed to pay their own bills. Nor can their children or grandchildren always sacrifice their own health and family budgets to meet this constant drain.

Social Security has long helped to meet the hardships of retirement, death and disability. I now urge that its coverage be extended without further delay to provide health insurance for the elderly.

EDUCATION

Equally important to our strength is the quality of our education. Eight million adult Americans are classified as functionally illiterate. This is a disturbing figure—reflected in Selective Service rejection rates —reflected in welfare rolls and crime rates. I shall recommend plans for a massive attack to *end this adult illiteracy.*

I shall also recommend bills to *improve educational quality,* to *stimulate the arts,* and, at the college level, to provide *federal loans for the construction of academic facilities and federally-financed scholarships.*

If this nation is to grow in wisdom and strength, then every able-bodied high school graduate should have the opportunity to develop his talents. Yet nearly half lack either the funds or the facilities to attend college. Enrollments are going to double in our colleges in the short space of ten years. The annual cost per student is skyrocketing to astronomical levels—now averaging $1,650 a year, although almost half of our families earn less than $5,000 a year. They cannot afford such costs—but this nation cannot afford to maintain its military power and neglect its brainpower.

But excellence in education must begin at the elementary level. I sent to the Congress last year a proposal for *federal aid to public school construction and teachers' salaries.* I believe that bill, which passed the Senate and received House Committee approval, offered the minimum amount required by our needs and—in terms of across-the-board aid —the maximum scope permitted by our Constitution. I therefore see no reason to weaken or withdraw that bill: and I urge its passage at this session.

"Civilization," said H. G. Wells, "is a race between education and catastrophe." It is up to you in this Congress to determine the winner of that race. These are not unrelated measures addressed to specific gaps or grievances in our national life. They are the pattern of our intentions and the foundation of our hopes. "I believe in democracy," said Woodrow Wilson, "because it releases the energy of every human being. The dynamic of democracy is the power and the purpose of the individual." And the policy of this Administration is to give to the individual the opportunity to realize his own highest possibilities.

Our program is to open to all the opportunity for steady and productive employment, to remove from all the handicap of arbitrary or irrational exclusion, to offer to all the facilities for education and health and welfare, to make society the servant of the individual and the individual the source of progress, and thus to realize for all the full promise of American life.

IV. OUR GOALS ABROAD

All of these efforts at home give meaning to our efforts abroad. Since the close of the Second World War, a global civil war has divided and tormented mankind. But it is not our military might, or our higher standard of living, that has most distinguished us from our adversaries. It is our belief that the state is the servant of the citizen and not his master.

This basic clash of ideas and wills is but one of the forces reshaping our globe—swept as it is by the tides of hope and fear, by crises in the headlines today that become mere footnotes tomorrow. Both the successes and the setbacks of the past year remain on our agenda of unfinished business. For every apparent blessing contains the seeds of danger—every area of trouble gives out a ray of hope—and the one unchangeable certainty is that nothing is certain or unchangeable.

Yet our basic goal remains the same: a peaceful world community of free and independent states—free to choose their own future and their own system, so long as it does not threaten the freedom of others.

Some may choose forms and ways we would not choose for ourselves—but it is not for us that they are choosing. We can welcome diversity—the Communists cannot. For we offer a world of choice— and they offer a world of coercion. And the way of the past shows

THE POWER TO RECOMMEND LEGISLATION

clearly that freedom, not coercion, is the wave of the future. At times our goal has been obscured by crisis or endangered by conflict—but it draws sustenance from five basic sources of strength:

the moral and physical strength of the United States;

the united strength of the Atlantic Community;

the regional strength of our Hemispheric relations;

the creative strength of our efforts in the new and developing nations; and

the peace-keeping strength of the United Nations.

V. OUR MILITARY STRENGTH

Our moral and physical strength begins at home as already discussed. But it includes our military strength as well. So long as fanaticism and fear brood over the affairs of men, we must arm to deter others from aggression.

In the past twelve months our military posture has steadily improved. We increased the previous defense budget by 15%—not in the expectation of war but for the preservation of peace. We more than doubled our acquisition rate of Polaris submarines—we doubled the production capacity for Minuteman missiles—and increased by 50% the number of manned bombers standing ready on a 15-minute alert. This year the combined force levels planned under our new Defense budget—including nearly three hundred additional Polaris and Minuteman missiles—have been precisely calculated to insure the continuing strength of our nuclear deterrent.

But our strength may be tested at many levels. We intend to have at all times the capacity to resist non-nuclear or limited attacks—as a complement to our nuclear capacity, not as a substitute. We have rejected any all-or-nothing posture which would leave no choice but inglorious retreat or unlimited retaliation.

Thus we have doubled the number of ready combat divisions in the Army's strategic reserve—increased our troops in Europe—built up the Marines—added new airlift and sealift capacity—modernized our weapons and ammunition—expanded our anti-guerrilla forces—and increased the active fleet by more than 70 vessels and our tactical air forces by nearly a dozen wings.

Because we needed to reach this higher long-term level of readiness more quickly, 155,000 members of the Reserve and National Guard were activated under the Act of this Congress. Some disruptions and distress were inevitable. But the overwhelming majority bear their burdens—and their nation's burdens—with admirable and traditional devotion.

In the coming years our reserve programs will be revised—two Army Divisions will, I hope, replace those Guard Divisions on duty—

and substantial other increases will boost our Air Force fighter units, the procurement of equipment, and our continental defense and warning efforts. The nation's first serious civil defense shelter program is underway, identifying, marking and stocking 50 million spaces; and I urge your approval of *federal incentives for the construction of public fall-out shelters in schools, hospitals and similar centers.*

VI. THE UNITED NATIONS

But arms alone are not enough to keep the peace—it must be kept by men. Our instrument and our hope is the United Nations—and I see little merit in the impatience of those who would abandon this imperfect world instrument because they dislike our imperfect world. For the troubles of a world organization merely reflect the troubles of the world itself. And if the organization is weakened, these troubles can only increase. We may not always agree with every detailed action taken by every officer of the United Nations, or with every voting majority. But as an institution, it should have in the future, as it has had in the past, since its inception, no stronger or more faithful member than the United States of America.

In 1961, the peace-keeping strength of the United Nations was reinforced. And those who preferred or predicted its demise, envisioning a troika in the seat of Hammarskjold—or Red China inside the Assembly—have seen instead a new vigor, under a new Secretary General and a fully independent Secretariat. In making plans for a new forum and principles on disarmament—for peace-keeping in outer space—for a decade of development effort—the UN fulfilled its Charter's lofty aims.

Eighteen months ago the tangled and turbulent Congo presented the UN with its gravest challenge. The prospect was one of chaos—or certain big-power confrontation, with all its hazards and all of its risks, to us and others. Today the hopes have improved for peaceful conciliation within a united Congo. This is the objective of our policy in this important area.

No policeman is universally popular—particularly when he uses his stick to restore law and order on his beat. Those members who are willing to contribute their votes and their views—but very little else—have created a serious deficit by refusing to pay their share of special UN assessments. Yet they do pay their annual assessments to retain their votes—and a *new UN Bond issue,* financing special operations for the next 18 months, is to be repaid with interest from these regular assessments. This is clearly in our interest. It will not only keep the UN solvent, but require all voting members to pay their fair share of its activities. Our share of special operations has long been much higher than our share of the annual assessment—and the bond issue will in effect reduce our disproportionate obligation. For these reasons, I am urging Congress to approve our participation.

With the approval of this Congress, we have undertaken in the past year a great new effort in outer space. Our aim is not simply to be first on the moon any more than Charles Lindbergh's real aim was to be first to Paris. His aim was to develop the techniques and the authority of this country and other countries in the field of the air and the atmosphere. And our objective in making this effort—which we hope will place one of our citizens on the moon—is to develop in a new frontier of science, commerce and cooperation, the position of the United States and the free world. This nation belongs among the first to explore it. And among the first, if not the first, we shall be.

We are offering know-how and cooperation to the United Nations. Our satellites will soon be providing other nations with improved weather observations. And I shall soon send to the Congress a measure to govern the financing and operation of an *International Communications Satellite system,* in a manner consistent with the public interest and our foreign policy.

But peace in space will help us naught once peace on earth is gone. World order will be secured only when the whole world has laid down these weapons which seem to offer us present security but threaten our future survival of the human race. That armistice day seems very far away. The vast resources of this planet are being devoted more and more to the means of destroying, instead of enriching, human life.

But the world was not meant to be a prison in which man awaits his executioner. Nor has mankind survived the tests and trials of thousands of years to surrender everything including its existence now. This nation has the will and the faith to make a supreme effort to break the log jam on disarmament and nuclear tests—and we will persist until we prevail, until the rule of law has replaced the ever-dangerous use of force.

VII. LATIN AMERICA

I turn now to a prospect of great promise: our hemispheric relations. The Alliance for Progress is being rapidly transformed from proposal to program. Last month in Latin America I saw for myself the quickening of hope, the revival of confidence, the new trust in our country—among workers and farmers as well as diplomats. We have pledged our help in speeding their economic, educational and social progress. The Latin American Republics have in turn pledged a new and strenuous effort of self-help and self-reform.

To support this historic undertaking I am proposing under the authority contained in the bills of the last session of Congress a *special long-term Alliance for Progress fund* of $3 billion. Combined with our Food for Peace, Export-Import Bank and other resources, this will provide more than $1 billion a year in new support for the Alliance. In addition, we have increased twelvefold our Spanish and Portuguese-language broadcasting in Latin America, and improved hemispheric trade and defense. And while the blight of communism has been increasingly exposed and isolated in the Americas, liberty has scored a gain. The people of the Dominican Republic, with our firm encouragement and help and those of our sister Republics of this hemisphere, are safely passing through the treacherous course from dictatorship through disorder toward democracy.

VIII. THE NEW AND DEVELOPING NATIONS

Our efforts to help other new or developing nations, and to strengthen their stand for freedom, have also made steady progress. A newly unified Agency for International Development is reorienting our foreign assistance to emphasize long-term development loans instead of grants, more economic aid instead of military, individual plans to meet the individual needs of the nations, and new standards on what they must do themselves to marshal their own resources.

A newly conceived Peace Corps is winning friends and helping people in fourteen countries—supplying trained and dedicated young men and women, to give these new nations a hand in building a society, and a glimpse of the best that is in our country. If there be a problem here, it is that we cannot supply the spontaneous and mounting demand.

A newly-expanded Food for Peace Program is feeding the hungry of many lands with the abundance of our productive farms—providing lunches for children in school, wages for economic development, relief for the victims of flood and famine, and a better diet for millions whose daily bread is their chief concern.

These programs help people; and, by helping people, they help freedom. The views of their governments may sometimes be very different from ours—but events in Africa, the Middle East and Eastern Europe teach us never to write off any nation as lost to the Communists. That is the lesson of our time. We support the independence of those newer or weaker states whose history, geography, economy or lack of power impels them to remain outside "entangling alliances" —as we did for more than a century. For the independence of nations is a bar to the Communists' "grand design"—it is the basis of our own.

In the past year, for example, we have urged a neutral and independent Laos—regained there a common policy with our major allies —and insisted that a cease-fire precede negotiations. While a workable formula for supervising its independence is still to be achieved, both

THE POWER TO RECOMMEND LEGISLATION

the spread of war which might have involved this country also, and a communist occupation have thus far been prevented.

A satisfactory settlement in Laos would also help to achieve and safeguard the peace in Viet Nam—where the foe is increasing his tactics of terror—where our own efforts have been stepped up—and where the local government has initiated new programs and reforms to broaden the base of resistance. The systematic aggression now bleeding that country is not a "war of liberation"—for Viet Nam is already free. It is a war of attempted subjugation—and it will be resisted.

IX. THE ATLANTIC COMMUNITY

Finally, the united strength of the Atlantic Community has flourished in the last year under severe tests. NATO has increased both the number and the readiness of its air, ground and naval units—both its nuclear and non-nuclear capabilities. Even greater efforts by all of its members are still required. Nevertheless our unity of purpose and will has been, I believe, immeasurably strengthened.

The threat to the brave city of Berlin remains. In these last six months the Allies have made it unmistakably clear that our presence in Berlin, our free access thereto, and the freedom of two million West Berliners would not be surrendered either to force or through appeasement—and to maintain those rights and obligations, we are prepared to talk, when appropriate, and to fight, if necessary. Every member of NATO stands with us in a common commitment to preserve this symbol of free men's will to remain free.

I cannot now predict the course of future negotiations over Berlin. I can only say that we are sparing no honorable effort to find a peaceful and mutually acceptable resolution of this problem. I believe such a resolution can be found, and with it an improvement in our relations with the Soviet Union, if only the leaders in the Kremlin will recognize the basic rights and interests involved, and the interest of all mankind in peace.

But the Atlantic community is no longer concerned with purely military aims. As its common undertakings grow at an ever-increasing pace, we are, and will increasingly be, partners in aid, trade, defense, diplomacy and monetary affairs.

The emergence of the new Europe is being matched by the emergence of new ties across the Atlantic. It is a matter of undramatic daily cooperation in hundreds of workaday tasks: of currencies kept in effective relation, of development loans meshed together, of standardized weapons, and concerted diplomatic positions. The Atlantic Community grows, not like a volcanic mountain by one mighty explosion, but like a coral reef from the accumulating activity of all.

Thus, we in the free world are moving steadily toward unity and cooperation, in the teeth of that old Bolshevik prophecy, and at the very time when extraordinary rumbles of discord can be heard across the Iron Curtain. It is not free societies which bear within them the seeds of inevitable disunity.

X. OUR BALANCE OF PAYMENTS

On one special problem, of great concern to our friends and to us, I am proud to give the Congress an encouraging report. Our efforts to safeguard the dollar are progressing. In the eleven months preceding last February 1, we suffered a net loss of nearly $2 billion in gold. In the eleven months that followed, the loss was just over a half a billion dollars. And our deficit in our basic transactions with the rest of the world—trade, defense, foreign aid, and capital, excluding volatile short-term flows—has been reduced from $2 billion for 1960 to about one-third that amount for 1961. Speculative fever against the dollar is ending—and confidence in the dollar has been restored.

We did not—and could not—achieve these gains through import restrictions, troop withdrawals, exchange controls, dollar devaluation or choking off domestic recovery. We acted not in panic but in perspective. But the problem is not yet solved. Persistently large deficits would endanger our economic growth and our military and defense commitments abroad. Our goal must be a reasonable equilibrium in our balance of payments. With the cooperation of the Congress, business, labor and our major allies, that goal can be reached.

We shall continue to attract foreign tourists and foreign investments to our shores, to seek increased military purchases here by our allies, to minimize the outflow of dollars involved in our own military efforts, to maximize foreign aid procurements from American firms, to urge increased aid from other fortunate nations to the less fortunate, to seek tax laws which do not favor investment in other industrialized nations or tax havens, and to urge coordination of allied fiscal and monetary policies so as to discourage large and disturbing capital movements.

TRADE

Above all, if we are to pay for our commitments abroad we must expand our exports. Our businessmen must be export-conscious and export-competitive. Our tax policies must spur modernization of our plants—our wage and price gains must be consistent with productivity to hold the line in prices—our export credit and promotion campaigns for American industry must continue to expand.

But the greatest challenge of all is posed by the growth of the European Common Market. Assuming the accession of the United Kingdom, there will arise across the Atlantic a trading partner behind a single external tariff similar to ours with an economy which nearly equals our own. Will we in this country adapt our thinking to these new prospects and patterns—or will we wait until events have passed us by?

This is the year to decide. The Reciprocal Trade Act is expiring. We need a new law—a wholly new approach—and a bold new instrument of American trade policy. Our decision could well affect the unity of the West, the course of the Cold War and the economic growth of our nation for a generation or more to come.

If we move decisively, our factories and farms can increase their sales to their richest, fastest-growing market. Our exports will increase. Our balance of payments position will improve. And we will have forged across the Atlantic a trading partnership with vast resources for freedom.

If, on the other hand, we hang back in deference to local economic pressures, we will find ourselves cut off from our major allies. Industries, and I believe this is most vital, will move their plants and jobs and capital inside the walls of the Common Market and jobs, therefore, will be lost in the United States if they cannot otherwise compete for its consumers.

Our farm surpluses and our balance of trade, as you all know, to Europe—the Common Market—in farm products is nearly 3 or 4 to 1 in our favor, amounting to one of the best earners of dollars in our balance-of-payments structure. And without entrance to this market—without the ability to enter it—our farm surpluses will pile up in the Middle West, tobacco in the South and other commodities which have gone to Western Europe for fifteen years.

Our balance of payments position will worsen. Our consumers will lack a wider choice of goods at lower prices. And millions of American workers—whose jobs depend on the sale or the transportation or the distribution of exports or imports, or whose jobs will be endangered by the movement of our capital to Europe, or whose jobs can be maintained only in an expanding economy—these millions of workers in your home states and mine will see their real interests sacrificed.

Members of the Congress: The United States did not rise to greatness by waiting for others to lead. This nation is the world's foremost manufacturer, farmer, banker, consumer and exporter. The Common Market is moving ahead at an economic growth rate twice ours. The Communist economic offensive is underway. The opportunity is ours—the initiative is up to us—and I believe that 1962 is the time.

To seize that initiative, I shall shortly send to the Congress a new five-year Trade Expansion Action, far-reaching in scope but designed with great care to make certain that its benefits to our people far outweigh any risks. The bill will permit the gradual elimination of tariffs here in the United States and in the Common Market on those items in which we together supply 80% of the world's trade—mostly items in which our own ability to compete is demonstrated by the fact that we sell abroad in these items substantially more than we import. This step will make it possible for our major industries to compete with their counterparts in Western Europe for access to European consumers.

On the other hand, the bill will permit a gradual reduction of duties up to 50%—permit bargaining by major categories—and provide for appropriate and tested forms of assistance to firms and employees adjusting to import competition. We are not neglecting the safeguards provided by peril points, an escape clause, or the National Security Amendment. Nor are we abandoning our non-European friends or our traditional "most-favored nation" principle. On the contrary, the bill will provide new encouragement for their sale of tropical agricultural products, so important to our friends in Latin America, who have long depended upon the European market and now find themselves faced with new challenges which we must join with them in overcoming.

Concessions, in this bargaining, must of course be reciprocal, not unilateral. The Common Market will not fulfill its own high promise unless its outside tariff walls are low. The dangers of restriction or timidity in our own policy have counterparts for our friends in Europe. For together we face a common challenge: to enlarge the prosperity of free men everywhere—to build in partnership a new trading community in which all free nations may gain from the productive energy of free competitive effort.

These various elements in our foreign policy lead, as I have said, to a single goal—the goal of a peaceful world of free and independent states. This is our guide for the present and our vision for the future —a free community of nations, independent but interdependent, uniting north and south, east and west, in one great family of man, outgrowing and transcending the hates and fears that rend our age.

We will not reach that goal today, or tomorrow. We may not reach it in our lifetime. But the quest is the greatest adventure of our century. We sometimes chafe at the burdens of our obligations, the complexity of our decisions, the agony of our choices. But there is no comfort or security for us in evasion, no solution in abdication, no relief in irresponsibility.

A year ago, in assuming the tasks of the Presidency, I said that few generations, in all history, had been granted the role of being the great defender of freedom in its hour of maximum danger. This is our good fortune; and I welcome it now as I did a year ago. For it is the fate of this generation—of you in the Congress and of me as President— to live with a struggle we did not start, in a world we did not make. But the pressures of life are not always distributed by choice. And while no nation has ever faced such a challenge, no nation has ever been so ready to seize the burden and glory of freedom, and in this high endeavor may God watch over the United States of America.

THE POWER
TO EXECUTE LAWS

DOCUMENT 8 EISENHOWER
DISPATCHES TROOPS
TO LITTLE ROCK

In a democratic society, most laws are essentially self-executing—
that is, all but a handful of citizens obey them because they reflect
the consensus of the community. The criminal code is therefore invoked to handle a small number of deliberate malefactors—and to
remind the ambivalent members of society that "crime does not pay."
In the United States, the great bulk of criminal prosecutions is disposed of by state courts operating under state law. The Supreme
Court intervenes from time to time to redefine or clarify responsibilities and jurisdictions of state courts, but in between, little tension
develops between state and federal jurisdictions.

However, since the Supreme Court held in 1954 that racial segregation could not be enforced in public schools without violating the
equal-protection clause of the Fourteenth Amendment—a decision
that has since been expanded to counter any state requirement of
racial discrimination—there have been an increasing number of con-
frontations between state authority and federal power. In these instances, the normal standards of law enforcement have been under-
mined by the resistance not of individual citizens, but of organized
units of state governmental power. The situation reached the boiling
point in 1957, when a federal court ordered the integration of the
public schools in Little Rock, Arkansas; Governor Faubus, backed by
his legislature, ordered state officers to defy the federal writ and
called out the state guard to prevent United States marshals from
enforcing the laws of the United States.

When efforts at compromise failed, President Eisenhower, faced
with a showdown, called on the Army to move into Little Rock and
enforce the court order. Five years later, in September 1962, President Kennedy, confronted with a similar problem at Oxford, Mississippi, was eventually forced to employ troops to protect a Negro

student who had been admitted under court order to the University of Mississippi. A year after that, in June 1963, federal troops were prepared to deal with the racial crisis in Alabama that arose because Governor Wallace, refusing to conform to the constitutional mandate, made an ultimately futile attempt to block the admission of two Negroes to the University of Alabama.

In this selection, President Eisenhower carefully notes that, ordinarily, the running of the American school system belongs strictly in the hands of state and local officials, but he argues that the presence of mob rule in Little Rock has made it a special case. He justifies his use of paratroops on the ground that it is a crucial responsibility of the President to ensure that the decisions of the Supreme Court are carried out.

Good Evening, My Fellow Citizens:

For a few minutes this evening I want to speak to you about the serious situation that has arisen in Little Rock. To make this talk I have come to the President's office in the White House. I could have spoken from Rhode Island, where I have been staying recently, but I felt that, in speaking from the house of Lincoln, of Jackson and of Wilson, my words would better convey both the sadness I feel in the action I was compelled today to take and the firmness with which I intend to pursue this course until the orders of the Federal Court at Little Rock can be executed without unlawful interference.

In that city, under the leadership of demagogic extremists, disorderly mobs have deliberately prevented the carrying out of proper orders from a Federal Court. Local authorities have not eliminated that violent opposition and, under the law, I yesterday issued a Proclamation calling upon the mob to disperse.

This morning the mob again gathered in front of the Central High School of Little Rock, obviously for the purpose of again preventing the carrying out of the Court's order relating to the admission of Negro children to that school.

Whenever normal agencies prove inadequate to the task and it becomes necessary for the Executive Branch of the Federal Government to use its powers and authority to uphold Federal Courts, the President's responsibility is inescapable.

In accordance with that responsibility, I have today issued an Execu-

FROM Radio and Television Address to the American People on the Situation in Little Rock by President Dwight D. Eisenhower, September 24, 1957, *Public Papers of the Presidents of the United States: Dwight D. Eisenhower, 1957* (Washington, D.C., Government Printing Office, 1958), pp. 689–94.

THE POWER TO EXECUTE LAWS

tive Order directing the use of troops under Federal authority to aid in the execution of Federal law at Little Rock, Arkansas. This became necessary when my Proclamation of yesterday was not observed, and the obstruction of justice still continues.

It is important that the reasons for my action be understood by all our citizens.

As you know, the Supreme Court of the United States has decided that separate public educational facilities for the races are inherently unequal and therefore compulsory school segregation laws are unconstitutional.

Our personal opinions about the decision have no bearing on the matter of enforcement; the responsibility and authority of the Supreme Court to interpret the Constitution are very clear. Local Federal Courts were instructed by the Supreme Court to issue such orders and decrees as might be necessary to achieve admission to public schools without regard to race—and with all deliberate speed.

During the past several years, many communities in our Southern States have instituted public school plans for gradual progress in the enrollment and attendance of school children of all races in order to bring themselves into compliance with the law of the land.

They thus demonstrated to the world that we are a nation in which laws, not men, are supreme.

I regret to say that this truth—the cornerstone of our liberties— was not observed in this instance.

It was my hope that this localized situation would be brought under control by city and State authorities. If the use of local police powers had been sufficient, our traditional method of leaving the problems in those hands would have been pursued. But when large gatherings of obstructionists made it impossible for the decrees of the Court to be carried out, both the law and the national interest demanded that the President take action.

Here is the sequence of events in the development of the Little Rock school case.

In May of 1955, the Little Rock School Board approved a moderate plan for the gradual desegregation of the public schools in that city. It provided that a start toward integration would be made at the present term in the high school, and that the plan would be in full operation by 1963. Here I might say that in a number of communities in Arkansas integration in the schools has already started and without violence of any kind. Now this Little Rock plan was challenged in the courts by some who believed that the period of time as proposed in the plan was too long.

The United States Court at Little Rock, which has supervisory responsibility under the law for the plan of desegregation in the public schools, dismissed the challenge, thus approving a gradual rather than an abrupt change from the existing system. The court found that the school board had acted in good faith in planning for a public school system free from racial discrimination.

Since that time, the court has on three separate occasions issued orders directing that the plan be carried out. All persons were instructed to refrain from interfering with the efforts of the school board to comply with the law.

Proper and sensible observance of the law then demanded the respectful obedience which the nation has a right to expect from all its people. This, unfortunately, has not been the case at Little Rock. Certain misguided persons, many of them imported into Little Rock by agitators, have insisted upon defying the law and have sought to bring it into disrepute. The orders of the court have thus been frustrated.

The very basis of our individual rights and freedoms rests upon the certainty that the President and the Executive Branch of Government will support and insure the carrying out of the decisions of the Federal Courts, even, when necessary with all the means at the President's command.

Unless the President did so, anarchy would result.

There would be no security for any except that which each one of us could provide for himself.

The interest of the nation in the proper fulfillment of the law's requirements cannot yield to opposition and demonstrations by some few persons.

Mob rule cannot be allowed to override the decisions of our courts.

Now, let me make it very clear that Federal troops are not being used to relieve local and state authorities of their primary duty to preserve the peace and order of the community. Nor are the troops there for the purpose of taking over the responsibility of the School Board and the other responsible local officials in running Central High School. The running of our school system and the maintenance of peace and order in each of our States are strictly local affairs and the Federal Government does not interfere except in a very few special cases and when requested by one of the several States. In the present case the troops are there, pursuant to law, solely for the purpose of preventing interference with the orders of the Court.

The proper use of the powers of the Executive Branch to enforce the orders of a Federal Court is limited to extraordinary and compelling circumstances. Manifestly, such an extreme situation has been created in Little Rock. This challenge must be met and with such measures as will preserve to the people as a whole their lawfully-protected rights in a climate permitting their free and fair exercise.

The overwhelming majority of our people in every section of the country are united in their respect for observance of the law—even in those cases where they may disagree with that law.

They deplore the call of extremists to violence.

The decision of the Supreme Court concerning school integration, of course, affects the South more seriously than it does other sections of the country. In that region I have many warm friends, some of them in the city of Little Rock. I have deemed it a great personal privilege to spend in our Southland tours of duty while in the military service and enjoyable recreational periods since that time.

So from intimate personal knowledge, I know that the overwhelming majority of the people in the South—including those of Arkansas and of Little Rock—are of good will, united in their efforts to preserve and respect the law even when they disagree with it.

They do not sympathize with mob rule. They, like the rest of our nation, have proved in two great wars their readiness to sacrifice for America.

A foundation of our American way of life is our national respect for law.

In the South, as elsewhere, citizens are keenly aware of the tremendous disservice that has been done to the people of Arkansas in the eyes of the nation, and that has been done to the nation in the eyes of the world.

At a time when we face grave situations abroad because of the hatred that Communism bears toward a system of government based on human rights, it would be difficult to exaggerate the harm that is being done to the prestige and influence, and indeed to the safety, of our nation and the world.

Our enemies are gloating over this incident and using it everywhere to misrepresent our whole nation. We are portrayed as a violator of those standards of conduct which the peoples of the world united to proclaim in the Charter of the United Nations. There they affirmed "faith in fundamental human rights" and "in the dignity and worth of the human person" and they did so "without distinction as to race, sex, language or religion."

And so, with deep confidence, I call upon the citizens of the State of Arkansas to assist in bringing to an immediate end all interference with the law and its processes. If resistance to the Federal Court orders ceases at once, the further presence of Federal troops will be unnecessary and the City of Little Rock will return to its normal habits of peace and order and a blot upon the fair name and high honor of our nation in the world will be removed.

Thus will be restored the image of America and of all its parts as one nation, indivisible, with liberty and justice for all.

Good night, and thank you very much.

FLORIDA
CONDEMNS
EISENHOWER

*The President is obliged to see that the laws are faithfully executed
and to prevent unlawful conspiracies and obstructions of national
authority. When the law of the land, as interpreted by the Supreme
Court, is challenged, it is the President's job to enforce these judicial
decisions. However, Presidential efforts to implement the Court's
1954 desegregation decision have met with policies of "massive resistance" in the states of the Deep South. Since no policy is complete
without a philosophy to justify it, great efforts have been made to
resurrect the doctrine of states' rights from its resting place in the
constitutional mummy room. President Eisenhower's decision to send
federal troops into Little Rock to enforce desegregation (see Document 8) triggered this shotgun indictment by the Florida state senate.*

*This selection contends that the President's powers are limited to
those specifically enumerated in the Constitution and that the states
have never surrendered to the President their right to exercise discretion in local matters as stipulated in the Tenth Amendment. Moreover, it charges that the Governor did not request federal help, that
no state of rebellion existed in Arkansas, and that the President acted
on the authority of an unconstitutional law. In short, the document
argues that President Eisenhower gravely abused his executive powers
by taking action without constitutional authority. The existence of the
Fourteenth Amendment is, of course, ignored.*

A memorial to the Congress of the United States to enact measures
tending to cause the withdrawal of federal military forces from the
occupation of Little Rock, Arkansas, and prevent the further intrusion
by federal military troops on the constitutional rights of the sovereign
states of the union, by withholding of appropriations and public funds
from such troops while so engaged, thereby guaranteeing the sovereign
states freedom from military rule as contemplated by the first four
articles [of] the Constitution.

Whereas, the Legislature of Florida, during the 1957 Legislative Session, through Senate Concurrent Resolution No. 72, unequivocally
expressed a firm and determined resolution to maintain and defend the
Constitution of the United States against every attempt, whether for-

FROM Florida State Senate Memorial Number 19X, October 29, 1957, *Race
Relations Law Reporter,* Vol. 2 (December 1957), No. 2, pp. 1171–73.

eign or domestic, to undermine and destroy the fundamental principles, embodied in our basic law, by which the liberty of the people and the sovereignty of the states, in their proper spheres, have long been protected and assured, and

Whereas, the Legislature of Florida doth hereby express a firm belief that the recent action of the President of the United States, in inflicting military rule upon the sovereign state of Arkansas, is a far more serious threat to the security of the Nation and our constitutional form of government than any possible threat from abroad, and

Whereas, the Legislature of Florida lately did explicitly and peremptorily assert that it viewed the powers of the federal government as resulting solely from the compact to which the states are parties, as limited by the plain sense and intention of the instrument creating that compact, which compact carefully expressed the limited powers of the President of the United States, and

Whereas, the Legislature of Florida did assert most clearly that the powers of the federal government, including those of the President, are valid only to the extent that such powers have been enumerated in the compact to which the various states assented originally and to which the states have assented in subsequent amendments validly adopted and ratified, and

Whereas, the Legislature of Florida did consider that the very nature of this basic compact, apparent upon its face, is that the ratifying states, parties thereto, have agreed voluntarily to surrender certain of their sovereign rights, but only certain of these sovereign rights, to a federal government thus constituted; and that all powers not delegated to the United States, including the President thereof, by the Constitution, or prohibited by it to the states, have been reserved to the states, respectively, or to the people, and

Whereas, the several sovereign states have at no time surrendered to the federal government their right under the Tenth Amendment to the Constitution to exercise their discretion in the regulation of matters of strictly local concern, and

Whereas, the sovereign states, in ratifying the Fourteenth Amendment to the Constitution, did not agree that the power to regulate matters of local concern be prohibited to them thereby, and

Whereas, the Legislature of Florida emphatically denies that the President of the United States had the right which he asserted recently to peremptorily use federal troops in the sovereign state of Arkansas to compel the enforcement of a questionable judicial edict requiring the enforced integration of the public schools therein, and

Whereas, the threats and coercive measures of the federal military troops occupying the sovereign state of Arkansas constitute a deliberate, palpable, and dangerous attempt by the President and the federal government to prohibit to the states certain rights and powers never surrendered by them, and

Whereas, the President of the United States, without the request, consent, and in the absence of the Governor, ordered federal troops to occupy a portion of the sovereign state of Arkansas, and such troops through the exercise of brute force and with the high-handed tactics reminiscent of Hitler's storm troopers declared their intention to rule the citizenry therein, and thereby proceeded to maliciously and unnecessarily enjoin the inherent and inalienable rights and powers of the citizens thereof, and

Whereas, the immediate military leader of such troops, arrogantly and with impunity and with the implied acquiescence of the President of the United States, entered the public schools of Arkansas and thrust his views upon the minds of the children therein, thereby indelibly impressing upon the minds and hearts of such children the imprint of Fascism and military arrogance, and

Whereas, the President of the United States, in ordering federal military troops to occupy Little Rock, Arkansas, cited as authority for such act a clearly unconstitutional law which was created by a vengeful Reconstruction Congress to give dictatorial powers to the President of the United States, and

Whereas, even if such law were constitutional its provisions were improperly invoked by the President in that no federal law was being breached, and

Whereas, the federal military forces occupying Little Rock, Arkansas, under the express order of the President of the United States are not in nature or fact a *posse comitatus* authorized by federal law to assist a federal marshal in enforcement of a federal law, and

Whereas, the President was without authority and jurisdiction to invoke federal military rule in the sovereign state of Arkansas because (1) the Governor of Arkansas did not provide the requisite request for military assistance, (2) a state of insurrection, rebellion, or need to repel an invasion, did not exist, (3) no federal law existed upon which a violation was predicated, and

Whereas, if the President of the United States had had jurisdiction and authority to invoke federal military rule in the sovereign state of Arkansas, he was powerless to interfere with the operation of the public schools therein because the Constitution of the United States does not confer upon the President, or the federal government, any power or authority over such schools or over the subject of education, jurisdiction over these matters being reserved to the states, nor did the states by the Fourteenth Amendment authorize any interference on the part of the President or any other department of the federal government with the operation by the states of such public schools as they might in their discretion see fit to establish and operate, and

Whereas, the President of the United States, by his recent action invoking military rule in the sovereign state of Arkansas, announced his power to adjudge state laws ineffectual and inoperative on the basis

THE POWER TO EXECUTE LAWS

of his opinion of such laws as tested by the existing climate of political expediency, and

Whereas, the President of the United States, by federalizing the State Militia of Arkansas, rendered the Governor thereof powerless to employ such agency of state government for the protection of the inhabitants thereof should an emergency arise within the State requiring their use, and

Whereas, if the President of the United States is permitted to exercise the power to determine the method of enforcing a federal decree, and thereby to invoke military rule because of the inconvenience attendant in the proper use of constitutional processes, the states will have been destroyed; and the indestructible union of indestructible states established by the Constitution of the United States will have ceased to exist, and in its stead the President will have created, without jurisdiction or authority from the people, a dictator form of government, possessing total, unrestricted power, and

Whereas, it is clear that the President of the United States has deliberately resolved to disobey the Constitution of the United States and to flout and defy the supreme law of the land. The duty and responsibility of protecting life, property and the priceless possession of freedom rests with each government of each individual state of the union, as to all those within their respective territorial limits. The state alone has this responsibility, and

Whereas, it is clearly evident to the Legislature of Florida that the President of the United States, by his action, in the sovereign state of Arkansas, and his general intent as inadvertently disclosed by the Pentagon to occupy southern states with military forces, is deserving of the censure of the Congress, and

Whereas, the Legislature of Florida asserts that whenever the President of the United States engages in the deliberate, palpable and dangerous exercise of powers not granted to him, the states who are parties to the compact have the right to expect and require that the Congress of the United States exercise the powers granted by the compact to arrest the progress of the evil, and maintain the constitutional guarantees of the several sovereign states under the Tenth Amendment to the United States Constitution, and

Whereas, a failure on the part of the Congress thus to assert its authority in this regard would be construed as acquiescence in the surrender thereof; and that such submissive acquiescence to the seizure of one right by the President would in the end lead to the surrender of all rights, and inevitably to the consolidation of all functions of government under one separate dictatorial head, contrary to the sacred compact by which this Union of States was created, *now, therefore, Be it resolved by the Legislature of the State of Florida:*

That the Congress of the United States be and it is hereby requested to:

1. withhold all funds and appropriations from any federal military forces directed to occupy any sovereign state without the express approval of the governor therein, and

2. enact legislation designed to assure the several sovereign states freedom from federal military control, and

3. enact an appropriate measure censuring the President of the United States for his deliberate interference with the constitutional guarantees of the citizens of Little Rock, Arkansas, and admonishing the President to recognize the Congress of the United States as the legally proper branch of the government charged with the responsibility of furnishing direction in matters relating to civil rights as contemplated by the language of Section 2 of the Fourteenth Amendment that "The Congress shall have power to enforce this article by appropriate legislation."

Be it further resolved, that copies of this Memorial be dispatched to the President of the United States, to the President of the United States Senate; to the Speaker of the United States House of Representatives; and to each of the congressional delegation in the United States Congress.

Filed in Office of Secretary of State October 29, 1957.

THE EMERGENCY POWERS

DOCUMENT 10   WARTIME ECONOMIC CONTROLS

Presidential power is not a fixed, clearly definable entity established once and for all by Article II of the Constitution. While the President was granted a wide range of authority, the checks and balances also written into the Constitution created potential limits that have often proved most effective. The Senate, for example, has to approve his top-level appointments; the Congress has to appropriate the funds necessary to put his program into effect; his veto can be overridden; and, as Document 11 demonstrates, the Supreme Court can exercise a post facto check by declaring his action unconstitutional. Thus, legally speaking, a strong President has no more authority than a weak one, and even a vigorous Chief Executive must, in Harry Truman's words, "sit here all day, trying to persuade people to do the things they ought to have sense enough to do without my persuading them." A strong President attains his status from his political talent, not from any special constitutional dispensation.

Nowhere is this more apparent than in connection with the so-called emergency powers, which can best be defined as the President's authority to act without specific constitutional or statutory mandate in times of national crisis. The first President to exercise emergency powers was Abraham Lincoln, who during the early weeks of the Civil War authorized extraordinary measures to put down the rebellion (suspension of the writ of habeas corpus, expenditure of public funds without Congressional approval, and so forth). In July 1861 Lincoln called Congress into special session, told it of his actions, and asked retroactive approbation. He received it; not until after the end of the war and after his assassination was Lincoln chastised (in Ex parte Milligan, 1866) by the Supreme Court for overreaching his constitutional jurisdiction.

In this selection, Franklin D. Roosevelt boldly informed Congress that if it did not legislate effective price controls, he would act under his emergency powers. This statement was not made in a vacuum: the farm bloc in Congress had been conducting a holding action to oppose price controls against tremendous national pressure, and Roosevelt succeeded brilliantly in mobilizing the necessary sense of urgency. After a number of speeches about the evils of dictatorship, the President's bill was enacted.

To the Congress of the United States:

Four months ago, on April 27, 1942, I laid before the Congress a seven-point national economic policy designed to stabilize the domestic economy of the United States for the period of the war. The objective of that program was to prevent any substantial further rise in the cost of living.

It is not necessary for me to enumerate again the disastrous results of a runaway cost of living—disastrous to all of us, farmers, laborers, businessmen—the Nation itself. When the cost of living spirals upward, everybody becomes poorer, because the money he has and the money he earns buys so much less. At the same time the cost of the war, paid ultimately from taxes of the people, is needlessly increased by many billions of dollars. The national debt, at the end of the war, would become unnecessarily greater. Indeed, the prevention of a spiraling domestic economy is a vital part of the winning of the war itself.

I reiterate the seven-point program which I presented April 27, 1942:

1. To keep the cost of living from spiraling upward, we must tax heavily, and in that process keep personal and corporate profits at a reasonable rate, the word "reasonable" being defined at a low level.

2. To keep the cost of living from spiraling upward, we must fix ceilings on the prices which consumers, retailers, wholesalers, and manufacturers pay for the things they buy; and ceilings on rents for dwellings in all areas affected by war industries.

3. To keep the cost of living from spiraling upward, we must stabilize the remuneration received by individuals for their work.

4. To keep the cost of living from spiraling upward, we must stabilize the prices received by growers for the products of their lands.

5. To keep the cost of living from spiraling upward, we must encourage all citizens to contribute to the cost of winning this war by purchasing War bonds with their earnings instead of using those earnings to buy articles which are not essential.

6. To keep the cost of living from spiraling upward, we must ration

FROM Message to Congress by President Franklin D. Roosevelt, September 7, 1942, *Congressional Record,* Seventy-Seventh Congress, second session (Washington, D.C., Government Printing Office, 1942), Vol. 88, pp. 7052–54.

THE EMERGENCY POWERS

all essential commodities of which there is a scarcity, so that they may be distributed fairly among consumers and not merely in accordance with financial ability to pay high prices for them.

7. To keep the cost of living from spiraling upward, we must discourage credit and installment buying, and encourage the paying off of debts, mortgages, and other obligations; for this promotes savings, retards excessive buying, and adds to the amount available to the creditors for the purchase of War bonds.

In my message of 4 months ago, I pointed out that in order to succeed in our objective of stabilization it was necessary to move on all seven fronts at the same time, but that two of them called for legislation by the Congress before action could be taken. It was obvious then, and it is obvious now, that unless those two are realized, the whole objective must fail. These are points numbered 1 and 4, namely, an adequate tax program and a law permitting the fixing of price ceilings on farm products at parity prices.

I regret to have to call to your attention the fact that neither of these two essential pieces of legislation has as yet been enacted into law. That delay has now reached the point of danger to our whole economy.

However, we are carrying out, by executive action, the other parts of the seven-point program which did not require congressional action.

Price ceilings have been fixed on practically all commodities—other than certain exempted agricultural products—and on rents in war production areas of the United States.

This process of keeping prices and rents at reasonable levels constitutes one of the most far-reaching economic steps that this Nation has ever taken—in time of peace or war.

Our experience during the last 4 months has proved that general control of prices is possible—but only if that control is all inclusive. If, however, the costs of production, including labor, are left free to rise indiscriminately, or if other major elements in the costs of living are left unregulated, price control becomes impossible. If markets are flooded with purchasing power in excess of available goods, without taking adequate measures to siphon off the excess purchasing power, price control becomes likewise impossible.

❖❖❖❖

It is impossible for the cost of living to be stabilized while farm prices continue to rise. You cannot expect the laborer to maintain a fixed wage level if everything he wears and eats begins to go up drastically in price. On the other hand, it is impossible to keep any prices stable—farm prices or other prices—if wage rates, one of the most important elements in the cost of production, continue to increase.

❖❖❖❖

The cost of all food used by wage earners—controlled and uncontrolled—has been going up at the rate of 1¼ percent per month since the price ceilings were set in May 1942. If this rise should be permitted to continue, the increased cost of food to wage earners next May would be more than 15 percent over the level which existed when the ceilings were set.

This would be equal to imposing a 15-percent sales tax on all food purchased by wage earners. Obviously no one would consider imposing such a tax.

This drastic increase has been caused, and will be caused chiefly by the fact that a number of food commodities are exempt under existing law.

In the case of these exempt commodities the increases are even more startling. The cost of such food used by wage earners has been rising at an average of 3¼ percent per month since May 1, 1942.

Prices received by farmers have risen 85 percent since the outbreak of the war in September 1939, and these prices are continuing to rise. Cash farm income, including Government payments, has increased from $8,700,000,000 in 1939 to substantially more than $15,000,-000,000 in 1942. This is an increase of about 75 percent.

✵✵✵✵

If wages should be stabilized and farm prices permitted to rise at any rate like the present rate, workers will have to bear the major part of the increase. This we cannot ask. The Congress must realize that unless the existing control over farm prices is strengthened we must abandon our efforts to stabilize wages and salaries and the cost of living. If that occurs, workers and farmers alike will not only suffer a reduction in real income but will bring upon themselves and the Nation the unparalleled disaster of unchecked inflation.

The reason why price ceilings have not already been imposed on all food products is, as you know, that paragraph 3 of the Emergency Price Control Act prohibits such ceilings until farm prices as a whole have gone up beyond parity prices—far beyond—as high as an average of 16 percent beyond.

✵✵✵✵

What is needed, therefore, is an overall stabilization of prices, salaries, wages, and profits. That is necessary to the continued production of planes and tanks and ships and guns at the present constantly increasing rate.

We cannot hold the actual cost of food and clothing down to approximately the present level beyond October 1. But no one can give any assurances that the cost of living can be held down after that date.

Therefore, I ask the Congress to pass legislation under which the President would be specifically authorized to stabilize the cost of living, including the price of all farm commodities. The purpose should be to hold farm prices at parity, or at levels of a recent date, whichever is higher.

I ask the Congress to take this action by the 1st of October. Inaction on your part by that date will leave me with an inescapable responsibility to the people of this country to see to it that the war effort is no longer imperiled by threat of economic chaos.

In the event that the Congress should fail to act, and act adequately, I shall accept the responsibility, and I will act.

At the same time that farm prices are stabilized, wages can and will be stabilized, also. This I will do.

The President has the powers, under the Constitution and under congressional acts, to take measures necessary to avert a disaster which would interfere with the winning of the war.

I have given the most thoughtful consideration to meeting this issue without further reference to the Congress. I have determined, however, on this vital matter to consult with the Congress.

There may be those who will say that, if the situation is as grave as I have stated it to be, I should use my powers and act now. I can only say that I have approached this problem from every angle, and that I have decided that the course of conduct which I am following in this case is consistent with my sense of responsibility as President in time of war, and with my deep and unalterable devotion to the processes of democracy.

The responsibilities of the President in wartime to protect the Nation are very grave. This total war, with our fighting fronts, all over the world, makes the use of Executive power far more essential than in any previous war.

If we were invaded the people of this country would expect the President to use any and all means to repel the invader.

The Revolution and the War between the States were fought on our own soil, but today this war will be won or lost on other continents and remote seas.

I cannot tell what powers may have to be exercised in order to win this war.

The American people can be sure that I will use my powers with a full sense of my responsibility to the Constitution and to my country. The American people can also be sure that I shall not hesitate to use every power vested in me to accomplish the defeat of our enemies in any part of the world where our own safety demands such defeat.

When the war is won, the powers under which I act automatically revert to the people—to whom they belong.

✤✤✤✤

THE STEEL-SEIZURE CASE

*The best constitutional rule on emergency powers seems to be that
the President can use them only when there is a real emergency, that
is, when in effective political terms the Congress and the nation are
convinced that the special authority is imperative. During World War
II, for example, President Franklin Roosevelt took over factories on
occasion with no stipulated legal justification (usually when there was
an insoluble labor-management dispute in an essential war industry).
It was always a temporary affair, and although those affected de-
nounced the action, there was little public concern and no judicial
interest: the courts were in judicious wartime hibernation.*

*In 1952, however, President Harry Truman attempted to reassert
the authority that Roosevelt had so successfully exercised, and the
story had another ending. Faced with a steel strike, and unwilling to
invoke the Taft-Hartley Act because he was convinced management
was at fault, the President declared that the requirements of the
Korean War had created an emergency that justified government seizure of the steel mills. His order was immediately challenged in Congress, in the press, and in the courts; after some lower-court litigation
a suit reached the Supreme Court claiming that the Chief Executive's
action was unconstitutional. The American people did not appear to
consider the Korean War a real emergency.*

*The Court held that the President went beyond his constitutional
sphere when he took over the steel industry, though the reader of the
decision may have some difficulty finding out the reasons for the
Court's judgment! This case is, in fact, a very interesting example of
a judicial body trying to come to grips with elusive political considerations—a factor that only Justice Jackson has the candor to discuss.*

MR. JUSTICE BLACK delivered the opinion of the Court.

We are asked to decide whether the President was acting within his
constitutional power when he issued an order directing the Secretary
of Commerce to take possession of and operate most of the Nation's
steel mills. The mill owners argue that the President's order amounts to

FROM Opinion by Mr. Justice Black, Concurring Opinions of Mr. Justices
Frankfurter, Douglas, Jackson, and Clark, and Dissenting Opinion of Chief
Justice Vinson, *Youngstown Sheet and Tube Company* v. *Sawyer,* 343 U.S.
579 (1952).

lawmaking, a legislative function which the Constitution has expressly confided to the Congress and not to the President. The Government's position is that the order was made on findings of the President that his action was necessary to avert a national catastrophe which would inevitably result from a stoppage of steel production, and that in meeting this grave emergency the President was acting within the aggregate of his constitutional powers as the Nation's Chief Executive and the Commander in Chief of the Armed Forces of the United States. The issue emerges here from the following series of events:

In the latter part of 1951, a dispute arose between the steel companies and their employees over terms and conditions that should be included in new collective bargaining agreements. Long-continued conferences failed to resolve the dispute. On December 18, 1951, the employees' representative, United Steelworkers of America, C.I.O., gave notice of an intention to strike when the existing bargaining agreements expired on December 31. The Federal Mediation and Conciliation Service then intervened in an effort to get labor and management to agree. This failing, the President on December 22, 1951, referred the dispute to the Federal Wage Stabilization Board to investigate and make recommendations for fair and equitable terms of settlement. This Board's report resulted in no settlement. On April 4, 1952, the Union gave notice of a nation-wide strike called to begin at 12:01 a.m. April 9. The indispensability of steel as a component of substantially all weapons and other war materials led the President to believe that the proposed work stoppage would immediately jeopardize our national defense and that governmental seizure of the steel mills was necessary in order to assure the continued availability of steel. Reciting these considerations for his action, the President, a few hours before the strike was to begin, issued Executive Order 10340 . . . . The order directed the Secretary of Commerce to take possession of most of the steel mills and keep them running. The Secretary immediately issued his own possessory orders, calling upon the presidents of the various seized companies to serve as operating managers for the United States. They were directed to carry on their activities in accordance with regulations and directions of the Secretary. The next morning the President sent a message to Congress reporting his action. . . . Twelve days later he sent a second message. . . . Congress has taken no action.

Obeying the Secretary's orders under protest, the companies brought proceedings against him in the District Court. Their complaints charged that the seizure was not authorized by an act of Congress or by any constitutional provisions. The District Court was asked to declare the orders of the President and the Secretary invalid and to issue preliminary and permanent injunctions restraining their enforcement. Opposing the motion for preliminary injunction, the United States asserted that a strike disrupting steel production for even a brief period would so endanger the well-being and safety of the Nation that the President had "inherent power" to do what he had done—power "supported by the Constitution, by historical precedent, and by court decisions." The Government also contended that in any event no preliminary injunction should be issued because the companies had made no showing that their available legal remedies were inadequate or that their injuries from seizure would be irreparable. Holding against the Government on all points, the District Court on April 30 issued a preliminary injunction restraining the Secretary from "continuing the seizure and possession of the plant . . . and from acting under the purported authority of Executive Order No. 10340." (103 F.Supp. 569.) On the same day the Court of Appeals stayed the District Court's injunction, 90 U.S.App.D.C. 416, 197 F.2d 582. Deeming it best that the issues raised be promptly decided by this Court, we granted certiorari on May 3 and set the cause for argument on May 12. (343 U.S. 937.)

Two crucial issues have developed: *First.* Should final determination of the constitutional validity of the President's order be made in this case which has proceeded no further than the preliminary injunction stage? *Second.* If so, is the seizure order within the constitutional power of the President?

I.

It is urged that there were non-constitutional grounds upon which the District Court could have denied the preliminary injunction and thus have followed the customary judicial practice of declining to reach and decide constitutional questions until compelled to do so. On this basis it is argued that equity's extraordinary injunctive relief should have been denied because (a) seizure of the companies' properties did not inflict irreparable damages, and (b) there were available legal remedies adequate to afford compensation for any possible damages which they might suffer. While separately argued by the Government, these two contentions are here closely related, if not identical. Arguments as to both rest in large part on the Government's claim that should the seizure ultimately be held unlawful, the companies could recover full compensation in the Court of Claims for the unlawful taking. Prior cases in this Court have cast doubt on the right to recover in the Court of Claims on account of properties unlawfully taken by government officials for public use as these properties were alleged to have been. See e.g., Hooe v. United States, 218 U.S. 322, 335–336; United States v. North American Co., 253 U.S. 330, 333. But see Larson v. Domestic & Foreign Corp., 337 U.S. 682, 701–702. Moreover, seizure and governmental operation of these going businesses were bound to result in many present and future damages of such nature as to be difficult, if not incapable, of measurement. Viewing the case this way, and in the light of the facts presented, the District Court saw no reason for delaying decision of the constitutional validity of the orders. We agree with the District Court and can see no reason why that question was not ripe for determination on the record presented. We shall therefore consider and determine that question now.

II.

The President's power, if any, to issue the order must stem either from an act of Congress or from the Constitution itself. There is no statute that expressly authorizes the President to take possession of property as he did here. Nor is there any act of Congress to which our attention has been directed from which such a power can fairly be implied. Indeed, we do not understand the Government to rely on statutory authorization for this seizure. There are two statutes which do authorize the President to take both personal and real property under certain conditions. [The Selective Service Act of 1948 and the Defense Production Act of 1950.] However, the Government admits that these conditions were not met and that the President's order was not rooted in either of the statutes. The Government refers to the seizure provisions of one of these statutes (§ 201b of the Defense Production Act) as "much too cumbersome, involved, and time-consuming for the crisis which was at hand."

Moreover, the use of the seizure technique to solve labor disputes in order to prevent work stoppages was not only unauthorized by any congressional enactment; prior to this controversy, Congress had refused to adopt that method of settling labor disputes. When the Taft-Hartley Act was under consideration in 1947, Congress rejected an amendment which would have authorized such governmental seizures in cases of emergency. Apparently it was thought that the technique of seizure, like that of compulsory arbitration, would interfere with the process of collective bargaining. Consequently, the plan Congress adopted in that Act did not provide for seizure under any circumstances. Instead, the plan sought to bring about settlements by use of the customary devices of mediation, conciliation, investigation by boards of inquiry, and public reports. In some instances temporary injunctions were authorized to provide cooling-off periods. All this failing, the union were left free to strike if the majority of the employees, by secret ballot, expressed a desire to do so.

It is clear that if the President had authority to issue the order he did, it must be found in some provisions of the Constitution. And it is not claimed that express constitutional language grants this power to the President. The contention is that presidential power should be implied from the aggregate of his powers under the Constitution. Particular reliance is placed on provisions in Article II which say that "the executive Power shall be vested in a President . . ."; that "he shall take Care that the Laws be faithfully executed"; and that he "shall be Commander in Chief of the Army and Navy of the United States."

The order cannot properly be sustained as an exercise of the President's military power as Commander in Chief of the Armed Forces. The Government attempts to do so by citing a number of cases upholding broad powers in military commanders engaged in day-to-day fighting in a theater of war. Such cases need not concern us here. Even though "theater of war" be an expanding concept, we cannot with faithfulness to our constitutional system hold that the Commander in Chief of the Armed Forces has the ultimate power as such to take possession of private property in order to keep labor disputes from stopping production. This is a job for the Nation's lawmakers, not for its military authorities.

Nor can the seizure order be sustained because of the several constitutional provisions that grant executive power to the President. In the framework of our Constitution, the President's power to see that the laws are faithfully executed refutes the idea that he is to be a lawmaker. The Constitution limits his functions in the law-making process to the recommending of laws he thinks wise and the vetoing of laws he thinks bad. And the Constitution is neither silent nor equivocal about who shall make laws which the President is to execute. The first section of the first article says that "All legislative Powers herein granted shall be vested in a Congress of the United States. . . ." After granting many powers to the Congress, Article I goes on to provide that Congress may "make all Laws which shall be necessary and proper for carrying into Execution the foregoing Powers and all other Powers vested by this Constitution in the Government of the United States, or in any Department or Officer thereof."

The President's order does not direct that a congressional policy be executed in a manner prescribed by Congress—it directs that a presidential policy be executed in a manner prescribed by the President. The preamble of the order itself, like that of many statutes, sets out reasons why the President believes certain policies should be adopted, proclaims these policies as rules of conduct to be followed, and again, like a statute, authorizes a government official to promulgate additional rules and regulations consistent with the policy proclaimed and needed to carry that policy into execution. The power of Congress to adopt such public policies as those proclaimed by the order is beyond question. It can authorize the taking of private property for public use. It can make laws regulating the relationships between employers and employees, prescribing rules designed to settle labor disputes, and fixing wages and working conditions in certain fields of our economy.

THE EMERGENCY POWERS

The Constitution does not subject this lawmaking power of Congress to presidential or military supervision or control.

It is said that other Presidents without congressional authority have taken possession of private business enterprises in order to settle labor disputes. But even if this be true, Congress has not thereby lost its exclusive constitutional authority to make laws necessary and proper to carry out the powers vested by the Constitution "in the Government of the United States, or any Department or Officer thereof."

The Founders of this Nation entrusted the lawmaking power to the Congress alone in both good and bad times. It would do no good to recall the historical events, the fears of power and the hopes for freedom that lay behind their choice. Such a review would but confirm our holding that this seizure order cannot stand.

The judgment of the District Court is
Affirmed.

MR. JUSTICE FRANKFURTER, concurring.

❈❈❈❈

The issue before us can be met, and therefore should be, without attempting to define the President's powers comprehensively. I shall not attempt to delineate what belongs to him by virtue of his office beyond the power even of Congress to contract; what authority belongs to him until Congress acts; what kind of problems may be dealt with either by the Congress or by the President or by both, cf. La Abra Silver Mine Co. v. United States, 175 U.S. 423; what power must be exercised by the Congress and cannot be delegated to the President. . . .

We must therefore put to one side consideration of what powers the President would have had if there had been no legislation whatever bearing on the authority asserted by the seizure, or if the seizure had been only for a short, explicitly temporary period, to be determined automatically unless Congressional approval were given. These and other questions, like or unlike, are not now here. I would exceed my authority were I to say anything about them.

The question before the Court comes in this setting. Congress has frequently—at least 16 times since 1916—specifically provided for executive seizure of production, transportation, communications, or storage facilities. In every case it has qualified this grant of power with limitations and safeguards. This body of enactments . . . demonstrates that Congress deemed seizure so drastic a power as to require that it be carefully circumscribed whenever the President was vested with this extraordinary authority. The power to seize has uniformly been given only for a limited period or for a defined emergency, or has been repealed after a short period. Its exercise has been restricted to particular circumstances such as "time of war or when war is imminent," the needs of "public safety" or of "national security or defense," or "urgent and impending need." The period of governmental operation has been limited, as, for instance, to "sixty days after the restoration of productive efficiency." Seizure statutes usually make executive action dependent on detailed conditions: for example, (a) failure or refusal of the owner of a plant to meet governmental supply needs or (b) failure of voluntary negotiations with the owner for the use of a plant necessary for great public ends. Congress often has specified the particular executive agency which should seize or operate the plants or whose judgment would appropriately test the need for seizure. Congress also has not left to implication that just compensation be paid; it has usually legislated in detail regarding enforcement of this litigation-breeding general requirement.

Congress in 1947 was again called upon to consider whether governmental seizure should be used to avoid serious industrial shutdowns. Congress decided against conferring such power generally and in advance, without special congressional enactment to meet each particular need. . . .

In adopting the provisions which it did, by the Labor Management Relations Act of 1947, for dealing with a "national emergency" arising out of a breakdown in peaceful industrial relations, Congress was very familiar with Government seizure as a protective measure. On a balance of considerations Congress chose not to lodge this power in the President. . . . Previous seizure legislation had subjected the powers granted to the President to restrictions of varying degrees of stringency. Instead of giving him even limited powers, Congress in 1947 deemed it wise to require the President, upon failure of attempts to reach a voluntary settlement, to report to Congress if he deemed the power of seizure a needed shot for his locker. The President could not ignore the specific limitations of prior seizure statutes. No more could he act in disregard of the limitation put upon seizure by the 1947 Act.

✦✦✦✦

By the Labor Management Relations Act of 1947, Congress said to the President, "You may not seize. Please report to us and ask for seizure power if you think it is needed in a specific situation." This of course calls for a report on the unsuccessful efforts to reach a voluntary settlement, as a basis for discharge by Congress of its responsibility—which it has unequivocally reserved—to fashion further remedies than it provided. But it is now claimed that the President has seizure power by virtue of the Defense Production Act of 1950 and its Amendments. And the claim is based on the occurrence of new events—Korea and the need for stabilization, etc.—although it was well known that seizure power was withheld by the Act of 1947, and although the President, whose specific requests for other authority were in the main granted by Congress, never suggested that in view of the new events he needed the power of seizure which Congress in its judgment had decided to withhold from him. . . .

The Defense Production Act affords no ground for the suggestion that the 1947 denial to the President of seizure powers has been impliedly repealed, and its legislative history contradicts such a suggestion. Although the proponents of that Act recognized that the President would have a choice of alternative methods of seeking a mediated settlement, they also recognized that Congress alone retained the ultimate coercive power to meet the threat of "any serious work stoppage."

That conclusion is not changed by what occurred after the passage of the 1950 Act. . . . The legislative history of the Defense Production Act and its Amendments in 1951 cannot possibly be vouched for more than Congressional awareness and tacit approval that the President had charged the Wage Stabilization Board with authority to seek voluntary settlement of labor disputes. . . .

Art. II, § 3. The nature of that authority has for me been comprehensively indicated by Mr. Justice Holmes. "The duty of the President to see that the laws be executed is a duty that does not go beyond the laws or require him to achieve more than Congress sees fit to leave within his power." (Myers v. United States, 272 U.S. 52, 177.) The powers of the President are not as particularized as are those of Congress. But unenumerated powers do not mean undefined powers. The separation of powers built into our Constitution gives essential content to undefined provisions in the frame of our government.

To be sure, the content of the three authorities of government is not to be derived from an abstract analysis. The areas are partly interacting, not wholly disjointed. The Constitution is a framework for government. Therefore the way the framework has consistently operated fairly establishes that it has operated according to its true nature. Deeply embedded traditional ways of conducting government cannot supplant the Constitution or legislation, but they give meaning to the words of a text or supply them. It is an inadmissibly narrow conception of American constitutional law to confine it to the words of the Constitution and to disregard the gloss which life has written upon them. In short, a systematic, unbroken, executive practice, long pursued to the knowledge of the Congress and never before questioned, engaged in by Presidents who have also sworn to uphold the Constitution, making as it were such exercise of power part of the structure of our government, may be treated as a gloss on "executive Power" vested in the President by § 1 of Art. II.

A scheme of government like ours no doubt at times feels the lack of power to act with complete, all-embracing, swiftly moving authority. No doubt a government with distributed authority, subject to be challenged in the courts of law, at least long enough to consider and adjudicate the challenge, labors under restrictions from which other governments are free. It has not been our tradition to envy such governments. In any event our government was designed to have such restrictions. The price was deemed not too high in view of the safeguards which these restrictions afford. I know no more impressive words on this subject than those of Mr. Justice Brandeis:

The doctrine of the separation of powers was adopted by the Convention of 1787, not to promote efficiency but to preclude the exercise of arbitrary power. The purpose was, not to avoid friction, but, by means of the inevitable friction incident to the distribution of the governmental powers among three departments, to save the people from autocracy. (Myers v. United States, 272 U.S. 52, 240, 293. . . .)

MR. JUSTICE DOUGLAS, concurring.

There can be no doubt that the emergency which caused the President to seize these steel plants was one that bore heavily on the country. But the emergency did not create power; it merely marked an occasion when power should be exercised. And the fact that it was necessary that measures be taken to keep steel in production does not mean that the President, rather than the Congress, had the constitutional authority to act. The Congress, as well as the President, is trustee of the national welfare. The President can act more quickly than the Congress. The President with the armed services at his disposal can move with force as well as with speed. All executive power —from the reign of ancient kings to the rule of modern dictators— has the outward appearance of efficiency.

Legislative power, by contrast, is slower to exercise. There must be delay while the ponderous machinery of committees, hearings, and debates is put into motion. That takes time; and while the Congress slowly moves into action, the emergency may take its toll in wages, consumer goods, war production, the standard of living of the people, and perhaps even lives. . . .

We therefore cannot decide this case by determining which branch of government can deal most expeditiously with the present crisis. The answer must depend on the allocation of powers under the Constitution.

❖❖❖❖

A determination that sanctions should be applied, that the hand of the law should be placed upon the parties, and that the force of the courts should be directed against them, is an exercise of legislative power. In some nations that power is entrusted to the executive branch as a matter of course or in case of emergencies. We chose another course. We chose to place the legislative power of the Federal Government in the Congress. The language of the Constitution is not ambiguous or qualified. It places not *some* legislative power in the Congress; Article I, Section 1 says "All legislative Powers herein granted shall be vested in a Congress of the United States, which shall consist of a Senate and House of Representatives."

The legislative nature of the action taken by the President seems to me to be clear.

****

If we sanctioned the present exercise of power by the President, we would be expanding Article II of the Constitution and rewriting it to suit the political conveniences of the present emergency. Article II which vests the "executive Power" in the President defines that power with particularity. Article II, Section 2 makes the Chief Executive the Commander in Chief of the Army and Navy. But our history and tradition rebel at the thought that the grant of military power carries with it authority over civilian affairs. Article II, Section 3 provides that the President shall "from time to time give to the Congress Information of the State of the Union, and recommend to their Consideration such Measures as he shall judge necessary and expedient." The power to recommend legislation, granted to the President, serves only to emphasize that it is his function to recommend and that it is the function of the Congress to legislate. Article II, Section 3 also provides that the President "shall take Care that the Laws be faithfully executed." But as Mr. Justice Black and Mr. Justice Frankfurter point out the power to execute the laws starts and ends with the laws Congress has enacted. . . .

We pay a price for our system of checks and balances, for the distribution of power among the three branches of government. It is a price that today may seem exorbitant to many. Today a kindly President uses the seizure power to effect a wage increase and to keep the steel furnaces in production. Yet tomorrow another President might use the same power to prevent a wage increase, to curb trade unionists, to regiment labor as oppressively as industry thinks it has been regimented by this seizure.

MR. JUSTICE JACKSON, concurring in the judgment and opinion of the Court.

****

We should not use this occasion to circumscribe, much less to contract, the lawful role of the President as Commander-in-Chief. I should indulge the widest latitude of interpretation to sustain his exclusive function to command the instruments of national force, at least when turned against the outside world for the security of our society. But, when it is turned inward, not because of rebellion but because of a lawful economic struggle between industry and labor, it should have no such indulgence. His command power is not such an absolute as might be implied from that office in a militaristic system but is subject to limitations consistent with a constitutional Republic whose law and policy-making branch is a representative Congress. The purpose of lodging dual titles in one man was to insure that the civilian would control the military, not to enable the military to subordinate the presidential office. No penance would ever expiate the sin against free government of holding that a President can escape control of executive powers by law through assuming his military role. What the power of command may include I do not try to envision, but I think it is not a military prerogative, without support of law, to seize persons or property because they are important or even essential for the military and naval establishment.

The third clause in which the Solicitor General finds seizure powers is that "he shall take Care that the Laws be faithfully executed . . . ." That authority must be matched against words of the Fifth Amendment that "No person shall be . . . deprived of life, liberty or property, without due process of law . . . ." One gives a governmental authority that reaches so far as there is law, the other gives a private right that authority shall go no farther. These signify about all there is of the principle that ours is a government of laws, not of men, and that we submit ourselves to rulers only if under rules.

The Solicitor General lastly grounds support of the seizure upon nebulous, inherent powers never expressly granted but said to have accrued to the office from the customs and claims of preceding administrations. The plea is for a resulting power to deal with a crisis or an emergency according to the necessities of the case, the unarticulated assumption being that necessity knows no law.

❉❉❉❉

The appeal, however, that we declare the existence of inherent powers *ex necessitate* to meet an emergency asks us to do what many think would be wise, although it is something the forefathers omitted. They knew what emergencies were, knew the pressures they engender for authoritative action, knew, too, how they afford a ready pretext for usurpation. We may also suspect that they suspected that emergency powers would tend to kindle emergencies. Aside from suspension of the privilege of the writ of habeas corpus in time of rebellion or invasion, when the public safety may require it, they made no express provision for exercise of extraordinary authority because of a crisis. I do not think we rightfully may so amend their work, and, if we could, I am not convinced it would be wise to do so, although many modern nations have forthrightly recognized that war and economic crises may upset the normal balance between liberty and authority. . . .

In the practical working of our Government we already have evolved a technique within the framework of the Constitution by which normal executive powers may be considerably expanded to meet an emergency.

THE EMERGENCY POWERS

Congress may and has granted extraordinary authorities which lie dormant in normal times but may be called into play by the Executive in war or upon proclamation of a national emergency. In 1939, upon congressional request, the Attorney General listed ninety-nine such separate statutory grants by Congress of emergency or war-time executive powers. They were invoked from time to time as need appeared. Under this procedure we retain Government by law—special, temporary law, perhaps, but law nonetheless. The public may know the extent and limitations of the powers that can be asserted, and persons affected may be informed from the statute of their rights and duties.

In view of the ease, expedition and safety with which Congress can grant and has granted large emergency powers, certainly ample to embrace this crisis, I am quite unimpressed with the argument that we should affirm possession of them without statute.

❖❖❖❖

MR. JUSTICE CLARK, concurring in the judgment of the Court.

❖❖❖❖

The limits of presidential power are obscure. However, Article II, no less than Article I, is part of "a constitution intended to endure for ages to come, and consequently, to be adapted to the various crises of human affairs." Some of our Presidents, such as Lincoln, "felt that measures otherwise unconstitutional might become lawful by becoming indispensable to the preservation of the Constitution through the preservation of the nation." Others, such as Theodore Roosevelt, thought the President to be capable, as a "steward" of the people, of exerting all power save that which is specifically prohibited by the Constitution or the Congress. In my view . . . the Constitution does grant to the President extensive authority in times of grave and imperative national emergency. In fact, to my thinking, such a grant may well be necessary to the very existence of the Constitution itself. As Lincoln aptly said, "[is] it possible to lose the nation and yet preserve the Constitution?" In describing this authority I care not whether one calls it "residual," "inherent," "moral," "implied," "aggregate," "emergency," or otherwise. I am of the conviction that those who have had the gratifying experience of being the President's lawyer have used one or more of these adjectives only with the utmost of sincerity and the highest of purpose.

I conclude that where Congress has laid down specific procedures to deal with the type of crisis confronting the President, he must follow those procedures in meeting the crisis; but that in the absence of such action by Congress, the President's independent power to act depends upon the gravity of the situation confronting the nation. I cannot sustain the seizure in question because here . . . Congress had prescribed methods to be followed by the President in meeting the emergency at hand.

✤✤✤✤

MR. CHIEF JUSTICE VINSON, with whom MR. JUSTICE REED and MR. JUSTICE MINTON join, dissenting.

The President of the United States directed the Secretary of Commerce to take temporary possession of the Nation's steel mills during the existing emergency because "a work stoppage would immediately jeopardize and imperil our national defense and the defense of those joined with us in resisting aggression, and would add to the continuing danger of our soldiers, sailors and airmen engaged in combat in the field." The District Court ordered the mills returned to their private owners on the ground that the President's action was beyond his powers under the Constitution.

This Court affirms. Some members of the Court are of the view that the President is without power to act in time of crisis in the absence of express statutory authorization. Other members of the Court affirm on the basis of their reading of certain statutes. Because we cannot agree that affirmance is proper on any ground, and because of the transcending importance of the questions presented not only in this critical litigation but also to the powers the President and of future Presidents to act in time of crisis, we are compelled to register this dissent.

In passing upon the question of Presidential powers in this case, we must first consider the context in which those powers were exercised.

Those who suggest that this is a case involving extraordinary powers should be mindful that these are extraordinary times. A world not yet recovered from the devastation of World War II has been forced to face the threat of another and more terrifying global conflict.

Accepting in full measure its responsibility in the world community, the United States was instrumental in securing adoption of the United Nations Charter, approved by the Senate by a vote of 89 to 2. The first purpose of the United Nations is to "maintain international peace and security, and to that end: to take effective collective measures for the prevention and removal of threats to the peace, and for the suppression of acts of aggression or other breaches of the peace, ..." In 1950, when the United Nations called upon member nations "to render every assistance" to repel aggression in Korea, the United States furnished its vigorous support. For almost two full years, our armed forces have been fighting in Korea, suffering casualties of over 108,000 men. Hostilities have not abated. The "determination of the United Nations to continue its action in Korea to meet the aggression" has been reaffirmed. Congressional support of the action in Korea has been manifested by provisions for increased military manpower and equipment and for economic stabilization, as hereinafter described.

✤✤✤✤

Congress recognized the impact of these defense programs upon the economy. Following the attack in Korea, the President asked for authority to requisition property and to allocate and fix priorities for scarce goods. In the Defense Production Act of 1950, Congress granted the powers requested and, *in addition,* granted power to stabilize prices and wages and to provide for settlement of labor disputes arising in the defense program. The Defense Production Act was extended in 1951, a Senate Committee noting that in the dislocation caused by the programs for purchase of military equipment "lies the seed of an economic disaster that might well destroy the military might we are straining to build." Significantly, the Committee examined the problem "in terms of just one commodity, steel," and found "a graphic picture of the over-all inflationary danger growing out of reduced civilian supplies and rising incomes." Even before Korea, steel production at levels above theoretical 100% capacity was not capable of supplying civilian needs alone. Since Korea, the tremendous military demand for steel has far exceeded the increases in productive capacity. This Committee emphasized that the shortage of steel, even with the mills operating at full capacity, coupled with increased civilian purchasing power, presented grave danger of disastrous inflation.

The President has the duty to execute the foregoing legislative programs. Their successful execution depends upon continued production of steel and stabilized prices for steel. Accordingly, when the collective bargaining agreements between the Nation's steel producers and their employees, represented by the United Steel Workers, were due to expire on December 31, 1951, and a strike shutting down the entire basic steel industry was threatened, the President acted to avert a complete shutdown of steel production. On December 22, 1951, he certified the dispute to the Wage Stabilization Board, requesting that the Board investigate the dispute and promptly report its recommendation as to fair and equitable terms of settlement. The Union complied with the President's request and delayed its threatened strike while the dispute was before the Board. After a special Board panel had conducted hearings and submitted a report, the full Wage Stabilization Board submitted its report and recommendations to the President on March 20, 1952.

The Board's report was acceptable to the Union but was rejected by plaintiffs. The Union gave notice of its intention to strike as of 12:01 a.m., April 9, 1952, but bargaining between the parties continued with hope of settlement until the evening of April 8, 1952. After bargaining had failed to avert the threatened shutdown of steel production, the President issued the . . . Executive Order . . . The next morning, April 9, 1952, the President addressed . . . Congress. . . .

Twelve days passed without action by Congress. On April 21, 1952, the President sent a letter to the President of the Senate in which he again described the purpose and need for his action and again stated his position that "The Congress can, if it wishes, reject the course of action I have followed in this matter." Congress has not so acted to this date.

Meanwhile, plaintiffs instituted this action in the District Court to compel defendant to return possession of the steel mills seized under Executive Order 10340.

❀❀❀❀

One is not here called upon even to consider the possibility of executive seizure of a farm, a corner grocery store or even a single industrial plant. Such considerations arise only when one ignores the central fact of this case—that the Nation's entire basic steel production would have shut down completely if there had been no Government seizure. Even ignoring for the moment whatever confidential information the President may possess as "the Nation's organ for foreign affairs," the uncontroverted affidavits in this record amply support the finding that "a work stoppage would immediately jeopardize and imperil our national defense."

❀❀❀❀

Accordingly, if the President has any power under the Constitution to meet a critical situation in the absence of express statutory authorization, there is no basis whatever for criticizing the exercise of such power in this case.

❀❀❀❀

In passing upon the grave constitutional question presented in this case, we must never forget, as Chief Justice Marshall admonished, that the Constitution is "intended to endure for ages to come, and, consequently, to be adapted to the various *crises* of human affairs," and that "[i]ts means are adequate to its ends." Cases do arise presenting questions which could not have been foreseen by the Framers. In such cases, the Constitution has been treated as a living document adaptable to new situations. But we are not called upon today to expand the Constitution to meet a new situation. For, in this case, we need only look to history and time-honored principles of constitutional law—principles that have been applied consistently by all branches of the Government throughout our history. It is those who assert the invalidity of the Executive Order who seek to amend the Constitution in this case.

A review of executive action demonstrates that our Presidents have on many occasions exhibited the leadership contemplated by the Framers when they made the President Commander in Chief, and imposed upon him the trust to "take Care that the Laws be faithfully executed." With or without explicit statutory authorization, Presidents have at such times dealt with national emergencies by acting promptly and resolutely to enforce legislative programs, at least to save those programs until Congress could act. Congress and the courts have responded to such executive initiative with consistent approval.

Our first President displayed at once the leadership contemplated by the Framers. When the national revenue laws were openly flouted in some sections of Pennsylvania, President Washington, without waiting for a call from the state government, summoned the militia and took decisive steps to secure the faithful execution of the laws. When international disputes engendered by the French revolution threatened to involve this country in war, and while congressional policy remained uncertain, Washington issued his Proclamation of Neutrality. Hamilton, whose defense of the Proclamation has endured the test of time, invoked the argument that the Executive has the duty to do that which will preserve peace until Congress acts and, in addition, pointed to the need for keeping the Nation informed of the requirements of existing laws and treaties as part of the faithful execution of the laws.

❖❖❖❖

Jefferson's initiative in the Louisiana Purchase, the Monroe Doctrine, and Jackson's removal of Government deposits from the Bank of the United States further serve to demonstrate by deed what the Framers described by word when they vested the whole of the executive power in the President.

Without declaration of war, President Lincoln took energetic action with the outbreak of the Civil War. He summoned troops and paid them out of the Treasury without appropriation therefor. He proclaimed a naval blockade of the Confederacy and seized ships violating that blockade. Congress, far from denying the validity of these acts, gave them express approval. The most striking action of President Lincoln was the Emancipation Proclamation, issued in aid of the successful prosecution of the Civil War, but wholly without statutory authority.

In an action furnishing a most apt precedent for this case, President Lincoln directed the seizure of rail and telegraph lines leading to Washington without statutory authority. Many months later, Congress recognized and confirmed the power of the President to seize railroads and telegraph lines and provided criminal penalties for interference with Government operation. This Act did not confer on the President any additional powers of seizure. Congress plainly rejected the view that the President's acts had been without legal sanction until ratified by the legislature. Sponsors of the bill declared that its purpose was only to confirm the power which the President already possessed. Opponents insisted a statute authorizing seizure was unnecessary and might even be construed as limiting existing Presidential powers.

❖❖❖❖

President Theodore Roosevelt seriously contemplated seizure of Pennsylvania coal mines if a coal shortage necessitated such action. In his autobiography, President Roosevelt expounded the "Stewardship

Theory" of Presidential power, stating that "the executive [is] subject only to the people, and, under the Constitution, bound to serve the people affirmatively in cases where the Constitution does not explicitly forbid him to render the service." Because the contemplated seizure of the coal mines was based on this theory, then ex-President Taft criticized President Roosevelt in a passage in his book relied upon by the District Court in this case. . . . In the same book, however, President Taft agreed that such powers of the President as the duty "to take care that the laws be faithfully executed" could not be confined to "express Congressional statutes." . . .

In 1909, President Taft was informed that government owned oil lands were being patented by private parties at such a rate that public oil lands would be depleted in a matter of months. Although Congress had explicitly provided that these lands were open to purchase by United States citizens, 29 Stat. 526 (1897), the President nevertheless ordered the lands withdrawn from sale "[i]n aid of proposed legislation." In United States v. Midwest Oil Co., 236 U.S. 459 (1915), the President's action was sustained as consistent with executive practice throughout our history. An excellent brief was filed in the case by the Solicitor General, Mr. John W. Davis, together with Assistant Attorney General Knaebel, later Reporter for this Court. In this brief, the situation confronting President Taft was described as "an emergency; there was no time to wait for the action of Congress." The brief then discusses the powers of the President under the Constitution in such a case:

Ours is a self-sufficient Government within its sphere. (Ex parte Siebold, 100 U.S. 271, 395; In re Debs, 158 U.S. 564, 578.) "Its means are adequate to its ends" (McCulloch v. Maryland, 4 Wheat., 316, 424), and it is rational to assume that its active forces will be found equal in most things to the emergencies that confront it. The function of making laws is peculiar to Congress, and the Executive can not exercise that function to any dregree. But this is not to say that all of the subjects concerning which laws might be made are perforce removed from the possibility of Executive influence. The Executive may act upon things and upon men in many relations which have not, though they might have, been actually regulated by Congress. In other words, just as there are fields which are peculiar to Congress and fields which are peculiar to the Executive, so there are fields which are common to both, in the sense that the Executive may move within them until they shall have been occupied by legislative action. These are not the fields of legislative prerogative, but fields within which the lawmaking power may enter and dominate whenever it chooses. This situation results from the fact that the President is the active agent, not of Congress, but of the Nation. As such he performs the duties which the Constitution lays upon him immediately, and as such, also, he executes the laws and regulations adopted by Congress. He is the agent of the people of the United States, deriving all his power from them and responsible directly to them. In no sense is he the agent of Congress. He obeys and executes the laws of Congress, not because Congress is enthroned in authority over him, but because the Constitution directs him to do so.

Therefore it follows that in ways short of making laws or disobeying them, the Executive may be under a grave constitutional duty to act for the national protection in situations not covered by the acts of Congress, and in which, even, it may not be said that his action is the direct expression of any particular one of the independent powers which are granted to him specifically by the Constitution. Instances wherein the President has felt and fulfilled such a duty have not been rare in our history, though, being for the public benefit and approved by all, his acts have seldom been challenged in the courts. We are able, however, to present a number of apposite cases which were subjected to judicial inquiry. . . . In none of those cases did the action of the President amount merely to the execution of some specific law.

Neither does any of them stand apart in principle from the case at bar, as involving the exercise of specific constitutional powers of the President in a degree in which this case does not involve them. Taken collectively, the provisions of the Constitution which designate the President as the official who must represent us in foreign relations, in commanding the Army and Navy, in keeping Congress informed of the state of the Union, in insuring the faithful execution of the laws and in recommending new ones, considered in connection with the sweeping declaration that the executive power shall be vested in him, completely demonstrate that his is the watchful eye, the active hand, the overseeing dynamic force of the United States.

This brief is valuable not alone because of the caliber of its authors but because it lays bare in succinct reasoning the basis of the executive practice which this Court approved in the Midwest Oil case.

During World War I, President Wilson established a War Labor Board without awaiting specific direction by Congress. With William Howard Taft and Frank P. Walsh as co-chairmen, the Board had as its purpose the prevention of strikes and lockouts interfering with the production of goods needed to meet the emergency. Effectiveness of War Labor Board decision was accomplished by Presidential action, including seizure of industrial plants. Seizure of the Nation's railroads was also ordered by President Wilson.

Beginning with the Bank Holiday Proclamation and continuing through World War II, executive leadership and initiative were characteristic of President Franklin D. Roosevelt's administration. In 1939, upon the outbreak of war in Europe, the President proclaimed a limited national emergency for the purpose of strengthening our national defense. By May of 1941, the danger from the Axis belligerents having become clear, the President proclaimed "an unlimited national emergency" calling for mobilization of the Nation's defenses to repel aggression. The President took the initiative in strengthening our defenses by acquiring rights from the British Government to establish air bases in exchange for overage destroyers.

In 1941, President Roosevelt acted to protect Iceland from attack by Axis powers when British forces were withdrawn by sending our forces to occupy Iceland. Congress was informed of this action on the same day that our forces reached Iceland. The occupation of Iceland was but one of "at least 125 incidents" in our history in which Presidents, "without Congressional authorization, and in the absence of a declaration of war, [have] ordered the Armed Forces to take action or maintain positions abroad."

Some six months before Pearl Harbor, a dispute at a single aviation plant [North American Aviation, Inc.] at Inglewood, California, interrupted a segment of the production of military aircraft. In spite of the comparative insignificance of this work stoppage to total defense production as contrasted with the complete paralysis now threatened by a shutdown of the entire basic steel industry, and even though our armed forces were not then engaged in combat, President Roosevelt ordered the seizure of the plant "pursuant to the powers vested in [him] by the Constitution and laws of the United States, as President of the United States of America and Commander in Chief of the Army and Navy of the United States." The Attorney General [Jackson] vigorously proclaimed that the President had the moral duty to keep this Nation's defense effort a "going concern." His ringing moral justification was coupled with a legal justification equally well stated:

The Presidential proclamation rests upon the aggregate of the Presidential powers derived from the Constitution itself and from statutes enacted by the Congress.

The Constitution lays upon the President the duty "to take care that the laws be faithfully executed." Among the laws which he is required to find means to execute are those which direct him to equip an enlarged army, to provide for a strengthened navy, to protect Government property, to protect those who are engaged in carrying out the business of the Government, and to carry out the provisions of the Lend-Lease Act. For the faithful execution of such laws the President has back of him not only each general law-enforcement power conferred by the various acts of Congress but the aggregate of all such laws plus that wide discretion as to method vested in him by the Constitution for the purpose of executing the laws.

The Constitution also places on the President the responsibility and vests in him the powers of Commander in Chief of the Army and of the Navy. These weapons for the protection of the continued existence of the Nation are placed in his sole command and the implication is clear that he should not allow them to become paralyzed by failure to obtain supplies for which Congress has appropriated the money and which it has directed the President to obtain. . . .

94

More recently, President Truman acted to repel aggression by employing our armed forces in Korea. Upon the intervention of the Chinese Communists, the President proclaimed the existence of an unlimited national emergency requiring the speedy build-up of our defense establishment. Congress responded by providing for increased manpower and weapons for our own armed forces, by increasing military aid under the Mutual Security Program and by enacting economic stabilization measures, as previously described.

This is but a cursory summary of executive leadership but it amply demonstrates that Presidents have taken prompt action to enforce the laws and protect the country whether or not Congress happened to provide in advance for the particular method of execution. At the minimum, the executive actions reviewed herein sustain the action of the President in this case. And many of the cited examples of Presidential practice go far beyond the extent of power necessary to sustain the President's order to seize the steel mills. The fact that temporary executive seizures of industrial plants to meet an emergency have not been directly tested in this Court furnishes not the slightest suggestion that such actions have been illegal. Rather, the fact that Congress and the courts have consistently recognized and given their support to such executive action indicates that such a power of seizure has been accepted throughout our history.

History bears out the genius of the Founding Fathers, who created a Government subject to law but not left subject to inertia when vigor and initiative are required.

Focusing now on the situation confronting the President on the night of April 8, 1952, we cannot but conclude that the President was performing his duty under the Constitution "to take care that the laws be faithfully executed"—a duty described by President Benjamin Harrison as "the central idea of the office."

The President reported to Congress the morning after the seizure that he acted because a work stoppage in steel production would immediately imperil the safety of the Nation by preventing execution of the legislative programs for procurement of military equipment. And, while a shutdown could be averted by granting the price concessions requested by plaintiffs, granting such concessions would disrupt the price stabilization program also enacted by Congress. Rather than fail to execute either legislative program, the President acted to execute both.

Much of the argument in this case has been directed at straw men. We do not now have before us the case of a President acting solely on the basis of his own notions of the public welfare. Nor is there any question of unlimited executive power in this case. The President himself closed the door to any such claim when he sent his Message to Congress stating his purpose to abide by any action of Congress, whether approving or disapproving his seizure action. Here, the President immediately made sure that Congress was fully informed of the temporary action he had taken only to preserve the legislative programs from destruction until Congress could act.

****

Whatever the extent of Presidential power on more tranquil occasions, and whatever the right of the President to execute legislative programs as he sees fit without reporting the mode of execution to Congress, the single Presidential purpose disclosed on this record is to faithfully execute the laws by acting in an emergency to maintain the status quo, thereby preventing collapse of the legislative programs until Congress could act. The President's action served the same purposes as a judicial stay entered to maintain the status quo in order to preserve the jurisdiction of a court. In his Message to Congress immediately following the seizure, the President explained the necessity of his action in executing the military procurement and anti-inflation legislative programs and expressed his desire to cooperate with any legislative proposals approving, regulating or rejecting the seizure of the steel mills. Consequently, there is no evidence whatever of any Presidential purpose to defy Congress or act in any way inconsistent with the legislative will.

In United States v. Midwest Oil Co., supra, this Court approved executive action where, as here, the President acted to preserve an important matter until Congress could act—even though his action in that case was contrary to an express statute. In this case, there is no statute prohibiting the action taken by the President in a matter not merely important but threatening the very safety of the Nation. Executive inaction in such a situation, courting national disaster, is foreign to the concept of energy and initiative in the Executive as created by the Founding Fathers. The Constitution was itself "adopted in a period of grave emergency. . . . While emergency does not create power, emergency may furnish the occasion for the exercise of power."

****

Faced with the duty of executing the defense programs which Congress had enacted and the disastrous effects that any stoppage in steel production would have on those programs, the President acted to preserve those programs by seizing the steel mills. There is no question that the possession was other than temporary in character and subject to congressional direction—either approving, disapproving or regulating the manner in which the mills were to be administered and returned to the owners. The President immediately informed Congress of his action and clearly stated his intention to abide by the legislative will. No basis for claims of arbitrary action, unlimited powers or dictatorial usurpation of congressional power appears from the facts of this case. On the contrary, judicial, legislative and executive precedents throughout our history demonstrate that in this case the President acted in full conformity with his duties under the Constitution. Accordingly, we would reverse the order of the District Court.

THE VETO POWER

**TRUMAN VETOES
THE INTERNAL
SECURITY ACT**

The great check that the President has on the activities of Congress is his power to veto legislation. Before Andrew Jackson's term of office, Chief Executives followed the precedent set by George Washington and utilized the veto only when they were convinced that a statute was unconstitutional; the veto was not, in other words, employed to implement a President's policy views. However, President Jackson took a different view and vetoed more bills than all his predecessors combined: he maintained that the President had every right to use the veto to attain his own policy objectives, a position that has not been seriously challenged since then. (Grover Cleveland, Franklin Roosevelt, and Harry Truman have accounted for more than three-quarters of the total vetoes in our history—F. D. R. alone used the veto 631 times.)

The veto is a clumsy weapon, but a potent one. Under normal political circumstances, it is very difficult to muster the two-thirds-of-a-quorum vote in both houses of Congress that is necessary to override a veto; however, legislators have devised techniques to inhibit the exercise of the President's negative: for example, they will attach a "rider," a proposal known to be objectionable to the White House, to a statute for which the President is clamoring. (There is no item veto: the Chief Executive must approve or disapprove the whole bill.) An informal system has developed in which the President informs Congress unofficially of his intention to veto a bill. (For example, a story "not for attribution" is leaked to New York Times columnist James Reston, who may note that according to "a high government source," the President finds a statute unacceptable in its present form.) Congressmen then attempt to counter the threat and build up a bargaining position of their own to persuade the President to let the bill pass—implicitly threatening to override his veto and/or sabotage other parts of his legislative program in return. Informal communications between the President and Congress allow both sides to find out what points are unacceptable to one side or the other, where areas of possible compromise lie, or at worst, what the penalties for one side will be for ignoring the interests of the other. In a sense, the actual use of the veto generally indicates that the President's informal connections with Congress have broken down.

Such was the case with President Truman and. the Congress elected in 1950. The Korean War and the rise of Communist power in China had created a deep sense of national insecurity and a concomitant demand, particularly from the McCarthyites, for strict internal-security legislation. President Truman took a different perspective and vetoed the proposed Internal Security Act. Congress read the message that accompanied his veto and then rapidly overrode his veto by huge majorities to enact the bill. Only ten Senators voted with the President. The following selection is President Truman's message to Congress.

To the House of Representatives:

I return herewith, without my aproval, H.R. 9490, the proposed Internal Security Act of 1950.

The ostensible purpose . . . is to prevent persons who would be dangerous to our national security from entering the country or becoming citizens. In fact, present law already achieves that objective.

What these provisions would actually do is to prevent us from admitting to our country, or to citizenship, many people who could make real contributions to our national strength. The bill would deprive our Government and our intelligence agencies of the valuable services of aliens in security operations. It would require us to exclude and to deport the citizens of some friendly non-Communist countries. Furthermore, it would actually make it easier for subversive aliens to become United States citizens. Only the Communist movement would gain from such actions . . . .

In brief, when all the provisions of H.R. 9490 are considered together, it is evident that the great bulk of them are not directed toward the real and present dangers that exist from communism. Instead of striking blows at communism, they would strike blows at our own liberties and at our position in the forefront of those working for freedom in the world . . . .

The idea of requiring Communist organizations to divulge information about themselves is a simple and attractive one. But it is about as practical as requiring thieves to register with the sheriff. Obviously, no such organization as the Communist Party is likely to register voluntarily . . . .

FROM Veto Message by President Harry S. Truman, September 22, 1950, *Congressional Record,* Eighty-First Congress, second session (Washington, D.C., Government Printing Office, 1950), Vol. 96, pp. 15629–32 *passim.*

Unfortunately, these provisions are not merely ineffective and unworkable. They represent a clear and present danger to our institutions.

Insofar as the bill would require registration by the Communist Party itself, it does not endanger our traditional liberties. However, the application of the registration requirements to so-called Communist-front organizations can be the greatest danger to freedom of speech, press and assembly, since the alien and sedition laws of 1798. This danger arises out of the criteria or standards to be applied in determining whether an organization is a Communist-front organization.

There would be no serious problem if the bill required proof that an organization was controlled and financed by the Communist Party before it could be classified as a Communist-front organization. However, recognizing the difficulty of proving those matters, the bill would permit such a determination to be based solely upon "the extent to which the positions taken or advanced by it from time to time on matters of policy do not deviate from those" of the Communist movement.

This provision could easily be used to classify as a Communist-front organization any organization which is advocating a single policy or objective which is also being urged by the Communist Party or by a Communist foreign government. In fact, this may be the intended result since the bill defines "organization" to include "a group of persons . . . permanently or temporarily associated together for joint action on any subject or subjects." Thus, an organization which advocates low-cost housing for sincere humanitarian reasons might be classified as a Communist-front organization because the Communists regularly exploit slum conditions as one of their fifth-column techniques.

It is not enough to say that this probably would not be done. The mere fact that it could be done shows clearly how the bill would open a Pandora's box of opportunities for official condemnation of organizations and individuals for perfectly honest opinions which happen to be stated also by Communists.

The basic error of these sections is that they move in the direction of suppressing opinion and belief. This would be a very dangerous course to take, not because we have any sympathy for Communist opinions, but because any governmental stifling of the free expression of opinion is a long step toward totalitarianism.

There is no more fundamental axiom of American freedom than the familiar statement: In a free country we punish men for the crimes they commit but never for the opinions they have. And the reason this is so fundamental to freedom is not, as many suppose, that it protects the few unorthodox from suppression by the majority. To permit freedom of expression is primarily for the benefit of the majority, because it protects criticism, and criticism leads to progress.

We can and we will prevent espionage, sabotage, or other actions endangering our national security. But we would betray our finest traditions if we attempted, as this bill would attempt, to curb the simple expression of opinion. This we should never do, no matter how distasteful the opinion may be to the vast majority of our people. The course proposed by this bill would delight the Communists, for it would make a mockery of the Bill of Rights and of our claims to stand for freedom in the world.

And what kind of effect would these provisions have on the normal expression of political views? Obviously, if this law were on the statute books, the part of prudence would be to avoid saying anything that might be construed by someone as not deviating sufficiently from the current Communist-propaganda line. And since no one could be sure in advance what views were safe to express, the inevitable tendency would be to express no views on controversial subjects.

The result could only be to reduce the vigor and strength of our political life—an outcome that the Communists would happily welcome, but that freemen should abhor.

We need not fear the expression of ideas—we do need to fear their suppression.

Our position in the vanguard of freedom rests largely on our demonstration that the free expression of opinion, coupled with government by popular consent, leads to national strength and human advancement. Let us not, in cowering and foolish fear, throw away the ideals which are the fundamental basis of our free society . . . .

There should be no room in our laws for such hysterical provisions. The next logical step would be to "burn the books." . . .

But far more significant—and far more dangerous—is their apparent underlying purpose. Instead of trying to encourage the free movement of people, subject only to the real requirements of national security, these provisions attempt to bar movement to anyone who is, or once was, associated with ideas we dislike and, in the process, they would succeed in barring many people whom it would be to our advantage to admit.

Such an action would be a serious blow to our work for world peace. We uphold—or have upheld till now, at any rate—the concept of freedom on an international scale. That is the root concept of our efforts to bring unity among the free nations and peace in the world.

The Communists, on the other hand, attempt to break down in every possible way the free interchange of persons and ideas. It will be to their advantage, and not ours, if we establish for ourselves an "iron curtain" against those who can help us in the fight for freedom.

Another provision of the bill which would greatly weaken our national security is section 25, which would make subversive aliens eligible for naturalization as soon as they withdraw from organizations required to register under this bill, whereas under existing law they must wait for a period of 10 years after such withdrawal before becoming eligible for citizenship. This proposal is clearly contrary to the national interest, and clearly gives to the Communists an advantage they do not have under existing law . . .

I do not undertake lightly the responsibility of differing with the majority in both Houses of Congress who have voted for this bill. We are all Americans; we all wish to safeguard and preserve our constitutional liberties against internal and external enemies. But I cannot approve this legislation, which instead of accomplishing its avowed purpose would actually interfere with our liberties and help the Communist against whom the bill was aimed.

This is a time when we must marshal all our resources and all the moral strength of our free system in self-defense against the threat of Communist aggression. We will fail in this, and we will destroy all that we seek to preserve, if we sacrifice the liberties of our citizens in a misguided attempt to achieve national security.

THE REMOVAL POWER

DOCUMENT 13 ## TRUMAN RELIEVES MacARTHUR OF COMMAND

In his capacity as Commander-in-Chief of the Armed Forces, the President is obliged to maintain the principle of civilian control over the military. While all top military appointments have to be approved by the Senate, the Chief Executive's removal power is absolute and unfettered—at least in constitutional terms. For example, during the Civil War, President Lincoln was under constant pressure to replace Democrats in high military command with Republicans. George Mc-Clellan, a Democrat, was particularly suspect in Republican Congressional circles as having political as well as military ambitions (and with some reason—he ran against Lincoln for President in 1864!). However, Lincoln held out in support of McClellan as general-in-chief for several months and did not demote him until he was convinced that the general was too cautious to win battles.

In political terms, however, removal by the Chief Executive may be very difficult indeed: a distinguished general often has a substantial national and Congressional following. The case of General Douglas MacArthur is most instructive. Clearly one of the great military strategists of the twentieth century, MacArthur was always involved in politics: his strategic principles in World War II coincided with the political priorities of the GOP leadership, namely the "Asia First" policy, which appealed enormously to the anti-European sentiments of the former isolationists. MacArthur saw this as a military, not as a political, concept and always denied that he was dabbling in politics —he was not responsible for political fallout from his strategic views. After the defeat of the Japanese, MacArthur took over as American viceroy in the Far East and, with passion and single-mindedness, argued for an Asia-oriented strategy.

The intervention of the Chinese armies in the Korean War in November 1950—after MacArthur had broken the North Korean forces and invaded North Korea in one of the most skillful amphibious operations of all time—brought this latent politico-military conflict to a head. While the President and the Joint Chiefs of Staff, concerned with the containment of Soviet power in Europe, decided to conduct a limited war in Korea, MacArthur publicly called for total victory in Asia at whatever risks were involved. President Truman summarily dismissed the general.

MESSAGE RELIEVING GENERAL MAC ARTHUR OF COMMAND, APRIL 10, 1951

I deeply regret that it becomes my duty as President and Commander in Chief of the United States military forces to replace you as Supreme Commander, Allied Powers; Commander in Chief, United Nations Command; Commander in Chief, Far East; and Commanding General, United States Army, Far East.

You will turn over your commands, effective at once, to Lt. Gen. Matthew B. Ridgway. You are authorized to have issued such orders as are necessary to complete desired travel to such place as you select.

My reasons for your replacement will be made public concurrently with the delivery to you of the foregoing order, and are contained in the next following message.

STATEMENT OF THE PRESIDENT RELATIVE TO THE RELIEF OF GENERAL MAC ARTHUR, APRIL 10, 1951

With deep regret I have concluded that General of the Army Douglas MacArthur is unable to give his wholehearted support to the policies of the United States Government and of the United Nations in matters pertaining to his official duties. In view of the specific responsibilities imposed upon me by the Constitution of the United States and the added responsibility which has been entrusted to me by the United Nations, I have decided that I must make a change of command in the Far East. I have, therefore, relieved General MacArthur of his commands and have designated Lt. Gen. Matthew B. Ridgway as his successor.

Full and vigorous debate on matters of national policy is a vital element in the constitutional system of our free democracy. It is fundamental, however, that military commanders must be governed by the policies and directives issued to them in the manner provided by our laws and Constitution. In time of crisis, this consideration is particularly compelling.

FROM *Military Situation in the Far East,* Hearings, Senate Committees on Armed Services and Foreign Relations, Eighty-Second Congress, first session (Washington, D.C., Government Printing Office, 1951), pp. 3179–80.

General MacArthur's place in history as one of our greatest commanders is fully established. The Nation owes him a debt of gratitude for the distinguished and exceptional service which he has rendered his country in posts of great responsibility. For that reason I repeat my regret at the necessity for the action I feel compelled to take in his case.

DOCUMENT 14 REMOVING CIVILIAN EMPLOYEES

The President's removal power is plenary with respect to military command and to purely executive officials who are outside of the coverage of the civil-service system. In dealing with the segment of the federal Administration that has civil-service protection (encompassing a couple of million positions, or over 95 per cent of the civilian establishment), the President can dismiss only by procedures and on grounds stipulated by Congress. (Not until 1963 did Congress provide that employees of the National Security Agency, like those of the Central Intelligence Agency, could be summarily fired without any of the normal procedural protections.) Civil-service legislation thus puts great checks on the Chief Executive's removal power—thereby limiting his use of patronage to cement party ranks: when the Eisenhower Administration took office in 1953, it discovered only a few thousand positions outside the protected zone, and the Kennedy Administration had the same experience in 1961.

The so-called quasi-legislative officials who are found on a number of regulatory agencies and other ad hoc bodies represent another gray area of the removal power. When President Roosevelt tried to remove William Humphrey from the Federal Trade Commission, the Supreme Court ruled in Humphrey's Executor v. United States (1935) that the President could remove appointees on political grounds only from purely executive jobs. It declared that since the functions of the FTC were quasi-judicial and quasi-legislative, the President could remove a member only for inefficiency or malfeasance, as stipulated by Congress.

As Justice Frankfurter's opinion indicates, President Eisenhower, searching for loaves and fishes for the Republican faithful, removed Mr. Wiener from the War Claims Commission in 1953 and replaced him with a GOP stalwart. Wiener asserted that, in effect, he did not work for the President but for Congress and that the legislature had not intended War Claims commissioners to work under a Presidential "sword of Damocles." The Court's decision reasserted the principle that Congress, when it sets up administrative and regulatory bodies, can severely limit the authority of the Chief Executive. This means that members of regulatory agencies such as the Federal Reserve Board, the Federal Communications Commission, or the Interstate Commerce Commission—to name only three—can be dismissed from office only on grounds stipulated by Congress: the President cannot fire them for even the most persistent and contumacious opposition to his political policies.

MR. JUSTICE FRANKFURTER delivered the opinion of the court:

This is a suit for back pay, based on petitioner's alleged illegal removal as a member of the War Claims Commission. The facts are not in dispute. By the War Claims Act of 1948, 62 Stat. 1240, Congress established that Commission with "jurisdiction to receive and adjudicate according to law," § 3, claims for compensating internees, prisoners of war, and religious organizations, §§ 5, 6 and 7, who suffered personal injury or property damage at the hands of the enemy in connection with World War II. The Commission was to be composed of three persons, at least two of whom were to be members of the bar, to be appointed by the President, by and with the advice and consent of the Senate. The Commission was to wind up its affairs not later than three years after the expiration of the time for filing claims, originally limited to two years but extended by successive legislation first to March 1, 1951, 63 Stat. 112, and later to March 31, 1952, 65 Stat. 28. This limit on the Commission's life was the mode by which the tenure of the Commissioners was defined, and Congress made no provision for removal of a Commissioner.

Having been duly nominated by President Truman, the petitioner was confirmed on June 2, 1950, and took office on June 8, following. On his refusal to heed a request for his resignation, he was, on December 10, 1953, removed by President Eisenhower in the following terms: "I regard it as in the national interest to complete the administration of the War Claims Act of 1948, as amended, with personnel of my own selection." The following day, the President made recess appointments to the Commission, including petitioner's post. After Congress assembled, the President, on February 15, 1954, sent the names of the new appointees to the Senate. The Senate had not confirmed these nominations when the Commission was abolished, July 1, 1954, by Reorganization Plan No. 1 of 1954, 68 Stat. 1279, issued pursuant to the Reorganization Act of 1949, 63 Stat. 203. Thereupon, petitioner brought this proceeding in the Court of Claims for recovery

FROM Opinion by Mr. Justice Frankfurter, *Wiener* v. *United States,* 357 U.S. 349 (1958).

THE REMOVAL POWER

of his salary as a War Claims Commissioner from December 10, 1953, the day of his removal by the President, to June 30, 1954, the last day of the Commission's existence. A divided Court of Claims dismissed the petition, 135 Ct. Cl. 827, 142 F. Supp. 910. We brought the case here, 352 U.S. 980, because it presents a variant of the constitutional issue decided in *Humphrey's Executor v. United States,* 295 U.S. 602.

Controversy pertaining to the scope and limits of the President's power of removal fills a thick chapter of our political and judicial history. The long stretches of its history, beginning with the very first Congress, with early echoes in the Reports of this Court, were laboriously traversed in *Myers v. United States,* 272 U.S. 52, and need not be retraced. President Roosevelt's reliance upon the pronouncements of the Court in that case in removing a member of the Federal Trade Commission on the ground that "the aims and purposes of the Administration with respect to the work of the Commission can be carried out most effectively with personnel of my own selection" reflected contemporaneous professional opinion regarding the significance of the *Myers* decision. Speaking through a Chief Justice who himself had been President, the Court did not restrict itself to the immediate issue before it, the President's inherent power to remove a postmaster, obviously an executive official. As of set purpose and not by way of parenthetic casualness, the Court announced that the President had inherent constitutional power of removal also of officials who have "duties of a quasi-judicial character . . . whose decisions after hearing affect interests of individuals, the discharge of which the President can not in a particular case properly influence or control." (*Myers v. United States, supra,* at 135.) This view of presidential power was deemed to flow from his "constitutional duty of seeing that the laws be faithfully executed." (*Ibid.*)

The assumption was short-lived that the *Myers* case recognized the President's inherent constitutional power to remove officials, no matter what the relation of the executive to the discharge of their duties and no matter what restrictions Congress may have imposed regarding the nature of their tenure. The versatility of circumstances often mocks a natural desire for definitiveness. Within less than ten years a unanimous Court, in *Humphrey's Executor v. United States,* 295 U.S. 602, narrowly confined the scope of the *Myers* decision to include only "all purely executive officers." (295 U.S., at 628.) The Court explicitly "disapproved" the expressions in *Myers* supporting the President's inherent constitutional power to remove members of quasi-judicial bodies. (295 U.S., at 626–627.) Congress had given members of the Federal Trade Commission a seven-year term and also provided for the removal of a Commissioner by the President for inefficiency, neglect of duty or malfeasance in office. In the present case, Congress provided for a tenure defined by the relatively short period of time during which the War Claims Commission was to operate—that is, it was to wind up not later than three years after the expiration of the time for filing of claims. But nothing was said in the Act about removal.

This is another instance in which the most appropriate legal significance must be drawn from congressional failure of explicitness. Necessarily this is a problem in probabilities. We start with one certainty. The problem of the President's power to remove members of agencies entrusted with duties of the kind with which the War Claims Commission was charged was within the lively knowledge of Congress. Few contests between Congress and the President have so recurringly had the attention of Congress as that pertaining to the power of removal. Not the least significant aspect of the *Myers* case is that on the Court's special invitation Senator George Wharton Pepper, of Pennsylvania, presented the position of Congress at the bar of this Court.

Humphrey's case was a *cause célèbre*—and not least in the halls of Congress. And what is the essence of the decision in Humphrey's case? It drew a sharp line of cleavage between officials who were part of the Executive establishment and were thus removable by virtue of the President's constitutional powers, and those who are members of a body "to exercise its judgment without the leave or hindrance of any other official or any department of the government," 295 U.S., at 625–626, as to whom a power of removal exists only if Congress may fairly be said to have conferred it. This sharp differentiation derives from the difference in functions between those who are part of the Executive establishment and those whose tasks require absolute freedom from Executive interference. "For it is quite evident," again to quote *Humphrey's Executor,* "that one who holds his office only during the pleasure of another, cannot be depended upon to maintain an attitude of independence against the latter's will." (295 U.S., at 629.)

Thus, the most reliable factor for drawing an inference regarding the President's power of removal in our case is the nature of the function that Congress vested in the War Claims Commission. What were the duties that Congress confided to this Commission? And can the inference fairly be drawn from the failure of Congress to provide for removal that these Commissioners were to remain in office at the will of the President? For such is the assertion of power on which petitioner's removal must rest. The ground of President Eisenhower's removal of petitioner was precisely the same as President Roosevelt's removal of Humphrey. Both Presidents desired to have Commissioners, one on the Federal Trade Commission, the other on the War Claims Commission, "of my own selection." They wanted these Commissioners to be their men. The terms of removal in the two cases are identical and express the assumption that the agencies of which the two Commissioners were members were subject in the discharge of their duties to the control of the Executive. An analysis of the Federal Trade Commission Act left this court in no doubt that such was not the conception of Congress in creating the Federal Trade Commission. The terms of the War Claims Act of 1948 leave no doubt that such was not the conception of Congress regarding the War Claims Commission.

The history of this legislation emphatically underlines this fact. The short of it is that the origin of the Act was a bill, H.R. 4044, 80th Cong., 1st Sess., passed by the House that placed the administration of a very limited class of claims by Americans against Japan in the hands of the Federal Security Administrator and provided for a Commission to inquire into and report upon other types of claims. . . . The Federal Security Administrator was indubitably an arm of the President. When the House bill reached the Senate, it struck out all but the enacting clause, rewrote the bill, and established a Commission with "jurisdiction to receive and adjudicate according to law" three classes of claims, as defined by § § 5, 6 and 7. The Commission was established as an adjudicating body with all the paraphernalia by which legal claims are put to the test of proof, with finality of determination "not subject to review by any other official of the United States or by any court, by mandamus or otherwise," § 11. Awards were to be paid out of a War Claims Fund in the hands of the Secretary of the Treasury, whereby such claims were given even more assured collectability than adheres to judgments rendered in the Court of Claims. . . . With minor amendment, . . . this Senate bill became law.

When Congress has for distribution among American claimants funds derived from foreign sources, it may proceed in different ways. Congress may appropriate directly; it may utilize the Executive; it may resort to the adjudicatory process. See *La Abra Silver Mining Co. v. United States,* 175 U.S. 423. For Congress itself to have made appropriations for the claims with which it dealt under the War Claims Act was not practical in view of the large number of claimants and the diversity in the specific circumstances giving rise to the claims. The House bill in effect put the distribution of the narrow class of claims that it acknowledged into Executive hands, by vesting the procedure in the Federal Security Administrator. The final form of the legislation, as we have seen, left the widened range of claims to be determined by adjudication. Congress could, of course, have given jurisdiction over these claims to the District Courts or to the Court of Claims. The fact that it chose to establish a Commission to "adjudicate according to law" the classes of claims defined in the statute did not alter the intrinsic judicial character of the task with which the Commission was charged. The claims were to be "adjudicated according to law," that is, on the merits of each claim, supported by evidence and governing legal considerations, by a body that was "entirely free from the control or coercive influence, direct or indirect," *Humphrey's Executor v. United States, supra,* 295 U.S., at 629, of either the Executive or the Congress. If, as one must take for granted, the War Claims Act precluded the President from influencing the Commission in passing on a particular claim, *a fortiori* must it be inferred that Congress did not wish to have hang over the Commission the Damocles' sword of removal by the President for no reason other than that he preferred to have on that Commission men of his own choosing.

For such is this case. We have not a removal for cause involving the rectitude of a member of an adjudicatory body, nor even a suspensory removal until the Senate could act upon it by confirming the appointment of a new Commissioner or otherwise dealing with the matter. Judging the matter in all the nakedness in which it is presented, namely, the claim that the President could remove a member of an adjudicatory body like the War Claims Commission merely because he wanted his own appointees on such a Commission, we are compelled to conclude that no such power is given to the President directly by the Constitution, and none is impliedly conferred upon him by statute simply because Congress said nothing about it. The philosophy of *Humphrey's Executor,* in its explicit language as well as its implications, precludes such a claim.

The judgment is reversed.

MORAL AUTHORITY
OR NAKED
POLITICAL POWER?

DOCUMENT 15 KENNEDY AND
THE STEEL INDUSTRY

In April 1962 President Kennedy found himself, like several of his predecessors, in a fierce scrimmage with the steel industry. As background to this encounter, it should be noted that the President had earlier brought great pressure to bear on the leaders of the Steelworkers union in the interest of a noninflationary wage settlement. With some grumbling, the union leadership endorsed the President's position that the inflationary spiral had to be stopped at the wage as well as the price level. President Kennedy had received a good deal of acclaim for his ability to influence the union when suddenly the steel companies announced a price increase. This action made the trade-union concessions look like a philanthropic gesture, as the union rank and file pointedly informed their leadership and as the union leaders pointed out to the President. The workers were prepared to restrain their demands in the interest of a national anti-inflation policy, but they were unwilling to do so if the steel companies were going to jack up profits and simultaneously spur inflation through a price increase.

Although the President has no express authority to fix prices, he can use the prestige of his office to persuade private industry that certain policies are essential for maintaining a stable economy. At his command are executive powers that can be used to exert indirect pressure on private industry. President Kennedy, hearing of the price increase and allegedly feeling he had been double-crossed, went into a towering rage. He mounted a many-pronged administrative assault on the steel companies (the "administrative version of the bum's rush" was the description of one commentator). The Administration conducted *a telephone campaign to discourage holdout steel companies from raising prices, while the Defense Department announced that government contracts would go only to companies not raising prices. Attorney-General Kennedy threatened grand-jury antitrust proceedings, Senator Kefauver and Representative Celler announced that their judiciary subcommittees would start Congressional investigations, and the Administration began drafting new antitrust legislation to submit to Congress. The steel companies hastily withdrew their price increases (which were not successfully reimposed until the spring of 1963—and then only on a selective basis).*

This selection demonstrates how Kennedy employed his press conference as a vehicle for mobilizing public support for executive intervention in price-setting by showing that the national interest demanded strong Presidential action.

[THE PRESIDENT:] Simultaneous and identical actions of United States Steel and other leading steel corporations increasing steel prices by some $6 a ton constitute a wholly unjustifiable and irresponsible defiance of the public interest.

In this serious hour in our Nation's history, when we are confronted with grave crises in Berlin and Southeast Asia, when we are devoting our energies to economic recovery and stability, when we are asking reservists to leave their homes and families for months on end and servicemen to risk their lives—and four were killed in the last two days in Vietnam—and asking union members to hold down their wage increases, at a time when restraint and sacrifice are being asked of every citizen, the American people will find it hard, as I do, to accept a situation in which a tiny handful of steel executives whose pursuit of private power and profit exceeds their sense of public responsibility can show such utter contempt for the interests of 185 million Americans.

If this rise in the cost of steel is imitated by the rest of the industry, instead of rescinded, it would increase the cost of homes, autos, appliances, and most other items for every American family. It would increase the cost of machinery and tools to every American businessman and farmer. It would seriously handicap our efforts to prevent an inflationary spiral from eating up the pensions of our older citizens, and our new gains in purchasing power.

FROM Press Conference by President John F. Kennedy, April 11, 1962, New York *Times,* April 12, 1962. Copyright by The New York Times. Reprinted by permission.

MORAL AUTHORITY OR NAKED POLITICAL POWER?

It would add, Secretary McNamara informed me this morning, an estimated $1 billion to the cost of our defenses, at a time when every dollar is needed for national security and other purposes. It would make it more difficult for American goods to compete in foreign markets, more difficult to withstand competition from foreign imports, and thus more difficult to improve our balance of payments position, and stem the flow of gold. And it is necessary to stem it for our national security, if we are going to pay for our security commitments abroad. And it would surely handicap our efforts to induce other industries and unions to adopt responsible price and wage policies.

The facts of the matter are that there is no justification for an increase in the steel prices. The recent settlement between the industry and the union, which does not even take place until July 1st, was widely acknowledged to be non-inflationary, and the whole purpose and effect of this Administration's role, which both parties understood, was to achieve an agreement which would make unnecessary any increase in prices. Steel output per man is rising so fast that labor costs per ton of steel can actually be expected to decline in the next 12 months. And in fact, the Acting Commissioner of the Bureau of Labor Statistics informed me this morning that, and I quote: "Employment costs per unit of steel output in 1961 were essentially the same as they were in 1958."

The cost of the major raw materials, steel scrap and coal, has also been declining, and for an industry which has been generally operating at less than two-thirds of capacity, its profit rate has been normal and can be expected to rise sharply this year in view of the reduction in idle capacity.

Their lot has been easier than that of 100,000 steel workers thrown out of work in the last three years. The industry's cash dividends have exceeded $600 million in each of the last five years, and earnings in the first quarter of this year were estimated in the February 28th Wall Street Journal to be among the highest in the history.

In short, at a time when they could be exploring how more efficient and better prices could be obtained [by] reducing prices in this industry in recognition of lower costs, their unusually good labor contract, their foreign competition and their increase in production and profits which are coming this year, a few gigantic corporations have decided to increase prices in ruthless disregard of their public responsibilities.

The Steelworkers union can be proud that it abided by its responsibilities in this agreement. And this government also has responsibilities which we intend to meet. The Department of Justice and the Federal Trade Commission are examining the significance of this action in a free, competitive economy. The Department of Defense and other agencies are reviewing its impact on their policies of procurement and I am informed that steps are underway by those members of the Congress who plan appropriate inquiries into how these price decisions are so quickly made and reached, and what legislative safeguards may be needed to protect the public interest.

Price and wage decisions in this country, except for very limited restrictions in the case of monopolies and national emergency strikes, are and ought to be freely and privately made, but the American people have a right to expect in return for that freedom, a higher sense of business responsibility for the welfare of their country than has been shown in the last two days.

Some time ago I asked each American to consider what he would do for his country. And I asked the steel companies. In the last 24 hours we had their answer.

✦✦✦✦

Q: Mr. President, in connection with the steel situation, again, is there not action that could be taken by the Executive Branch in connection with direct procurement of steel under the administration of the Agency for International Aid—I mean the Agency—for example, I think the Government buys about a million tons of steel. Could not the Government decide that only steel—that steel should be purchased only at the price, say, of yesterday, rather than today?

THE PRESIDENT: That matter was hinted, as a matter of fact, in a conversation between the Secretary of Defense and myself last evening, but at that time we were not aware that nearly the entire industry was about to come in, and, therefore, the amount of choice we have is somewhat limited.

IDENTICAL STEEL BIDS

Q: Sir, part two on this thing in the case of identical bids which the Government is sometimes confronted with, they decide to choose the smaller business unit rather than the larger.

THE PRESIDENT: I am hopeful that there will be those who will not participate in this parade and will meet the principle of the private enterprise competitive system in which every one tries to sell at the lowest price commensurate with their interests. And I am hopeful that there will be some who will decide that they shouldn't go in the way of U.S. Steel. But we have to wait and see on that, because they are coming very fast.

BIG STEEL ANTI-KENNEDY?

Q: Mr. President, two years ago after the settlement, I believe steel prices were not raised.

MORAL AUTHORITY OR NAKED POLITICAL POWER?

THE PRESIDENT: That is right.

Q: Do you think there was an element of political discrimination in the behavior of the industry this year?

THE PRESIDENT: I would not—and if there was, it doesn't really—if it was, if that was the purpose, that is comparatively unimportant to the damage that—the country is the one that suffers. If they do it in order to spite me, it really isn't so important.

STEEL PRICE COMMITMENTS

Q: Mr. President, to carry a previous question just one step further, as a result of the emphasis that you placed on holding the price line, did any word or impression come to you from the negotiations that there would be no price increase under the type of agreement that was signed?

THE PRESIDENT: I will say that in our conversations in which—we asked no commitments in regard to the details of the agreement or in regard to any policies of the union or the company. Our central thrust was that price stability was necessary and that the way to do it was to have a responsible agreement, which we got.

Now, at no time did any one suggest that if such an agreement was gained, that it would be still necessary to put up prices. That word did not come until last night.

****

Q: Mr. President, the steel industry is one of a half dozen which has been expecting tax benefits this summer through revision of the depreciation schedules. Does this price hike affect the Administration's actions in this area?

THE PRESIDENT: Well, it affects our budget. Secretary Dillon and I discussed it this morning. Of course, all this matter is being very carefully looked into now.

Q: Mr. President, the unusually strong language which you used in discussing the steel situation would indicate that you might be considering some pretty strong action. Are you thinking in terms of requesting or reviving the need for wage-price controls?

THE PRESIDENT: I think that my statement states what the situation is today. This is a free country. In all the conversations which were held by members of this Administration and myself with the leaders of the steel union and the companies, it was always very obvious that they could proceed with freedom to do what they thought was best within the limitations of law. But I did very clearly emphasize on every occasion that my only interest was that in trying to secure an agreement which would not provide an increase in prices, because I thought that price stability in steel would have the most far-reaching consequences for industrial and economic stability and for our position abroad, and price instability would have the most-far-reaching consequences in making our lot much more difficult.

When the agreement was signed—and the agreement was a moderate one and within the range of productivity increases, as I have said—actually, there will be reduction in cost per unit during the next year—I thought, I was hopeful, we had achieved our goal. Now the actions that will be taken will be—are being now considered by the Administration. The Department of Justice is, particularly in view of the very speedy action of the companies who have entirely different economic problems facing them than did United States steel, the speed with which they moved, it seems to me to require an examination of our present laws, and whether they are being obeyed, by the Federal Trade Commission, and by the Department of Justice. I am very interested in the respective investigations that will be conducted in the House and Senate, and whether we shall need additional legislation, which I would come to very reluctantly. But I must say the last 24 hours indicates that those with great power are not always concerned about the national interest.

TALKS WITH BLOUGH

Q: In your conversation with Mr. Blough yesterday, did you make a direct request that this price increase be either deferred or rescinded?

THE PRESIDENT: I was informed about the price increase after the announcement had gone out to the papers. I told Mr. Blough of my very keen disappointment and what I thought would be the most unfortunate effects of it. And of course we were hopeful that other companies who I have said, have a different situation in regard to profits and all of the rest than U.S. Steel. They all have somewhat different economic situations. I was hopeful particularly in view of the statement in the paper by the President of Bethlehem in which he stated—although now he says he is misquoted—that there should be no price increase and we are investigating that statement. I was hopeful that the others would not follow the example and therefore the pressures of the competitive marketplace would bring United States Steel back to their original prices. But the parade began. But it came to me after the decision was made, there was no prior consultation or information given to me.

Q: Mr. President, if I could get back to steel for a minute, you mentioned an investigation into the suddenness of the decision to increase prices. Did you—is it the position of the Administration that it believed it had the assurance of the steel industry at the time of the recent labor agreement that it would not increase prices? Is that a breach of their . . . .

THE PRESIDENT: We did not ask either side to give us any assurance, because there is a very proper limitation to the power of the Government in this free economy. All we did in our meetings was to emphasize how important it was that there be price stability, and we stressed that our whole purpose in attempting to persuade the union to begin to bargain early and to make an agreement which would not affect prices, of course, was for the purpose of maintaining price stability. That was the thread that ran through every discussion which I had or Secretary Goldberg had. We never at any time asked for a commitment in regard to the terms, precise terms of the agreement, from either Mr. McDonald or Mr. Blough, representing the steel company, because in our opinion that would be passing over the line of propriety. But I don't think that there was any question that our great interest in attempting to secure the kind of settlement that was finally secured was to maintain price stability, which we regard as very essential at this particular time. That agreement provided the price stability up until yesterday.

✦✦✦✦

Q: Mr. President, on your statement on the steel industry, sir, you mentioned a number of instances which would indicate that the cost of living will go up for many people if this price increase were to remain effective. In your opinion, does that give the steelworkers the right to try to obtain some kind of a wage increase to catch up?

THE PRESIDENT: Rather interestingly, the last contract was signed on Saturday at Great Lakes so that the steel union is bound for a year, and of course, I am sure would have felt like going much further if the matters had worked out as we all hoped. But they have made their agreement and I am sure they are going to stick with it, but it does not provide for the sort of action you have mentioned.

REGULATED STEEL PRICES

Q: Still on steel, Senator Gore advocated today legislation to regulate steel prices somewhat in the manner that public utilities prices are regulated and his argument seemed to be that the steel industry had sacrificed some of the privileges of the free market because it wasn't really setting its prices on supply and demand, but what he called "administered prices." Your statement earlier, and your remarks since, indicate a general agreement with that kind of approach. Is that correct?

THE PRESIDENT: No, Mr. Morgan, I don't think that I have stated that. I would have to look and see what Senator Gore has suggested. I am not familiar with it. What I said was that we should examine what can be done to try to minimize the impact on the public interest of these decisions, although we had, of course, always hoped that those involved would recognize that. I would say that what must disturb Senator Gore and Congressman Celler and others, and Senator Kefauver, will be the suddenness by which every company in the last few hours, one by one as the morning went by, came in with their almost, if not identical, almost identical price increases which isn't really the way we expect the competitive private enterprise system to always work.

❖❖❖❖

DOCUMENT 16 THE GOP LISTS "POLICE STATE" METHODS

The extent to which the President can use the powers of the federal government to persuade private industry to uphold the "national interest" is a subject that was under hot debate during the 1962 steel-pricing dispute, discussed in Document 16. Although Kennedy was victorious over the steel companies, Republican leaders argued that neither the Constitution nor any law gave him the right to set prices; not only was his intervention unconstitutional, they charged, but the pressures he applied were inherently anti-democratic. The Senate-House Republican leadership issued a furious pronouncement, reproduced here, calling the attention of the American people to this "police state" action.

We, the members of the Joint Senate-House Republican Leadership, deplore the necessity for issuing this statement, but the issues involved are too compelling to be ignored.

Beyond the administrative operations of the Federal Government, it is a proper function of a President, in fact it is a duty, to help American private enterprise maintain a stable economy. In our free society he must usually find his way by persuasion and the prestige of his office.

Last week President Kennedy made a determination that a 3½ per cent increase [in the price of steel would] throw the American economy out of line on several fronts. In the next twenty-four hours the President directed or supported a series of Governmental actions that

FROM Statement by Joint Senate-House Republican leadership, April 19, 1962, New York *Times,* April 20, 1962. Copyright by The New York Times. Reprinted by permission.

MORAL AUTHORITY OR NAKED POLITICAL POWER?

imperiled basic American rights, went far beyond the law, and were more characteristic of a police state than a free government.

We, the members of the Joint Senate-House Republican Leadership, believe that a fundamental issue has been raised: should a President of the United States use the enormous powers of the Federal Government to blackjack any segment of our free society into line with his personal judgment without regard to law?

SEE CUMULATIVE EFFECT

Nine actions which followed President Kennedy's press conference of Wednesday, April 11, were obviously a product of White House direction or encouragement and must be considered for their individual and cumulative effect. They were:

1. The Federal Trade Commission publicly suggested the possibility of collusion, announced an immediate investigation and talked of $2,000 a day penalties.

2. The Justice Department spoke threateningly of antitrust violations and ordered an immediate investigation.

3. Treasury Department officials indicated they were at once reconsidering the planned increase in depreciation rates for steel.

4. The Internal Revenue Service was reported making a menacing move toward U.S. Steel's incentive benefits plan for its executives.

5. The Senate Antitrust and Monopoly subcommittee began subpoenaing records from twelve steel companies, returnable May 14.

6. The House Antitrust subcommittee announced an immediate investigation, with hearings opening May 2.

7. The Justice Department announced it was ordering a grand jury investigation.

8. The Department of Defense, seemingly ignoring laws requiring competitive bidding, publicly announced it was shifting steel purchases to companies that had not increased prices, and other Government agencies were directed to do likewise.

9. The F.B.I. began routing newspaper men out of bed at 3:00 A.M. on Thursday, April 12, in line with President Kennedy's press conference assertion that "we are investigating" a statement attributed to a steel company official in the newspapers.

"NAKED POLITICAL POWER"

Taken cumulatively these nine actions amount to a display of naked political power never seen before in this nation.

Taken singly these nine actions are punitive, heavyhanded and frightening.

Although the President at his press conference made it clear that "price and wage decisions in this country . . . are and ought to be freely and privately made," there was nothing in the course of action which he pursued that supported this basic American doctrine.

Indeed, if big government can be used to extra-legally reverse the economic decisions of one industry in a free economy, then it can be used to reverse the decisions of any business, big or small, of labor, of farmers, in fact, of any citizen.

Most disturbing in its implications was the use of the F.B.I. Since the days of our founding fathers, this land has been the haven of millions who fled from the feared knock on the door in the night.

We condone nothing in the actions of the steel companies except their right to make an economic judgment without massive retaliation by the Federal Government.

Temporarily President Kennedy may have won a political victory, but at the cost of doing violence to the fundamental precepts of a free society.

This nation must realize that we have passed within the shadow of police state methods. We hope that we never again step into those dark regions whatever the controversy of the moment, be it economic or political.

part two

THE EXECUTIVE BRANCH AND FOREIGN POLICY

FOREIGN-POLICY INSTITUTIONS

DOCUMENT 17 THE ROLE OF THE PRESIDENT

Under the Articles of Confederation, the conduct of foreign affairs was supervised first by a Congressional committee and then by a Secretary of Foreign Affairs appointed by Congress. The Constitution, however, created a strong executive branch, and it was clearly the intention of the Founding Fathers that the President should exercise control over the conduct of foreign policy. Discussing the treaty power in the sixty-fourth Federalist paper, John Jay noted, "So often and so essentially have we heretofore suffered from the want of secrecy and dispatch that the Constitution would have been inexcusably defective if no attention had been paid to those object[ive]s. . . . For these the President will find no difficulty to provide."

Although the President is allowed enormous latitude in foreign policy, constitutional provisions and political imperatives both demand that he work out his programs in conjunction with Congress. The President must keep one eye on Congressional response not only because he needs its help in setting up and implementing his policies, but also because the opinions expressed within Congress provide a rough barometer of American attitudes in general. In constitutional terms, the Founding Fathers provided that the President must get the advice and consent of two-thirds of the Senate on all treaties, and they suggested that the President might employ that body as an advisory council in the formulation of policy. George Washington tried this once in connection with an Indian treaty, but the Senate stood on its prerogatives and informed him that it would discuss the matter privately and give him its judgment. Washington departed in high dudgeon, and thus ended the first and last effort formally to enlist the upper house in the preliminaries of negotiation.

But it is politically wise for a President to attempt informally to associate influential Senators with his policies in foreign affairs in order to build up a bipartisan consensus for his programs. Efforts to bypass Congress may make the action in question a partisan issue that will probably defeat the pending question and may hurt the party in power as well. For example, President Wilson's failure to include any politically significant Republicans in the delegation to Versailles in 1919 is often considered his major blunder, one that contributed to the defeat of the treaty in the Senate.

And to take another example, President Truman's response to the invasion of South Korea was initially very popular in the United States. Yet from the outset, influential Republicans in Congress declared that he had violated the Constitution by not asking the legislature for a declaration of war. Subsequently, as the Korean War became increasingly unpopular, Truman and the Democrats were accused of being the "war party"—a charge that hurt them badly in the 1952 elections. President Eisenhower, confronted by the same international problems that Truman had faced, went to extraordinary lengths to placate Congress, refusing, for example, to support the French in Indochina (because of the unpopularity of French colonialism), and later asking Congress for advance authorization of any emergency actions he might feel were necessary in the defense of Formosa and the Middle East.

Congress not only exercises the power of approval of the President's foreign-policy negotiations, but since the implementation of foreign policy costs money, it wields the power of the purse strings as well. As early as 1795 an argument developed (featuring James Madison and Alexander Hamilton, coauthors with John Jay of the Federalist papers, on opposite sides of the fence) as to whether the House of Representatives was bound to provide funds to implement the Jay treaty with Britain that had been approved by the Senate. Madison lost the battle—the necessary funds were appropriated—but he won the war: never since has the approval of the House of Representatives been taken for granted. (In 1812, President Madison had his own problems with Congress: when he asked for a declaration of war on Great Britain, the Senate took ten days to discuss the proposal before agreeing by a vote of 19 to 13!)

The following selection provides Justice Sutherland's classic formulation of Presidential jurisdiction in foreign policy. Congress may have great influence on the terms the President offers and accepts, but it cannot itself invade the arena of negotiations. The document sets out the premise that while Congress must be consulted—even cajoled—in putting programs into effect, ultimately the President alone is responsible for the conduct of American foreign policy.

MR. JUSTICE SUTHERLAND delivered the opinion of the Court.

✻✻✻✻

Not only, as we have shown, is the federal power over external affairs in origin and essential character different from that over internal affairs, but participation in the exercise of the power is significantly limited. In this vast external realm, with its important, complicated, delicate and manifold problems, the President alone has the power to speak or listen as a representative of the nation. He *makes* treaties with the advice and consent of the Senate; but he alone negotiates. Into the field of negotiation the Senate cannot intrude; and Congress itself is powerless to invade it. As Marshall said in his great argument of March 7, 1800, in the House of Representatives, "The President is the sole organ of the nation in its external relations, and its sole representative with foreign nations." . . . The Senate Committee on Foreign Relations at a very early day in our history (February 15, 1816), reported to the Senate, among other things, as follows:

The President is the constitutional representative of the United States with regard to foreign nations. He manages our concerns with foreign nations and must necessarily be most competent to determine when, how, and upon what subjects negotiations may be urged with the greatest prospect of success. For his conduct he is responsible to the Constitution. The committee consider this responsibility the surest pledge for the faithful discharge of his duty. They think the interference of the Senate in the direction of foreign negotiations calculated to diminish that responsibility and thereby to impair the best security for the national safety. The nature of transactions with foreign nations, moreover, requires caution and unity of design, and their success frequently depends on secrecy and dispatch. . . .

It is important to bear in mind that we are here dealing not alone with an authority vested in the President by an exertion of legislative power, but with such an authority plus the very delicate, plenary and exclusive power of the President as the sole organ of the federal government in the field of international relations—a power which does not require as a basis for its exercise an act of Congress, but which, of course, like every other governmental power, must be exercised in subordination to the applicable provisions of the Constitution. It is quite apparent that if, in the maintenance of our international relations, embarrassment—perhaps serious embarrassment—is to be avoided and success for our aims achieved, congressional legislation

FROM Opinion by Mr. Justice Sutherland, *United States* v. *Curtiss-Wright Export Corporation*, 299 U.S. 304 (1936).

which is to be made effective through negotiation and inquiry within the international field must often accord to the President a degree of discretion and freedom from statutory restriction which would not be admissible were domestic affairs alone involved. Moreover, he, not Congress, has the better opportunity of knowing the conditions which prevail in foreign countries, and especially is this true in time of war. He has his confidential sources of information. He has his agents in the form of diplomatic, consular and other officials. Secrecy in respect of information gathered by them may be highly necessary, and the premature disclosure of it productive of harmful results. Indeed, so clearly is this true that the first President refused to accede to a request to lay before the House of Representatives the instructions, correspondence and documents relating to the negotiation of the Jay Treaty—a refusal the wisdom of which was recognized by the House itself and has never since been doubted. In his reply to the request, President Washington said: *SECRECY*

The nature of foreign negotiations requires caution, and their success must often depend on secrecy; and even when brought to a conclusion a full disclosure of all the measures, demands, or eventual concessions which may have been proposed or contemplated would be extremely impolitic; for this might have a pernicious influence on future negotiations, or produce immediate inconveniences, perhaps danger and mischief, in relation to other powers. The necessity of such caution and secrecy was one cogent reason for vesting the power of making treaties in the President, with the advice and consent of the Senate, the principle on which that body was formed confining it to a small number of members. To admit, then, a right in the House of Representatives to demand and to have as a matter of course all the papers respecting a negotiation with a foreign power would be to establish a dangerous precedent. . . .

The marked difference between foreign affairs and domestic affairs in this respect is recognized by both houses of Congress in the very form of their requisitions for information from the executive departments. In the case of every department except the Department of State, the resolution *directs* the official to furnish the information. In the case of the State Department, dealing with foreign affairs, the President is *requested* to furnish the information "if not incompatible with the public interest." A statement that to furnish the information is not compatible with the public interest rarely, if ever, is questioned.

When the President is to be authorized by legislation to act in respect of a matter intended to affect a situation in foreign territory, the legislator properly bears in mind the important consideration that the form of the President's action—or, indeed, whether he shall act at all—may well depend, among other things, upon the nature of the confidential information which he has or may thereafter receive, or upon the effect which his action may have upon our foreign relations. This consideration, in connection with what we have already said on the subject, discloses the unwisdom of requiring Congress in this field of governmental power to lay down narrowly definite standards by which the President is to be governed. As this court said in *Mackenzie v. Hare*, 239 U.S. 299, 311,

 CURTAILMENT

IS
B
A
D

As a government, the United States is invested with all the attributes of Sovereignty. As it has the character of nationality it has the powers of nationality, especially those which concern its relations and intercourse with other countries. *We should hesitate long before limiting or embarrassing such powers.* (Italics supplied.)

In the light of the foregoing observations, it is evident that this court should not be in haste to apply a general rule which will have the effect of condemning legislation like that under review as constituting an unlawful delegation of legislative power. The principles which justify such legislation find overwhelming support in the unbroken legislative practice which has prevailed almost from the inception of the national government to the present day.

❋❋❋❋

DOCUMENT 18 **RELATIONS OF THE EXECUTIVE BRANCH AND CONGRESS**

In the following selection, the Hoover Commission discusses the difficulty of making a clear-cut distinction between the jurisdictions of the President and Congress in foreign affairs, and it describes the intermeshing of de facto authority between the two branches. It evaluates the proper role of the President as initiator, formulator, negotiator, and coordinator of policies, noting the increased scope of his personal participation because of recent technological advances. It stresses that while the President is ultimately responsible for conducting foreign policy, legislative-executive cooperation is increasingly required both in determining objectives and in formulating and executing policies.

The basic pattern for the conduct of foreign affairs is fixed in the first instance by the Constitution. It is frequently assumed that under the Constitution the President is solely responsible for the conduct of foreign affairs. This statement is always subject to the qualification that, under the constitutional system of separation of powers, not only the determination of United States objectives in world affairs but also the formulation and execution of foreign policies is, in the main, divided between the executive and legislative branches.

This constitutional division is not at all clear-cut in its assignment of foreign affairs powers to the President and the Congress. Indeed, one commentator has remarked:

Article II is the most loosely drawn chapter of the Constitution. To those who think that a constitution ought to settle everything beforehand, it should be a nightmare; by the same token, to those who think that constitution makers ought to leave considerable leeway for the future play of political forces, it should be a vision realized.

In the case of the President this lack of precision is especially true because his power over foreign relations to a considerable extent must be derived from general grants of executive power. Aside from the provisions in article II, sections 2 and 3, relating to the presidential power "by and with the advice and consent of the Senate to make treaties" and to appoint ambassadors, ministers, and consuls and to the power to receive "ambassadors and other public ministers," no reference is made by the Constitution to specific presidential powers in the foreign affairs field. Hence the basic source of the President's powers lies in the general provisions of article II vesting "the Executive power" in the President, making the President the Commander in Chief of the Army and Navy, authorizing the President to require written opinions from the principal officers of the executive departments, directing the President to "take care that the laws be faithfully executed" and authorizing the President to "commission all the officers of the United States."

The President undoubtedly derives additional authority in the field of foreign affairs by reason of the distinction between the powers of the Federal Government with respect to foreign affairs and domestic affairs. As observed by Mr. Justice Sutherland in *United States* v. *Curtiss-Wright Export Corp.*, in domestic affairs, the Constitution reserves to the States those powers not vested in the National Government. In foreign affairs, the various States never possessed powers of external sovereignty and the National Government does not depend upon affirmative grants of such powers by the Constitution. Conse-

FROM *The Organization of the Government for the Conduct of Foreign Affairs,* Commission on Organization of the Executive Branch of the Government (Washington, D.C., Government Printing Office, 1949), pp. 46–52.

quently, with respect to foreign affairs, the Constitution has left a great area of unassigned powers in which someone must act for the United States from time to time, and in the absence of any other assignment the President, in his capacity as Executive, is the only one able to act.

The powers of the Congress, on the other hand, are somewhat more precisely set forth by the Constitution. The explicit confirmation power of the Senate with respect to treaties and the appointment of ambassadors and ministers has been referred to above. The express power to regulate foreign as well as domestic commerce, to fix import duties, and to declare war gives the Congress a further foothold in the field of foreign affairs. Most important of all for present purposes is the congressional power to appropriate funds, the exclusive character of which has been clear ever since 1795 when, in connection with the Jay treaty, the Congress almost failed to appropriate funds to carry out the treaty notwithstanding its ratification by the Senate. As the United States during and after World War II assumed an active part in the affairs of the world and as domestic and foreign affairs came more and more to involve the same or closely related issues, these congressional powers assumed correspondingly greater significance. Indeed, after a long period of substantial domination of the conduct of foreign affairs by the executive branch, which led one authority to say in 1917 that the outcome of the executive-legislative contest was "decisively and conspicuously in favor of the President," we are now in a period of strong counterassertion of legislative authority.

While the initiative in the conduct of foreign affairs still lies largely with the executive branch, the Congress comes in at many levels of the process. The necessity for its approbation of the objectives of the United States in world affairs has never been more clearly demonstrated than by the Fulbright and Connally resolutions placing both the Senate and the House of Representatives on the record as favoring United States participation in an international peace organization, followed in 1945 by congressional approval of the United Nations charter. Similarly, under the appropriations power, the Congress has put its essential stamp of approval on programs of economic assistance for Europe, such as the British loan in 1946, the Greek-Turkish aid program in 1947, and the European recovery program in 1948. In the last-named instance, it should be noted, congressional participation went beyond the mere objective and extended beyond the formulation of policy to the dictation of the form of organization through which the economic assistance program should be administered and by provisions for the auditing of such administration by the creation of a special "watchdog" committee.

Other instances of present-day congressional participation in the conduct of foreign affairs are to be found on all sides. Under its constitutional power to impose tariffs, it has shared since 1934 in the reciprocal trade-agreement programs. Through its power over immigration it has played a part in policy formulation on the entrance of displaced persons. By the National Security Act of 1947 it has prescribed the process of policy formulation and coordination with respect to the utilization of the instrument of force in the conduct of foreign affairs.

With the line between present-day domestic and foreign affairs so indistinct, various departments which were created primarily to perform functions in the domestic sphere now find themselves, in part by reason of the exercise of their basic statutory powers, vitally involved in foreign affairs. Hence, just as the Congress recently determined the location in the executive branch of ECA as an instrument of financial assistance, so also has it in some measure fixed the location of other instruments through which United States foreign affairs are conducted.

To recapitulate, under the Constitution the President has an area in the conduct of foreign affairs in which he is independent of the Congress. The present character of the United States position in the world, however, has tended to restrict this sphere. The result is that while to a very considerable extent the initiative remains with the President, the Government-wide conduct of foreign affairs requires joint legislative-executive cooperation, both in determination of objectives and to a lesser extent in formulation and execution of policies.

The role of the President in the conduct of foreign affairs must be appraised in the light of his personal participation and of his institutional aids. Among the latter are not only the official White House group but also the Department of State, numerous other departments and agencies, and the new interdepartmental advisory bodies . . . .

As a personal participant, the President's present role is fundamentally the same as in the past. Under the Constitution, to paraphrase the title of a current book, the President has always been and today "is many men." Some Presidents in the past, like Franklin D. Roosevelt from about 1938 on, have personally been extremely active in the foreign field. Others, like most of the Presidents, have delegated the major responsibilities and intervened only on occasion. In either case the President nonetheless remains the one elected official in the executive branch, the only official who must account to the people of the United States.

The presidency, as such, by and large, has no formal organization for the conduct of foreign affairs. The President, in his role as initiator, formulator, negotiator, and coordinator, acts mainly in a personal capacity, and the principal problems arise out of his personal relationships with the Congress, the State Department, the other departments, and agencies, and interdepartmental councils and committees. . . .

Within the framework of the Constitution, the President has the ultimate responsibility for the conduct of foreign affairs. As the only elected official in the executive branch, he can be held accountable by the electorate for the manner in which he discharges his responsibility. This is true whether the President acts personally or through a deputy.

The Congress has been singularly conscious of the President's special role in foreign affairs under the Constitution. The Department of State, for example, has never had either its duties of organization prescribed by the Congress, its organic act merely providing that the Secretary of State shall perform such specified duties as the President from time to time may assign to him. Where other departments or agencies are given an explicit role in the foreign field, as in the case of the Economic Cooperation Administration, Congress has been careful to make clear that they are subject to the direction of the President.

In the conduct of foreign affairs, the President may personally participate in a great variety of ways. He may address messages to rulers of other countries, and he may meet the heads of other governments in conferences. He appoints the American diplomats to foreign countries, and he determines the eligibility of foreign diplomats sent to the United States. In addition to formal representation of the United States abroad, he may appoint personal agents for special foreign missions. At home he appoints the principal domestic officers concerned with foreign affairs. He controls the recognition of foreign governments, and he may make treaties subject to Senate confirmation, and may make Executive agreements which may or may not require congressional backing. Through his press conference and through messages to Congress and the public, he is able to initiate and to give direction to the course of our foreign policy.

Throughout American history the President has participated personally by the means described above. Today the scope of his personal participation has been remarkably increased by recent developments in communication and transportation. World War II saw the telephone become a powerful stimulus to the President's personal participation through Franklin D. Roosevelt's special transatlantic wire to Winston S. Churchill. The radio has enormously increased the numbers of the electorate able to hear discussions of foreign policy by the President. The airplane, moreover, has immensely facilitated the personal participation of the President as well as his deputies in diplomatic activities abroad.

The President's chief personal role in the conduct of foreign affairs today involves the functions of initiation or formulation of foreign policies and of negotiation and other action to implement foreign policies already decided upon. In addition, it may involve coordination of the entire executive branch so as to make sure that all requisite views are taken into account in formulating foreign policies, and that in carrying out these policies the segments of the executive branch which are concerned are working as [a] team and not at cross-purposes.

CONCLUSIONS

The conclusions to be drawn as to the President's personal role in the conduct of foreign affairs and his relationships therein with the executive branch involve, in the main, two types of judgments. The one relates to the manner of the President's personal participation in the conduct of foreign affairs and the other to the heavy burdens which today he must necessarily assume in connection with this participation. . . .

The personal participation of the President in the conduct of foreign affairs, particularly in the role of policy initiator and formulator, is marked with many pitfalls. History, as well as the present, bears witness to the validity of the principle that the President should consult his foreign policy advisers in the executive branch before committing the United States to a course of action. One example is William H. Taft's decision in his Presidency to initiate and carry out negotiations with President Diaz of Mexico. Diaz was ousted from the presidency within 18 months after the Taft-Diaz meeting. Taft did not consult the State Department, and thereby Taft did not obtain specialized knowledge which might have pointed out the precarious nature of the Diaz regime and which might have led Taft to adopt more cautious tactics. Similarly the Secretary of State should be consulted on the sending of special emissaries abroad, and the Secretary of Defense as well as the Secretary of State should be consulted before initiation of a policy involving national security risks.

In carrying out foreign policies as a negotiator, the President should likewise consult with his advisers in the executive branch. Furthermore, when a President either personally formulates a foreign policy or personally by negotiation carries a policy into execution, the Secretary of State and other officials in whose sphere the subject matter lies should be kept informed. . . .

In the coordination of the foreign affairs work of the executive branch, the President, except in unusual circumstances, such as existing wartime, must personally be the arbiter of high-level disputes. Successful coordination, however, involves more than settlement of disputes. The President should also, through appropriate machinery, see that unresolved disputes are brought up for resolution. . . . Even more important, through appropriate coordinating devices the President should see that he gets properly integrated advice on all important questions of national affairs. Today the advisory mechanism is out of balance, with the Presidency "overorganized" for foreign affairs advice in certain fields and "underorganized" in other areas of vital concern to the Nation. . . .

FOREIGN-POLICY INSTITUTIONS

The second type of conclusion involves the workload of the President. In foreign affairs today, as in other business of the Government, the President is overburdened. The solution is not to be found by removing from the President any of his basic functions. Such a remedy is precluded by the Constitution and, in any event, it is undesirable to take functions away from the only member of the executive branch who is responsible to the electorate. Furthermore, distinctive advantages in the conduct of foreign affairs can be obtained only by the President's personal participation. Hence the President's present workload in both foreign and domestic affairs must be reduced through the careful addition of new institutional aids to provide staff assistance and by improving the quality of all staff assistance to the President.

DOCUMENT 19 THE EXECUTIVE OFFICE

The authority to conduct foreign relations is one thing; the ability to do so is another. In the early 1790's, Secretary of State Thomas Jefferson had no difficulty administering the State Department with a handful of assistants; in the 1960's, coordinating the activities within the State Department is a major endeavor. In addition, the problems created by the participation of other agencies in the foreign-policy field are so numerous that the President may have almost as much trouble synchronizing his own officials as he has in coping with foreign chancelleries.

This predicament is a relatively new phenomenon—in real terms, the United States did not join the world until the outbreak of World War II. Moreover, the changing character of international conflict has brought about the proliferation of agencies with foreign responsibilities: the view that we are engaged in a "war of ideas" with the Communists has, for example, led to a new emphasis on ideological warfare and to the creation of the United States Information Agency, with a worldwide span of activities. And, of course, the objectives of these different agencies often clash. The Defense Department and the Central Intelligence Agency have often been accused of running their own foreign policies, even, on occasion, in direct conflict with the State Department: the Defense Department, for example, may push a crash program to provide arms to India for defense against the Chinese, while the State Department tries to convince the aroused Pakistanis that the United States will not aid the Indians against them.

The President alone can mediate these internal squabbles and attempt to provide over-all consistency for our foreign policy. In this selection, a Brookings Institution task force examines the instruments at the President's disposal in his efforts at policy management.

The President is the central figure in American foreign relations. Responsibility is fixed upon him. He has great authority, and the constitutional system, as well as the constitutional document, has given him the function of leadership. He may play his part well and wisely, or not; but he cannot escape it. This is a fundamental constitutional principle, understood by all, and most of all by the President. His effective leadership is essential.

The President's responsibility and authority, however, are not exclusive; they are shared. The nature of "foreign relations" today, in contrast with times past, has increased the sharing. As "international" relations have become "intranational" relations, and as social, economic, and defense activities of impressive proportions have become important in American foreign policy, they have brought the Congress more and more into the process of authorizing programs, appropriating funds, and appraising operations. The interaction of measures which are intended to have an effect abroad and those which are intended to have a domestic effect has increased, thus adding to the joint task of the President and Congress in rationally adjusting objectives, timing, and methods on a wide front of national policy.

The President and the Congress are also dependent upon others, as well as upon each other—for information, advice, and new ideas as well as for performance. The business of conducting foreign relations has become a big dynamic enterprise with a prodigious demand for alertness, imagination, professional and technical skill, cultural empathy, courage, vitality, and dedication. Busily engaged in this vast enterprise are political executives, Foreign Service officers, career civil servants, men plucked out of their normal pursuits in education, industry, or agriculture, and private citizens as employees of contractors, scattered over the United States and the rest of the world.

A. THE NATURE OF THE ADMINISTRATIVE LOAD

The President, the Congress, and the public have a special interest in the basic features of administrative organization at the highest levels. Here administrative organization provides the structure to support the

FROM The Brookings Institution, "The Formulation and Administration of United States Foreign Policy," *United States Foreign Policy: Compilation of Studies,* Number 9, Senate Committee on Foreign Relations, Eighty-Sixth Congress, second session (Washington, D.C., Government Printing Office, 1960), Vol. 2, pp. 838–44.

FOREIGN-POLICY INSTITUTIONS

principal responsibilities of democratic government. It establishes political and public responsibility as well as administrative accountability. It symbolizes the status and relationship of responsible officials and of important programs. It is almost the only means by which the citizen can visualize even in an approximate sense what his Government is up to. A well-conceived and well-understood top structure also is not without its symbolic uses to President, Congress, and even the humbler employees who work within it.

Essentially foreign policy as an administrative problem presents three questions and an overriding imperative: What to do? How to do it? When to do it? And to do it and get it done. Administrative experience must feed back into the revision and perfection of policy. This contribution to the legislative process, broadly conceived, is vital if the process is not to be shut off from its biggest and most productive source of information and ideas.

There have always been questions of ends and of means, of timing and of followthrough. Why do they seem so difficult today? Perhaps it is the vast scale of operations. President Jefferson had to communicate with only a few ministers in foreign capitals, and these by letter infrequently. Perhaps it is the variety of endeavors which employ civil servants at home and abroad, the Military Establishment, and contractors ramifying throughout American life. President Washington worked hard at his job, but he had to direct only three departments, with the assistance of a part-time Attorney General. Perhaps it is the swift tempo or the overwhelming flood of information. Washington and Jefferson dealt with information on a few handwritten sheets of paper from limited sources, in contrast with machine-tabulated, mass-produced data, assembled almost instantaneously by mechanized media from literally multitudinous sources, private as well as public. Perhaps it is the urgency. At only a few brief periods in American history have responsible officials felt that mistakes could be fatal to their country.

Whatever the causes, the administration of national affairs, in general terms, today presents an exacting list of requirements:

1. Vision to determine ultimate goals that will retain their basic value and appeal in a changing world for which the past is by no means a complete guide; and foresight to anticipate difficulties not now readily seen.

2. Alertness and flexibility to pick the limited objectives that will lead to the ultimate goals, and to revise them as needed.

3. Multiple coordination of objectives, programs, operations that otherwise might conflict and neutralize each other, or leave embarrassing lacunae.

4. Timing—to act at the opportune moment, phasing into each other activities that may be sequentially dependent.

5. Conduct of technically advanced and complex operations on a large scale at low cost and with normal efficiency.

6. Contraction and expansion of enterprises which in their nature are not easily adaptable to this accordion movement.

7. Awareness of the aspirations, feelings, and reactions of people steeped in cultures foreign to ours, living amidst conditions it is difficult for us to comprehend, and with traditions that may be beyond our ken.

8. Bringing to this process a personal enthusiasm and dedication which go far beyond the kind of commitment that one would expect in a land where the success of what the Government attempted did not seem very important to very many people not very long ago.

There is almost no variety of administrative problem known to man which does not exist in some form today to be dealt with by the President, Congress, and Federal administrators; and "foreign relations" now are an integral and major part of this total process.

B. ADJUSTMENT TO THE LOAD—
CYCLES AND DILEMMAS

Looking back over the period of growth in the national administration it is possible to note a cyclical process of adjustment.

New activities and new programs came into existence; and more often than not in recent years, they came into existence in new executive agencies—independent of the executive departments. In due course some of the programs were moved into executive departments, and others became new executive departments. But despite periodic revision in this way the revisions have tended to be rather modest adjustments. Additional programs lead to new agencies, and the total number of executive agencies continues to be large.

The Presidents, meanwhile, confronted with an ever-increasing volume of business, have sought assistance for the White House. First, they borrowed assistants from the executive departments, the President's "secretaries" were increased to three, military aids were put to work, and after 1939 the precedent of six administrative assistants was followed in the steady increase of assistants to the President, deputy assistants, and special assistants. The assistants had to have assistants, and in due course the several ranks of assistants were more or less organized under certain of their number: the assistant to the President; special assistants to the President, e.g., the Special Assistant for National Security Affairs; the staff secretary; and the secretary to the Cabinet.

In 1939 the Executive Office of the President was conceived and established. Within it were brought or created staff agencies—"staff" in the sense that they assisted or acted for the Chief Executive but normally did not administer substantive programs. Not all survived; but some have come to be sturdy members in the machinery of government, e.g., the Bureau of the Budget. To these have been added "councils" with their own groups of employees—the Council of Economic Advisers; the National Security Council (the latter with its subordinate Operations Coordinating Board and Central Intelligence Agency); the National Aeronautics and Space Council; and temporary, advisory committees, e.g., the President's Advisory Committee on Government Organization.

While the number of staff assistants and agencies in the Executive Office was increasing, their functions were also evolving—from handling records, to supplying information, to reviewing and analyzing documents (and situations), to advising, to negotiating, and to following up decisions or actions. A full-blown staff function has developed.

In this natural and not irrational evolutionary adjustment to the administrative load, two dilemmas and dangers are apparent.

The creation of new "independent" agencies immediately responsible to the President, often motivated by the desire to enhance their status and make sure that the Chief Executive will be actively responsible for them, in time makes it certain that they will have very little executive attention from the President. Increasing the Chief Executive's responsibility for direct supervision tends to make it a fiction.

When the adjustment takes the form of increasing the staff of assistants and assisting agencies in the Executive Office, at what point does the staff's attention substitute for the President's, and the President's direction of his own assistants and assisting agencies become only nominal? The Executive Office of the President has grown tremendously in both number of employees and scope of activities since it was established in 1939. Today the total personnel embraced by the Executive Office numbers more than 2,700. If the only escape from purely pro forma direction of too many executive departments and agencies is to a form of staff supervision, there may be a net gain, but there may also be overly centralized administration with little increase in the participation of the Chief Executive.

This brings the discussion back to the main focus of this analysis, the President's responsibility for foreign policy and for the administration of foreign relations. The President is dependent upon the machinery of government to make good in his responsibilities. The machinery of 1800, or 1900, or even 1940 will not do for the Government of 1960. This is recognized, and new machinery has been added, piece by piece, since the Second World War, specifically to deal with matters of national security and foreign policy. . . .

As the machinery of government has evolved, efforts to cope with new burdens have taken the form of added or new types of executive assistance, now chiefly within the Executive Office of the President, or of reorganization of the operating departments and agencies as new programs have been established or modified.

❋❋❋❋

C. THE ROLE OF EXECUTIVE ASSISTANCE

Closest to the President is the White House Office of some 400 persons. It includes an assistant to the President, a deputy assistant, two secretaries, a special counsel, various special and administrative assistant, a staff secretary, a secretary to the Cabinet, and a household staff. Within this organization are located the President's Special Assistants for National Security Affairs, Security Operations Coordination, and Foreign Economic Policy. The Assistant to the President has come to be recognized as a virtual chief of staff. Another aid has been designated Staff Secretary and is responsible for a variety of secretariat functions including supervision of the preparation and flow of White House paperwork, checking on the implementation of Presidential decisions, marshaling the daily intelligence, and preparing "staff notes" to alert the President to emerging problems and events. Another innovation has been the appointment of a Secretary to the Cabinet who organizes the preparatory and followup work surrounding Cabinet deliberations.

Not part of the White House Office (and one degree farther removed from the President) but part of the Executive Office are the Bureau of the Budget (1921), the Council of Economic Advisers (1946), the National Security Council (1947), the Office of Civil and Defense Mobilization (1953, 1958), the National Aeronautics and Space Council (1958), and the President's Advisory Committee on Government Organization (1953).

Together these Executive Office agencies represent efforts to equip the Chief Executive to deal with basic managerial decisions, to fix the President's responsibility for leadership in planning, and to involve him personally in formal interdepartmental consultations. These agencies themselves must coordinate their efforts, while attempting officially to aid the President to fulfill his executive role with reference to the executive departments and agencies.

The National Security Council which has a statutory basis in the National Security Act of 1947, as amended, is, in fact, an inner Cabinet for national security policy rather than a staff agency. In formal terms, it is the highest committee in the Government for the resolution of national security questions. The statutory members of the Council include the President, the Vice President, the Secretary of State, the Secretary of Defense, and the Director of the Office of Civil and Defense Mobilization. The President may, and does, also invite any other official who he feels should participate in the discussion of particular matters. Those who attend most frequently on this basis include the Secretary of the Treasury, the Director of the Bureau of the Budget, the Attorney General, and the Chairman of the Atomic Energy Commission. The Chairman of the Joint Chiefs of Staff and the Director of the Central Intelligence Agency serve as statutory advisers on military and intelligence matters.

The next level of officials of Assistant Secretary rank has, since 1953, been called the Planning Board; previously it was known as the Senior Staff. The Planning Board is aided by a lower echelon group of officials called Board assistants who meet regularly and do much of the preliminary work. The Special Assistant to the President for National Security Affairs acts as Chairman of the Planning Board, works closely with the small staff attached to the National Security Council and is, as his title implies, a key link between the Council and the President.

A major addition to this structure was the creation of the Operations Coordinating Board in 1953. It was an outgrowth of the Psychological Strategy Board, established in 1951, and consists of Cabinet agency officials of Under Secretary rank together with certain agency heads corresponding to the general composition of the National Security Council. The prescribed function of the Board is to advise the agencies concerned in their development, in more specific operational detail, of the general policies developed within the National Security Council structure and approved by the President, to facilitate a voluntary acceptance of specific responsibilities by the several departments and agencies, and to report periodically on the progress made. The Board has its own staff, separate from the National Security Council–Planning Board staff and, since 1957, a Presidential Special Assistant for Security Operations Coordination. It also has its own group of Board assistants. Its approximately 50 interdepartmental working groups oversee the execution of policy dealing with particular regional and functional problems.

In the Executive Office there are also several interdepartmental committees that operate in the area of foreign economic policy and will be discussed later in this report.

Finally, there have been numerous ad hoc study groups, such as the recent Committee To Study the U.S. Military Assistance Program (the "Draper Committee").

The Executive Office is in part the result of efforts to assist the President to fulfill his Chief Executive functions and in part the product of a determination to impose particular tasks as well as responsibilities upon him. The Presidents successively have sought some additions to and modifications of the Executive Office. Others have been thrust upon them. An example of the latter is the National Aeronautics and Space Act of 1958 which, by congressional choice rather than Presidential request, established a Cabinet-level Space Council, chaired by the President, to deal with policy problems in the field of peaceful and military exploitation of outer space. This Council is distinctive in that it has several private citizens as statutory members.

In the aggregate this is a formidable development of "executive assistance" in 20 years. The evolution may be expected to continue. No administration could function without similar machinery today.

****

DOCUMENT 20 **THE STATE DEPARTMENT AND ITS COMPETITORS**

The State Department is charged with the primary responsibility, under the President, for the definition and elaboration of foreign policy. However, for historical reasons, the department has always labored under Congressional suspicion. In political terms, it has no constituency, and it keeps sending big bills to Congress. A Senator who attacks the Commerce Department will be blasted in return by the agency's business friends; a Representative who assaults the Labor Department will hear from the trade unions; but the State Department is fair game for any unfulfilled demagogue. At best the Secretary will be defended by the President and the League of Women Voters, plus, of course, a number of nonvoting foreigners.

This political vulnerability has undoubtedly contributed to the diffusion over recent years of the responsibility for implementing foreign policy. Most of the agencies handling foreign economic aid have been virtually free of State Department control since the time of the Marshall Plan. (This proliferation of administrative agencies may also be due to the fact that it is much easier to get a huge appropriation for foreign aid through Congress by cutting it into several agency budgets.) In addition, there is reason to believe that the increase in the authority of the Defense Department in foreign-aid matters has been in large part an outgrowth of the relative political invulnerability of the military establishment: Congress is more apt to grant economic aid, for example, if it is disguised as "defense support." If a State Department "bureaucrat" told Congress that economic development of, say, Greece was essential to the development of a stable democratic regime, he would be greeted with skepticism, while the testimony of a three-star general that "defense support" was essential in Greece would be met with sympathy and deference. Even Congressmen do not like to argue with three-star generals about the national interest.

One of the first rules of administration is that budgetary control is essential to policy control. Congress, by controlling appropriations, exercises over-all budgetary control; then each executive agency, by

FOREIGN-POLICY INSTITUTIONS

administering the funds for a specific program like Point Four or the Marshall Plan, controls "foreign policy" as it concerns that program. The State Department may have the abstract power to determine policy, but without control of the purse strings, this is often empty rhetoric. The following selection discusses in broad terms the activities and responsibilities of the State Department and its "competitors."

The most striking present-day feature of the organization of the United States Government for the conduct of foreign affairs is the participation in all its phases of departments and agencies other than the State Department. This participation consists of furnishing advice to aid in the formulation of foreign policies and of insuring coordinated action in the execution of these policies. It has resulted in the creation of new interdepartmental organizational arrangements, including an elaborate structure of interdepartmental committees.

In the past the State Department constituted the principal source of advice to the President on foreign policy formulation within the executive branch. Consequently Government-wide integration of advice was a process for which there was little need. This is not to say that the President did not seek advice and aid on international matters from sources other than the State Department, and American history is replete with instances where he has turned to Secretaries other than the Secretary of State and to individuals outside the Government. These sources, however, were utilized primarily because of personal or political relationships, whereas the State Department was a source of advice and aid in an institutional sense.

The requirement of coordinated action in the conduct of foreign affairs, furthermore, is not an historical feature of American foreign relations. In large measure foreign policies in earlier periods were carried into execution by the President, either in the role of negotiator or through the Secretary of State. On the relatively infrequent occasions when other parts of the executive branch were involved, consistent and integrated action was obtained through informal liaison frequently at, or just below, the Secretary level. A request from the Secretary of State in days past carried with it a quality of Olympian majesty which usually evoked a quick response. Today, in sharp contrast, coordinated action by the State Department and the 45 other units of the executive branch having roles in foreign affairs is a sine qua non for the effective conduct of the varied and numerous United States foreign affairs activities.

FROM *The Organization of the Government for the Conduct of Foreign Affairs,* Commission on Organization of the Executive Branch of the Government (Washington, D.C., Government Printing Office, 1949), pp. 56–62.

A. THE STATUTORY FRAMEWORK

The statutory authority of the State Department and that of the other departments and agencies in the conduct of foreign affairs is markedly different. The role of the State Department has never been prescribed by the Congress. Its organic statute of 1789, which is still its basic charter, did not specify the duties of the Secretary of State. It provided:

The Secretary of State shall perform such duties as shall from time to time be enjoined or entrusted to him by the President relative to correspondences, commissions, or instructions to or with public ministers or consuls from the United States, or to negotiations with public ministers from foreign states or princes, or to memorials or other applications from foreign public ministers or other foreigners, or to such other matters respecting foreign affairs as the President of the United States shall assign to the department, and he shall conduct the business of the department in such manner as the President shall direct.

This statute clearly fixed the role of the Secretary of State as an arm of the President for the conduct of foreign affairs. Since 1789 his basic authority has remained fundamentally unchanged, the Congress has been careful to leave the duties of the State Department largely undefined, and in grants of substantive power to the Secretary of State it has explicitly recognized on many occasions the special prerogatives of the President by provisions that the Secretary of State shall act under the direction of the President. The great bulk of congressional grants of authority to the State Department will be found to be ministerial in character. As one authority has said: "The whole question of the Secretary's powers was left to the President and the way left open for the 'impulse to action' to come solely from that source."

The participation of the other departments and agencies in the conduct of foreign affairs, in sharp contrast, arises largely from direct grants of authority from the Congress. In many instances the Congress appears to have granted these powers with the domestic situation primarily in mind. The result today, with the disappearance of the line of demarcation between domestic and foreign affairs, is that these other departments and agencies have been carried into the foreign field. In other cases the Congress has made direct grants of foreign-affairs powers as such or has appropriated funds to these other departments and agencies. An example of the former is the extension of the Agriculture Department's domestic duties to the foreign field in connection with the foot-and-mouth disease in Mexico.

Examples of the second type include the powers of the Export-Import Bank with regard to loans for international purposes, and the Civil Aeronautics Board's powers of recommendation to the President with respect to authority for United States air carriers to operate internationally and for foreign air carriers to serve the United States.

The powers granted by the Congress to the Department of State are intrinsically different in character from those granted to the other departments and agencies. The State Department's organic statute gives it power over the means of conducting foreign relations; the organic statutes of the other departments and agencies provide them with substantive powers, i.e., powers with regard to fissionable materials, loans, communications, shipping, hydroelectric power, exports, etc.

B. FOREIGN AFFAIRS ACTIVITIES OF THE OTHER AGENCIES

The roles in foreign affairs of the other departments, agencies, commissions, boards, and interdepartmental councils differ in substance and importance. At one extreme are the Economic Cooperation Administration (ECA), the Departments of Agriculture, Treasury, and Commerce, and such interdepartmental bodies as the National Security Council and the National Advisory Council. These organizations have powers in the exercise of which highly significant decisions affecting foreign policy are made and executed. At the other extreme are agencies like the Securities and Exchange Commission and the Smithsonian Institution with relatively minor influence on the conduct of foreign affairs.

The variety of foreign affairs activities carried on in the executive branch, exclusive of the State Department, may best be indicated by a few illustrations:

1. The Agriculture Department, in order to meet United States sugar consumption requirements, establishes quotas for foreign states;

2. The Commerce Department administers export control and the China Trade Act;

3. The Interior Department takes the initiative in obtaining coordination and unification of Federal policy and administration with respect to activities relating to petroleum carried on by various Federal agencies;

4. The Fish and Wildlife Service of the Interior Department takes censuses of waterfowl population in certain Caribbean countries;

5. The Office of Alien Property of the Justice Department vests the property of foreign nationals and liquidates vested property;

6. The Treasury Department collects and evaluates data as to the international financial position of the countries with which the United States is concerned;

7. The Bureau of Federal Supply of the Treasury Department purchases strategic and critical materials for the national stock pile, as well

as commodities for the ECA and for the Greek-Turkish aid program;

8. The Labor Department, through the Bureau of Labor Statistics, obtains and publishes information on foreign labor conditions;

9. The Atomic Energy Commission purchases or otherwise acquires fissionable material or any interest therein outside the United States;

10. The Civil Aeronautics Board recommends issuance of foreign carrier permits;

11. The Federal Communications Commission regulates foreign commerce in communication by wire and radio;

12. The Export-Import Bank makes loans for international purposes;

13. The Public Health Service controls the export and import of biological materials applicable to the treatment of human diseases;

14. The Maritime Commission determines the ocean services, routes and lines from points in the United States to foreign markets, and determines the size of the American merchant marine; and

15. The Federal Reserve Board charters and supervises foreign banking corporations in the United States.

The role of these other departments and agencies in the conduct of United States foreign affairs is one that is not fully understood either within the Government or by the American public. A query representative of certain elements in the State Department is: "Who, other than the President and the State Department, has any interest in the conduct of foreign affairs?" This view is unrealistic, for it fails to recognize the significant role in the Government's total foreign affairs activities of the other departments and agencies. A clear appreciation of this participation is, of course, a prerequisite to effective organization and administration.

C. THE FOREIGN AFFAIRS TASK

The phrase "foreign affairs" or "foreign policy" eludes precise definition. The intrinsic difficulty can be shown most clearly by asking a representative question: "Is a governmental decision to permit the export of steel or of building materials to France at the present time a foreign policy decision or one of domestic policy"? The answer to this question, and to countless others, is that it is neither one nor the other, but it is a matter of national policy, involving consideration of both foreign and domestic requirements. From an organizational and administrative viewpoint, it thus becomes clear that the problem is to formulate and carry out foreign policies within a framework of national policies, which integrate in a consistent manner both the foreign and domestic objectives and requirements of the Nation.

The process of formulating foreign affairs policies and programs is the subject of consideration here. As stressed earlier, the conduct of foreign affairs is composed of several different major steps: (1) The determination of fundamental foreign policy objectives; (2) the formulation of policies and programs to achieve those objectives; (3) the execution of these various and variegated policies and programs; and (4) the support of all three of the foregoing by integration and coordination throughout the executive branch.

There is on occasion a lack of appreciation in the high councils of Government of the necessity of these steps and of the role of the President, the State Department, and the other departments and agencies in each of these steps. As an illustration, there is the statement by a high official of the State Department before a congressional committee in 1946, in part as follows:

The Department of State, under the direction of the President, in cooperation with the Congress is responsible for the achievement of our foreign policy objectives. Other Government agencies, such as War, Navy, Treasury, Commerce, and Agriculture departments, are also concerned with foreign relations. . . . Effective coordination under the Department of State of all foreign relations activities is essential if we are to achieve our foreign policy objectives.

This statement, perhaps because of its capsule quality, is deficient in many respects. First, the State Department may or may not be "responsible for the achievement" of United States' foreign policy objectives. It is in the achievement of objectives that departments and agencies other than the State Department play their most significant part. Second, the statement does not even attempt to define how the other departments and agencies are "concerned with foreign relations." Third, it says that coordination of "all foreign relations activities" is the job of the State Department. Yet in fact other departments and agencies may have the prime responsibility for coordination of specific foreign affairs activities between departments and agencies, as in the case of the National Advisory Council in international financial affairs. Furthermore, when several units within a single department or agency are concerned with problems having foreign aspects, internal coordination of the activities of those units must be achieved by the appropriate department or agency head.

D. RESPONSIBILITY FOR CONDUCT
OF FOREIGN AFFAIRS

Where, in fact, does the ultimate responsibility lie within the executive branch for the conduct of foreign affairs? In the President. He alone is ultimately responsible for defining foreign-policy objectives, for initiating policies and programs designed to realize these objectives, and for effecting the necessary coordination between the operative programs.

Since he cannot perform all these activities in his own person, he must, as the chief executive, establish such machinery and processes as the Congress permits that will aid him in fulfilling his gigantic responsibility.

Today the machinery and processes currently available for determining foreign-policy objectives are informal and highly unsystematic. If the President should desire to reconsider and review the broad aims of the United States vis-à-vis, for example, Brazil, he could turn to the Secretary of State. The inadequacy of this move is apparent when one realizes that a determination of objectives with respect to Brazil involves a multiplicity of specialized knowledge scattered throughout the executive branch. Financial data are in Treasury, trade and commerce data in State, Commerce and the Tariff Commission, agricultural information in Agriculture, and military data in the National Military Establishment, to cite only a few obvious illustrations. Unless the Secretary of State sees fit to call in these agencies—and the heads of the State Department have not always sought close collaboration with the other departments and agencies on matters of "high" foreign policy —their knowledge and viewpoints will not be brought to bear upon the issue. Moreover, by turning only to the Secretary of State the President would be acting on the false assumption that our foreign-policy objectives toward Brazil could be intelligently formulated without regard to their impact upon our domestic scene. This observation need not be labored, for it is obvious that such an objective, for example, as aiding in the industrialization of Brazil, would have consequences on United States trade and manufactures far different from an objective that contemplated aiding Brazil to develop its agriculture along new and different lines. And no objective could last for long if the consequences to the American public had not been calculated reasonably carefully and adjudged to be acceptable.

The machinery and processes for formulating specific policies and programs are little, if any, more adequate than those now available for advising the President on foreign-policy objectives. When Secretary of State Marshall made his address on European recovery in June 1947, he, in effect, proposed a program of United States economic assistance. Whatever discussions within the executive branch preceded his announcement, it is clear that they were not geared into any interdepartmental mechanism which would assure systematic consideration of all the major pros and cons. That such consideration would have been desirable is apparent if one takes cognizance of the possible effects of the policy on security or military plans and policies, on Federal fiscal and budgetary policies, and on domestic economic policies. That the Secretary of State alone could not be expected to pass judgment on all these matters needs no argument. Events of this kind dramatize the administrative inadequacies in the determination of foreign policies and programs, inadequacies that are largely due to mechanical defects which, happily, are readily subject to improvement.

Ultimate responsibility for the coordination of foreign-affairs policies and programs within the executive branch also resides in the Chief Executive. It is this coordination which constitutes a problem of major proportions because it must comprehend so many programs and must proceed on a day-to-day basis.

❖❖❖❖

DOCUMENT 21 THE FLOW OF POLICY-MAKING IN THE STATE DEPARTMENT

Although the participation of roughly forty-five executive agencies in the administration of foreign affairs, as discussed in Document 20, has relieved the State Department of much of its original responsibility, it has by no means reduced the complexity of its operation. The following selection indicates the wide range of demands made on the State Department during a typical day.

The Department of State is an organism that is constantly responding to a vast assortment of stimuli. A new Soviet threat to Berlin, a forthcoming conference of Foreign Ministers of the Organization of American States, a request from Poland for credit, a solicitation for support of a candidacy for the Presidency of the United Nations General Assembly, a plea from an ambassador that the head of the government to which he is accredited be invited to visit the United States officially, a refusal by another government to permit the duty-free importation of some official supplies for a U.S. consulate, a request from the White House for comment on the foreign affairs section of a major presidential address, an earthquake in the Aegean

FROM The Brookings Institution, "The Formulation and Administration of United States Foreign Policy," Appendix C, *United States Foreign Policy: Compilation of Studies,* Number 9, Senate Committee on Foreign Relations, Eighty-Sixth Congress, second session (Washington, D.C., Government Printing Office, 1960), Vol. 2, pp. 970–75.

creating hardships which it appears the U.S. Navy might be able to alleviate, a request for a speaker from a foreign policy association in California, a transmittal slip from a Member of Congress asking for information with which to reply to a letter from a constituent protesting discriminatory actions against his business by a foreign government, letters from citizens both supporting and deploring the policy of nonrecognition of Communist China, a continuing inquiry by a press correspondent who has got wind of a top secret telegram from Embassy Bonn on the subject of German rearmament and is determined to find out what is in it, a demand by a Protestant church group that the Department take steps to prevent harassment of their coreligionists in a foreign country, a request by a delegation of a federation of women's clubs for a briefing on southeast Asia and suggestions as to how its members might be useful in their planned tour of the area, a request from Consulate General Brazzaville for a revision of cost-of-living allowances, a visit by a commission of inquiry into the operations of U.S. foreign aid programs, a notification from the staff of the National Security Council that a revision of the National Security Council paper on dependent areas is due, a telegram from a U.S. embassy in the Near East declaring that last night's flareups make a visit by the Assistant Secretary for Near Eastern and South Asian Affairs, now in mid-Atlantic, inopportune at the moment, a warning by a European Foreign Minister of the consequences should the United States fail to support his nation's position in the Security Council, and a counterwarning by an African representative at the United Nations of the consequences should the United States do so—this is a sample of the requirements made of the Department of State in a typical day. Of course it does not include the oceans of informational reports that come into the Department by telegram and air pouch or the countless periodicals from all parts of the world that arrive by sea.

What is required to begin with is that the flow be routed into the right channels. This does not apply to press correspondents and foreign embassy officials; they usually know where to go without being directed. For the rest, almost every piece of business—every requirement or opportunity for action—comes within the Department's ken first as a piece of paper. These pieces of paper—telegrams, dispatches (or "despatches," as the Department prefers to call them), letters—must be gotten as speedily as possible into the hands of the officers who will have to do something about them or whose jobs require that they know about them.

The telegram and mail branches of the Division of Communication Services, a part of the Bureau of Administration, receive the incoming material and, after decoding and reproducing the telegrams, indicate on each communication the distribution it should receive among the bureaus or equivalent components of the Department. If, in the case of a letter or a dispatch, there are not enough copies to go around, the recipients are listed one after another and receive it consecutively, the original going first to the bureau responsible for taking whatever action the document requires. With telegrams, the deliveries are simultaneous. Several score copies of a telegram may be run off. A yellow copy, called the action copy, like the original of a dispatch or letter, goes to the bureau responsible for taking any necessary action; white copies go to all others interested.

A telegram (No. 1029, let us say) from a major U.S. embassy in Western Europe reports the warning of the Foreign Minister of X country that a grave strain would be imposed on relations between X and the United States should the latter fail to vote with X on a sensitive colonial issue in the United Nations General Assembly. Such a telegram would have a wide distribution. The action copy would go to the Bureau of European Affairs. The action copy of a telegram to the same purpose from the U.S. delegation to the United Nations in New York, quoting the X delegation, would go to the Bureau of International Organization Affairs. This is a matter of convention.

Information copies of a telegram of such importance would go to all officers in the higher echelons—the Secretary of State (via the executive secretariat), the Under Secretaries, the Deputy Under Secretaries, the counselor. They would also go to the Policy Planning Staff, to the Bureau of African Affairs because of the involvement of certain territories within its jurisdiction, to the Bureau of Far Eastern Affairs and the Bureau of Near Eastern and South Asian Affairs because the telegram concerns the incendiary question of European peoples' ruling non-European peoples, and of course to the Bureau of Intelligence and Research. Other copies would go to the Department of Defense and the Central Intelligence Agency. The executive secretariat would doubtless make certain that the Secretary would see the telegram. In addition, its staff would include a condensation in the secret daily summary, a slim compendium distributed in the Department on a need-to-know basis. If classified top secret, it would be included in the top secret daily staff summary, or black book, which goes only to Assistant Secretary-level officials and higher.

In the bureaus, incoming material is received by the message centers. There a further and more refined distribution would be made of telegram 1029. Copies would go to the Office of the Assistant Secretary (the so-called front office), to the United Nations adviser, to the public affairs adviser (since the United States is going to be in for trouble with public opinion in either one part of the world or the other), and to whatever geographic office or offices may seem to have the major interest. In the Bureau of International Organization Affairs, this would be the Office of United Nations Political and Security Affairs, Another copy, however, might go to the Office of Dependent Area Affairs.

In the Bureau of European Affairs, the yellow action copy of the telegram goes to the Office of Western European Affairs and thence to the X country desk, where it is the first thing to greet the desk officer's eye in the morning. As it happens, the desk officer was out the evening before at an official function where he discussed at length with the first secretary of the X embassy the desirability of avoiding any extremes of action in the United Nations over the territory in question. In the front office of the Bureau, the staff assistant has entered in his records the salient details of the problem the Bureau is charged with and has passed the telegram on to the Assistant Secretary.

The following scenes are now enacted:

The X country desk officer crosses the hall to the office of his superior, the officer-in-charge, and the two together repair to the office of the Director of the Office of Western European Affairs. The three officers put in a call to the Assistant Secretary for European Affairs and tell his secretary that they would like as early an appointment as possible.

The Director of the Office of United Nations Political and Security Affairs (UNP) telephones the Director of the Office of Western European Affairs (WE). He says he assumes WE will be drafting an instruction to the U.S. embassy in X to try to dissuade the Foreign Office from its course, and that UNP would like to be in on it. He adds that they had thought of getting the U.S. delegation to the United Nations (US Del) to present this view to the X mission in New York but that there seemed to be no point in doing so since the latter would already be advising its government to take account of world opinion.

After the Secretary's morning staff conference, where the matter is discussed briefly, a conference is held in the Office of the Assistant Secretary for European Affairs to decide on a line to take with the X government. The X desk officer is designated to prepare the first draft of a telegram embodying it. The draft is reviewed and modified by his officer-in-charge and the Office Director for Western European Affairs.

The telegram instructs the U.S. embassy in X to make clear to the X government our fear that its projected course of action "will only play into hands extremists and dishearten and undermine position elements friendly to West" and suggests that the X government emphasize its policy to take account of the legitimate aspirations of the indigenous population of the territory in order to improve the atmosphere for consideration of the problem by the General Assembly. The Assistant Secretary, after scrutinizing and approving the telegram, finds it necessary only to add the Bureau of Near Eastern and South Asian Affairs to the clearances. Those already listed for clearance are the Deputy Under Secretary for Political Affairs, the Bureau of International Organization Affairs, and the Bureau of African Affairs. He says it can be left to the Deputy Under Secretary for Political Affairs to sign the telegram; he does not see that the telegram need go higher.

It remains for the drafting officer to circulate the telegram for approval by those marked for clearance. In the Bureau of African Affairs the telegram is termed extremely gentle to the X government but is initialed as it stands. The Office of United Nations Political and Security Affairs (UNP) wishes to remind X that the United States, setting an example of its adherence to the principle of affording the widest latitude to the General Assembly, had even accepted on occasion the inscription of an item on the agenda accusing the United States of aggression. The X desk officer states, however, that WE would not favor such an addition, which might only further antagonize the X government. Thereupon, UNP, yielding on this point, requests deletion of a phrase in the telegram seeming to place the United States behind the X contention that the question is not appropriate for discussion in the United Nations. The drafter of the telegram telephones the Director of the Office of Western European Affairs who authorizes the deletion, having decided that he can do so on his own without referring the question to his superior, the Assistant Secretary.

With that, the Director of the Office of United Nations Political and Security Affairs initials the telegram for his Bureau, and the X desk officer "hand carries" the telegram (in the departmental phrase), with telegram 1029 attached, to the Office of the Deputy Under Secretary for Political Affairs and leaves it with his secretary. At 6 o'clock he is informed by telephone that the Deputy Under Secretary has signed the telegram (that is, signed the Secretary's name with his own initials beneath) without comment. The desk officer goes to the fifth floor, retrieves it, and takes it to the correspondence review staff of the executive secretariat, where the telegram is examined for intelligibility, completion of clearances, conformity with departmental practices, etc., before being sped to the Telegram Branch for enciphering and transmission.

The next morning, all offices of the Department participating in the framing of the telegram receive copies of it hectographed on pink outgoing telegram forms. The telegram, bearing the transmission time of 8:16 p.m., has entered history as the Department's No. 736 to the embassy in X. The X desk officer writes "telegram sent," with the date, in the space indicated by a rubber stamp on the yellow copy of the original telegram 1029, and the staff assistant in the front office makes an equivalent notation in his records. The yellow copy is then sent on to the central files, whence in time it will probably be consigned to the National Archives. Only the white copies may be kept in the Bureau's files.

In this case, however, no one is under any illusion that the matter has been disposed of. Scarcely 24 hours later comes a new telegram 1035 from the embassy in X reporting that, while the X government may possibly make some concessions, it will certainly wage an all-out fight against inscription of the item and will expect the United States to exert itself to marshal all the negative votes possible. The question is, what position will the United States in fact take and how much effort will it make to win adherents for its position? No one supposes for a moment that this explosive question can be decided on the bureau level. Only the Secretary can do so—as the Secretary himself unhappily realizes.

At the end of a staff meeting on Berlin, the Secretary turns to the Assistant Secretary for Policy Planning and asks him to give some thought within the next few days to the alternatives open on the question. The official addressed sets the wheels in motion at once. A meeting is called for the next morning. Attending are: the Assistant Secretary for Policy Planning himself and several members of his staff (including the European and African specialists), the Director of the Office of United Nations Political and Security Affairs, the Western European officer-in-charge, the X desk officer, a member of the policy guidance and coordination staff of the Bureau of Public Affairs, and two intelligence specialists, namely, the Director of the Office of Research and Analysis for Western Europe and the Director of the Office of Research and Analysis for the Near East, South Asia, and Africa.

The discussion explores all ramifications of the issues involved and is generally detached and dispassionate. The object of the meeting is to help clarify the issues so that the Policy Planning Staff may be sure all relevant considerations are taken into account in the staff paper it will prepare for the Secretary.

The Secretary is in a difficult position. The President's views on what course of action to take are somewhat different from his. The Congress is also of divided view, with some Members impressed by the irresistible force of nationalism among dependent peoples, others by the essential role of X in NATO and European defense. The ambassadors of some countries pull him one way, others another. One of the Nation's leading newspapers editorially counsels "restraint, understanding and vision." At the staff meeting he calls to arrive at a decision, the Secretary perceives that his subordinates are as deeply divided as he feared. He takes counsel with each—the Assistant Secretaries for Policy Planning, European Affairs, African Affairs, and Near Eastern and South Asian Affairs. At the end he sums up and announces his decision. Thereupon the following things happen:

The Assistant Secretaries take the news back to their bureaus.

An urgent telegram is sent to the U.S. Embassy in X reporting the decision.

Telegrams are sent to embassies in important capitals around the world instructing the ambassador to go to the Foreign Office and present the U.S. case in persuasive terms.

A similar telegram is sent to the U.S. delegation in New York for its use in talks with the delegations of other United Nations members.

Conferences attended by representatives of the geographic bureaus concerned, of the Bureau of Public Affairs, and of the U.S. Information Agency, are held. Afterward, the representatives of the U.S. Information Agency return to their headquarters to draft guidances to the U.S. Information Service establishments all over the world. Such guidances tell how news of the U.S. decision is to be played when it breaks.

The more important the problem, the more the upper levels of the Department become involved. In a crisis—one brought about, say, by the overthrow of A, a Western-oriented government in the Middle East—the Secretary himself will take over. However, the bulk of the Department's business is carried on, of necessity, by the lower ranking officers. Even when a crisis receives the Secretary's personal, day-to-day direction, the desk officer and the officer-in-charge are always at hand to provide the detailed information only specialists possess, while in the intelligence bureau, country analysts and branch chiefs will be putting in 10-hour days and 6- or 7-day weeks. Generally, moreover, the crisis will have been preceded by a good deal of work on the part of lower level officials.

In the case suggested, it was apparent for sometime that all was not well in A. The U.S. Embassy in A was aware of growing discontent with the regime through its indirect contacts with opposition political elements, from information from Cairo, from evidences of tension, from clandestine publications. Additional straws in the wind were supplied by the public affairs officer in A both to the embassy and to the U.S. Information Agency because of his special contacts among professional groups. On the strength of these reports and of dispatches from American foreign correspondents in the area, and equipped with analyses from the Bureau of Intelligence and Research, all pointing in the same direction, the desk officer at a staff meeting of the Office of Near Eastern Affairs imparts his disquiet. He is directed to prepare a memorandum which, if convincing in its presentation, the Office Director undertakes to put before the Assistant Secretary.

What the desk officer has in mind will require national action, so what he drafts takes the form of a memorandum to the Secretary. It embodies a statement of the problem, the actions recommended, a review of the facts bearing upon the problem, and a conclusion. At the end are listed the symbols of the offices of the Department from which concurrences must be sought. Backing up the memorandum will be supporting documents, especially telegrams from the embassy, each identified by a tab. The mass fills a third of an in-box.

The problem is defined as that of strengthening the present pro-Western regime of A. By way of recommendation, the desk officer is especially sensitive to the problems and needs of the country for which he is responsible. He calls for more detachment of the United States from A's rival, B, expediting U.S. arms deliveries to A and the supply of certain recoilless rifles and jet fighter planes the A government has been requesting, support for A's membership in various United Nations agencies, a Presidential invitation to the Prime Minister of A to visit the United States. Much of what the memorandum recommends has to be fought out in the Bureau and even in the Office since it conflicts with the claims of countries (and the desk officers responsible for them) in the same jurisdiction. While neither the Office Director nor the Assistant Secretary doubts that support of B is a handicap in the region, they consider that a proposal for a radical departure would simply doom the memorandum by preventing anyone from taking it seriously.

As it finally leaves the Bureau with the Assistant Secretary's signature, the memorandum is considerably revised, and further change awaits it. The Department of Defense cannot provide the desired recoilless rifles and jet fighters. The Bureau of International Organization Affairs cannot offer any undertaking at this stage with respect to the question of membership in United Nations agencies. The Deputy Under Secretary for Political Affairs rules out a request of the President to invite the A Prime Minister for an official visit because the number of those invited is already too large.

Among recommendations in memorandums to the Secretary, as among salmon battling their way upstream to the spawning grounds, mortality is heavy. Almost everywhere in the world, things are far from satisfactory, but the United States cannot be doing everything everywhere at the same time. And A, far from seeming to cry out for attention, looks like the one Middle Eastern country about which it is not necessary to worry.

Then the uprising occurs in A. Early in the morning, the officer-in-charge of A and one other country is awakened by the ringing of the telephone. In a flash, before his feet have touched the floor, he has visualized every conceivable disaster that could have befallen his area and has picked the overthrow of the monarchy in C as the most likely. Or did the security people find a top secret document under his desk?

On the telephone, the watch officer at the Department tells him that a "Niact" (a night action telegram, which means "Get this one read immediately even if you have to rout someone out of bed") is coming off the machine and it looks serious—he had better come down. En route, the officer-in-charge turns on his car radio and picks up a news broadcast, but nothing is said about A. Uncle Sam has beaten the press agencies.

At the Department, he finds the telegram wholly decoded and reads the hectograph master. There is revolution in A. The top leadership has been either murdered or banished. The officer-in-charge could legitimately awaken the Assistant Secretary, but for the moment it seems there is nothing that can be done, so he decides to hold off until 6 a.m. and then call the Office Director and put it up to him. He does, however, call the A desk officer and tell him to get on his way. To share his vigil beside the watch officer's window there is a representative of the executive secretariat, who will have the telegram ready for the Secretary to read immediately on his arrival. In the Bureau of Intelligence and Research—it being now after 4 o'clock—the morning briefers have arrived to go over the night's take and write up items of importance, with analyses, for the Director's use in briefing the Secretary's morning staff conference. The briefer for the Office of Research and Analysis for the Near East, South Asia and Africa—a GS-11 specialist on India—takes one look at the Niact on A and gets on the telephone to the A analyst.

By the time the Secretary has stepped from his black limousine and headed for the private elevator a good deal has happened. In the Bureau of Near Eastern and South Asian Affairs, everyone concerned with A from the Assistant Secretary down, and including the officer-in-charge of Baghdad Pact and Southeast Asia Treaty Organization affairs and the special assistant who serves as a policy and planning adviser, has been in conference for an hour laying out the tasks requiring immediate attention. Two more Niacts have come in from A, one reporting that so far no Americans are known to have been injured but offering little assurance with respect to the future. The Assistant Secretary has already put in a call to the Director of Intelligence Research to ask that all possible information on the new leader of A and his connections be marshaled and that the Central Intelligence Agency be informed of the need. For the rest, the following represent the Assistant Secretary's conception of what should be done first:

1. The Department of Defense must be apprised of the Department of State's anxiety and be requested to have transport planes in readiness at nearby fields for the evacuation of Americans if necessary in accordance with prearranged plans. There must be consultation on what instruments are available if American lives have to be protected by force.

2. The U.S. embassy in C, a friendly neighbor of A's to which the Niacts have been repeated, will be heard from at any moment, and the Special Assistant for Mutual Security Coordination in the Office of the Under Secretary for Economic Affairs and, also, the Office of International Security Affairs in the Department of Defense will have to be alerted to the possibility of emergency military assistance for C.

3. Anything in the pipeline for A should be held up. The Special Assistant for Mutual Security Coordination must be advised of this.

4. The possibility of a demonstration by the U.S. 6th Fleet in support of C's independence and integrity will have to be discussed with the Department of Defense.

5. A crash national intelligence estimate will be requested of the Central Intelligence Agency, provided the Agency does not consider the situation too fluid for a formal estimate to be useful.

6. The public affairs adviser will get in touch with the Bureau of Public Affairs, the departmental spokesman and the U.S. Information

Agency to agree on the kind of face the United States will put on the affair.

7. The B Ambassador will probably have to be called in and apprised of the critical need for his government's acquiescence in overflights of B for the purpose of getting supplies to C. The B and C desk officers had better get busy immediately on a draft telegram to embassy B (repeat to C) setting forth the case the ambassador should make urgently to the B Foreign Office.

At 9:12, anticipating that he will be called to accompany the Secretary to the White House, the Assistant Secretary instructs his secretary to cancel all his appointments for the day, including one with the dentist but excepting his appointment with the C ambassador. ("Mr. Ambassador, you may assure His Majesty that my Government remains fully determined to support the sovereignty and territorial integrity of his nation.")

At 9:14, 1 minute before the scheduled commencement of the staff meeting, the Assistant Secretary joins his colleagues in the Secretary's anteroom, prepared to hear the estimate of the Director of Intelligence and Research and to give his own appraisal and submit his plan of action.

DOCUMENT 22 THE DEFENSE DEPARTMENT AND FOREIGN POLICY

The diffusion of responsibility for implementing foreign policy, as discussed in Document 21, has been brought about as much by the demands of the international situation as by any political considerations. Because the position of the United States in world affairs rests largely on the efficacy of its actual or potential military commitment, military decisions and foreign-policy decisions are becoming more and more entwined. The following selection discusses the relationship between the military establishment and the civilian foreign-policy agencies—and more specifically, between the State and Defense Departments.

❖❖❖❖

No development affecting the contemporary organization of foreign policymaking is more significant than the impact of military affairs

FROM The Brookings Institution, "The Formulation and Administration of United States Foreign Policy," *United States Foreign Policy: Compilation of Studies,* Number 9, Senate Committee on Foreign Relations, Eighty-Sixth Congress, second session (Washington, D.C., Government Printing Office, 1960), Vol. 2, pp. 878–85.

on the daily relations between the United States and other governments. This is unprecedented in times of relative peace, and the trend is likely to continue in future years. It is obviously infeasible, of course, to consider joining the military and foreign policy organizations within a unified department. At the same time, it is clear that there should be the closest possible collaboration between the Department of Defense and the foreign policy apparatus, but this need is not being adequately met at the present time. Much has been done to improve the situation, but this relationship remains one of the weaker links in the foreign policy process.

The most striking inadequacies lie in the area of those military planning and decisionmaking activities which have critical implications for foreign policy but are often not subjected to adequate consideration by foreign policy officials. Obvious examples are the fundamental choices regarding weapons systems with which the military forces are to be equipped, the size, organization, and distribution of the forces, and military planning for various future international contingencies that may confront the United States. Under modern conditions, these are as much the concern of officials responsible for the Nation's foreign policy as major political decisions are rightfully the concern of military policymakers.

In addition to the systematic integration of military and foreign policy and the organizational specifications set forth at the beginning of this study, there are several other criteria of basic relevance in evaluating the participation of the Military Establishment in foreign policymaking. One such criterion is the traditional American concept of civilian supremacy. Unfortunately, as with other venerable concepts, the term has sometimes been used with more emotion than clarity. Essentially, it means that, both theoretically and effectively, the ultimate controlling policy decisions should be made by the politically responsibile civilian leadership, executive and legislative. It must be added, however, that there is no set of institutional and organizational arrangements that can insure this condition. Providing the Secretary of Defense with numerous Assistant Secretaries is no guarantee of civilian control. Implied in this concept is the belief that national security policy should not be overweighted in the direction of military concepts and military instruments of policy. There is also the idea that the professional officer corps should be protected from political involvement. Career personnel should eschew the partisan arena; their prestige with the Congress and the public should not be exploited for partisan purposes.

A. MILITARY ORGANIZATION
IN RELATION TO FOREIGN POLICY

The significant role of the Military Establishment is reflected in the fact that the Secretary of Defense is a statutory member of the

National Security Council, and that the Chairman of the Joint Chiefs of Staff attends Council meetings as an adviser. On the National Security Council Planning Board the Secretary is represented by the "Defense Member" and the Joint Chiefs of Staff by an "adviser." There is also Defense Establishment representation on the Operations Coordinating Board and its working groups.

In reaching his conclusions on major foreign policy and international security questions, the Secretary of Defense has at least two major sources of advice. First, there is an Assistant Secretary of Defense for International Security Affairs who has a combined military-civilian professional staff of approximately 140 people working for him. The Office of International Security Affairs is the official, authorized channel for communication between the Military Establishment and the Department of State.

Second, the Joint Chiefs of Staff are the other major source of advice to the Secretary. Their statutory responsibilities as military advisers to the President, the National Security Council, and the Secretary of Defense are well known. Under the Defense Reorganization Act of 1958, their power was increased, giving them operational control over the commanders of unified and specified forces in the field. However, orders to such commanders are to be issued by the President or the Secretary of Defense, or by the Joint Chiefs of Staff by authority and direction of the Secretary of Defense. The Joint Staff supports the Joint Chiefs of Staff in discharging their responsibilities but has no executive authority. To make it possible for them to carry out these increased responsibilities, the authorized strength of the Joint Staff that serves them has been doubled, from 200 to 400 officers.

The Secretary of Defense also has available to him the advice of the civilian secretaries of the three military departments as well as other Assistant Secretaries within the Office of the Secretary of Defense, such as the Comptroller and the General Counsel, but the Assistant Secretary of Defense for International Security Affairs and the Joint Chiefs of Staff are the most important advisers on foreign policy questions.

I. OFFICE OF INTERNATIONAL SECURITY AFFAIRS

The Office of International Security Affairs is a relatively recent unit. An official formally designated as Special Assistant to the Secretary for International Security Affairs was first appointed in December 1950. He was elevated to Assistant Secretary rank in 1953. This office has been given clear responsibility for, and control over, policy and programing for the military assistance program. In performing this function, the office is supported by strategic military guidance provided by the Joint Chiefs of Staff. Under the overall policy guidance developed by the Office of International Security

Affairs, the military services and overseas commands actually conduct the operations of providing material, training and other assistance to foreign countries. At the present time, this program absorbs about one-half of the time and energies of the staff of the Office of International Security Affairs, including its regional desk officers who deal with the Department of State daily on foreign policy problems involving military responsibilities and forces.

The second major function of the Office of International Security Affairs is coordinating and supporting the Department of Defense representation on the National Security Council, its Planning Board, and the Operations Coordinating Board. The Joint Chiefs of Staff have their own staff to advise them in support of the role of their Chairman as statutory adviser to the National Security Council. The officer who heads this group is the representative of the Joint Chiefs of Staff on the Planning Board. The Joint Chiefs, however, are not separately represented on the Operations Coordinating Board. The Assistant Secretary of Defense for International Security Affairs acts as alternate to the Deputy Secretary of Defense on the Operations Coordinating Board and is the Defense Department representative on the Planning Board. The Office of International Security Affairs currently supplies roughly one-third of the Military Establishment representatives on Operations Coordinating Board working groups; the rest come from the individual services and the Joint Staff.

The third major function of the International Security Affairs Office, and in a sense the most basic of its responsibilities, is to develop Department of Defense policy positions on a broad range of politico-military problems in United States relations with other nations. Examples would be the varied and complex problems arising from United States membership in regional security organizations like the North Atlantic Treaty Organization and the Southeast Asia Treaty Organization, the arrangements involved in stationing of United States forces in many foreign countries, and the international disarmament negotiations.

II. JOINT CHIEFS OF STAFF

In addition to their participation in the National Security Council process and their role as advisers to the President and the Secretary of Defense, the Joint Chiefs of Staff meet on a fairly regular weekly basis with several high officials of the Department of State, including at least one person at the Deputy Under Secretary level. While the substance of these discussions is privileged, the focus is apparently on what might be termed current operational questions. Examples might include international situations in which military forces are involved or military implications loom large, such as the recent Lebanon, Quemoy, and Berlin crises. The Assistant Secretary of Defense for International Security Affairs is present at these meetings.

At a lower level, there are weekly meetings of an informal nature between members of the Policy Planning Staff of the Department of State on the one hand and the director of the Joint Staff and several Office of International Security Affairs officials on the other. In addition, there is some consultation between other Joint Staff officers and the Department of State officials which flows from the new relationship between the Joint Chiefs of Staff and the unified and specified commanders.

It should be emphasized, however, that the main portion of Department of Defense contact with the Department of State is conducted by the Office of International Security Affairs. While the Joint Staff exchanges information with the unified commands on foreign policy issues, the Assistant Secretary of Defense for International Security Affairs and his office retain executive authority in this area through functions delegated by the Secretary of Defense to the Assistant Secretary.

Mention should also be made of the activities of the three service staffs. It seems to be generally understood, though not formally included in any directive, that there is to be no direct contact between the Department of State and the individual services beyond what is absolutely necessary. In practice, this principle is interpreted liberally. Officials on both sides are naturally inclined to deal directly with whoever seems to be in the best position to help solve a particular problem. Those who operate in this fashion usually feel that they keep the Office of International Security Affairs and other relevant offices sufficiently informed.

B. RELATIONS BETWEEN THE MILITARY ESTABLISHMENT AND CIVILIAN FOREIGN POLICY AGENCIES

Because there is still disagreement concerning the relationship between the Departments of Defense and State, it is well to consider the issue: How can the relationship between the Military Establishment and the principal foreign policy organization be strengthened?

Before turning to the several aspects of this issue, some basic premises should be stated. There can be no clearcut or fixed boundary between military policies and those of the civilian foreign policy organization. Each agency has its own assigned functions, and these should be as carefully and clearly defined as possible. It is obvious, however, that they must overlap to a considerable extent. Examples can be found in the broad range of factors involved in the North Atlantic Treaty Organization relationship or in such recent situations as those concerning Lebanon and Berlin.

Major foreign policy guidelines should be set by the primary foreign policy agency within the general strategy approved by the President. Because the general foreign policy organization and the Military Establishment must deal with a considerable number of situations jointly or at least with some recognition of common interest, there must be close and continuing working relations between them at all levels from the National Security Council to the lowest action officer.

Leaving other elements aside, the very differences in the responsibilities and functions of the Military Establishment and the foreign affairs agency make disagreement between them at times inevitable and, under certain circumstances, even desirable. It is not disagreement per se that is undesirable; what is important is the availability of means for prompt and decisive resolution of disagreements.

Those who are concerned that the primacy of civilian leadership be maintained in the foreign policy field should recognize that this cannot be insured by organizational arrangements. It must flow chiefly from the vigorous and creative leadership of the civilian personnel.

These points seem reasonably well accepted. There are others not so well established; these provide the basis for the major issues discussed below.

It is generally acknowledged that military considerations are so closely intertwined with broader foreign policy questions that military perspectives, information and expertise must be brought to bear regularly on a broad range of foreign policy questions. As suggested above, it is by no means clear that the opposite side of the coin, stemming with equal logic from the original premises, is as widely accepted. It is the position of this report that major military decisions —including those affecting force levels, composition and balance of forces, choice of weapons systems—be systematically examined and evaluated in relation to their political implications, with the regular participation of relevant civilian foreign policy personnel.

In an era when the position of the United States in world affairs rests so substantially on the nature and strength of its military posture and when the pace of weapons development is so swift, it is foolhardy for major military decisions to be made without the most searching consideration of their political and economic implications. For example, decisions made today regarding the choice of weapons systems to be developed are likely to have the most important consequences for the foreign policy position of the United States 5 years hence. Thus the broader foreign policy viewpoint must be brought to bear on military problems when fundamental choices are being made and basic planning is being done rather than when it is too late to affect such choices—when the weapons are being put into the hands of the troops.

This concept calls for some well-established relationship between at least the primary foreign policy leaders and the major military decision makers. Such an arrangement is likely to meet considerable resistance in some military quarters; equally reluctant may be those on the other side who assume that closer association may mean less independence.

The military are understandably concerned to protect their freedom of action based on their special role and competence. There are the inevitable time pressures in their work which are not likely to be alleviated by adding still another group to the process. There are interservice rivalries to be resolved in developing plans and making major policy decisions; presumably this can be done more easily without nonmilitary representatives present. And the military feel a special responsibility to protect the integrity of certain information crucial to the security of the United States.

There is the additional question of where the boundary line should be drawn between those decisions concerning which civilian participation would be appropriate and those regarding which it would be unnecessary or undesirable. It should be noted that this is a question equally relevant to military participation in the making of general foreign policy. There is no simple answer to this problem, but the evidence gathered for this study would suggest that there should be both more extensive and more intensive consultation between the civilian and military staffs.

*****

DOCUMENT 23 THE NATIONAL SECURITY COUNCIL

Since the Secretary of State does not have his hands on all the levers that operate policy, it has become essential to devise an administrative mechanism where all those who share power can thrash out their differences and standardize policies on matters of national urgency. The standard device at lower levels of the government is a "coordinating committee" to which each agency concerned with a specific facet of foreign affairs (for example, monetary policy, atomic energy, or economic aid) sends a legate. The executive department is littered with these bodies, which have the unfortunate characteristic of being useful precisely where they are least needed—on unimportant matters. Their authority rests on voluntary compliance, and when a really important problem emerges where the different departments have compelling interests, nobody wants to be coordinated. Each agency wants to triumph, and eventually the decision has to be made by the one man with final authority. As the sign on Harry Truman's desk put it, "The Buck Stops Here."

President Roosevelt detested committee meetings and thus dealt directly and privately with the parties to a dispute—a technique that created difficulties of its own: on occasion, each of the combatants left his office convinced that F. D. R. had given him the victory! President Truman, perhaps because of his Senate training, had more faith in the committee mechanism, and it was during his administration that the super-coordinating committee, the National Security Council, was established. The NSC met faithfully throughout the Eisenhower years, but was (in Washington parlance) a "talk shop" where little decision-making was accomplished. Secretary of State Dulles refused to take it seriously (he seems to have considered it a nest of hostile critics) and worked directly with the President. It was revived by the Kennedy Administration, but it was promptly streamlined with the creation of an informal "executive committee," a body including the Attorney-General (who is not a statutory member of the NSC) and excluding the Vice-President. This small group coordinated the President's confrontation with the U.S.S.R. over Cuba in October 1962. This selection discusses the development of the NSC up to the beginning of the Kennedy Administration.

As background for the main body of this study, the present account sets forth in relatively brief compass the organization and procedures of the National Security Council and the subordinate units attached to it.

A. STATUTORY BASIS

The statutory basis of the Council is the National Security Act of 1947, as amended and as supplemented by various Executive orders and memorandums. The function of the Council, as stated in the act, is: "To advise the President with respect to the integration of domestic, foreign, and military policies relating to the national security so as to enable the military services and the other departments and agencies of the Government to cooperate more effectively in matters involving the national security." There is also a paragraph dealing with the Council's responsibility "to assess and appraise the objectives, com-

FROM The Brookings Institution, "The Formulation and Administration of United States Foreign Policy," Burton M. Sapin, Appendix B, *United States Foreign Policy: Compilation of Studies,* Number 9, Senate Committee on Foreign Relations, Eighty-Sixth Congress, second session (Washington, D.C., Government Printing Office, 1960), Vol. 2, pp. 960–68.

mitments and risks of the United States in relation to our actual and potential military power, in the interest of national security, for the purpose of making recommendations to the President in connection therewith . . . ."

The membership provided for in the statute includes: The President, Vice President, Secretary of State, Secretary of Defense, and the Director of the Office of Civil and Defense Mobilization. It is also provided in the act that the following are to attend as advisers to the Council: The Chairman of the Joint Chiefs of Staff and the Director of the Central Intelligence Agency. The Central Intelligence Agency is made directly responsible to the Council.

Before proceeding to a more detailed description of the Council machinery, it should be emphasized that, in the 12 years of its existence, the Council has undergone considerable change and adjustment in its purposes and functions, in its organizational structure, and in its procedures. Furthermore, growth and development still continue. Primary attention in this paper will be given to the present pattern although major trends will be noted.

B. PRESENT ORGANIZATION BRIEFLY DESCRIBED

The National Security Council is a part of the Presidential staff organization known as the Executive Office of the President. The Council has always had a small professional staff attached to it, headed by an executive secretary, performing the following functions —analyzing policy questions independently and in cooperation with relevant agencies, arranging the agenda for meetings, providing and distributing the supporting papers including records of the actions taken at Council meetings, and facilitating negotiations among the participants. While the essential function of the staff is to service the Council, it also provides for the President's Special Assistant for National Security Affairs an "objective analysis of every policy paper that goes through the Planning Board to the Council." While it "does not itself make policy recommendations, it does scrutinize departmental proposals and suggest policy alternatives or additions that merit consideration."

Mr. Cutler [the President's Special Assistant for National Security Affairs] refers to the staff as having 11 "think people" who are "scrupulously nonpolitical and nonpolicymaking. They form the backbone of continuity, the reservoir of past knowledge and the staff assistance required by the special assistant in discharging his responsibilities to the President."

****

Since 1950 the Council has had a second-level group connected with it which has done much of the work involved in preparing for its consideration policy papers which, if favorably received by the Council and approved by the President, become official policy. This group was known as the Senior Staff under President Truman and became the Planning Board under President Eisenhower. Each member of the National Security Council is represented on the Planning Board, usually by an official of Assistant Secretary rank. In recent years, these officials have relied on a group of their subordinates, the Planning Board assistants, to do much of the detailed drafting.

In late 1953, in part as an outgrowth of a concern to maximize the psychological impact of U.S. policy, still another unit, the Operations Coordinating Board, was made a part of the national security organization, but it was not formally added to the National Security Council structure until July 1957. In brief, its function is to advise with the agencies concerned to ensure that the interagency execution of policies and programs in various functional and geographical areas is integrated to achieve maximum advantage. The Board is chaired by the Under Secretary of State; other designated members are the Deputy Secretary of Defense, the Director of the Central Intelligence Agency, and the Director of the U.S. Information Agency and the International Cooperation Administration. The Joint Chiefs of Staff are not directly represented.

The Operations Coordinating Board has its own professional staff, headed by an Executive Officer and somewhat separate from the staff of the National Security Council–Planning Board structure. Since 1957, there has also been a Presidential Special Assistant for Security Operations Coordination, who is designated Vice Chairman of the Board. This official also attends the meetings of the National Security Council and serves as an adviser to the Planning Board. The Coordinating Board members also have their Board assistants to do preliminary labors for them. Detailed scrutiny of policy execution in various geographical and functional areas is actually carried out by approximately 50 Operations Coordinating Board working groups, Interdepartmental committees of working-level officials with 1 professional staff person from the Board's staff also sitting in as a member.

One of President Eisenhower's important innovations in the National Security Council system was to establish in 1953 as part of his own immediate staff the position of Special Assistant to the President for National Security Affairs. This official plays a key role in the meetings of the Council, sits as Chairman of the Planning Board (a role previously played by the Executive Secretary of the Council staff), and is a member of the Operations Coordinating Board.

C. MEMBERSHIP AND MEETING PROCEDURE OF THE COUNCIL

In addition to the statutory members, the Secretary of the Treasury, under both President Truman and President Eisenhower, has had virtually regular membership status. At present, the Director of the Bureau of the Budget and the Chairman of the Atomic Energy Commission also attend the Council meetings on a regular basis. A considerable number of other officials normally are present. Some are staff aids and sit in the outer circle. Mr. Gordon Gray, the present Special Assistant for National Security Affairs, recently provided the following list of these other officials:

The Assistant to the President; the Director, U.S. Information Agency; the Under Secretary of State; the Special Assistants to the President for Foreign Economic Policy and Science and Technology; the White House Staff Secretary; the Special Assistant to the President for Security Operations Coordination; the Executive Secretary and the Deputy Executive Secretary, National Security Council. For agenda items which are the subject of official interest to them, the Attorney General and the Administrator, National Aeronautics and Space Administration, are invited. Of course, for any agenda items that the President may determine, ad hoc members participate.

For example, when matters relating to the Military Establishment are under discussion, the Chiefs of Staff and civilian Secretaries of the three services are likely to be present. The total of those now regularly in attendance at Council meetings is 20.

The Council regularly meets each Thursday at 9 a.m. Meetings normally do not exceed 2 hours. Special Council meetings are called by the Special Assistant for National Security Affairs at the request of the President. The agenda for a Council meeting is determined by the President, acting through the Special Assistant for National Security Affairs.

One feature of every Council meeting is a regular briefing by the Director of Central Intelligence. He gives a summary of important developments that are occurring throughout the world, and he gives particular attention to those areas which are on the Council agenda that day.

Under President Truman, the Council, particularly in its early years, did not meet quite so regularly or frequently, although during the Korean war it began to meet on a regular weekly basis. As Mr. Cutler has pointed out, President Truman attended the meetings less regularly than President Eisenhower, who has rarely missed a meeting since he has been in office, aside from his periods of illness.

The Council may have one item on its agenda or as many as four or five. There are no formal votes; the usual procedure is to take "the sense of the meeting." The nature of the Council's procedures in dealing with the papers that come before it is discussed below.

D. RELATIONSHIP OF THE COUNCIL TO OTHER UNITS

Since there are other advisory councils and committees at the presidential level and other units in the Executive Office of the President, the question of the Council's relations with them and the division of labor on national security problems is an important one.

The Cabinet is supposed to concern itself with all domestic matters not bearing "directly and primarily" on national security. This is not always an obvious or simple distinction, and there are certainly possibilities for jurisdictional dispute. Mr. Robert Cutler indicates how the question has been dealt with under the Eisenhower administration:

The complexity of modern times often makes it difficult to draw a clear line between the two categories; but in practice a rational accommodation has invariably been worked out between the Secretary of the Cabinet and the Special Assistant for National Security Affairs.

In other words, the fact that the President now has on his immediate staff both a Special Assistant for the Council and a secretary to the Cabinet provides the opportunity for close cooperation and apparently, under present circumstances, satisfactory working relations.

The question of division of labor also arises regarding those national security matters that might be termed current operational questions and those with important longer term policy aspects and implications, the latter presumably being the special province of the National Security Council. Here again, the present system seems to operate satisfactorily because of good working relationships between the Special Assistant for National Security Affairs and officials like the President's Staff Secretary, who is largely responsible for White House liaison with the Military Establishment on current operational matters.

As to other high-level advisory councils and committees in the foreign policy—national security field, no significant difficulties of integration and coordination seem to have arisen. The National Aeronautics and Space Council, formally chaired by the President, has not been in existence long enough for any important patterns to develop. Both the National Advisory Council on International Monetary and Financial Problems and the Council on Foreign Economic Policy seem to have fairly well-defined areas of responsibility which either have not interfered with any important National Security Council responsibilities or have been brought into the Security Council when this seemed desirable.

In any event, according to the accounts of Mr. Gray and Mr. Cutler, the present President is inclined to give major national security policy-making responsibilities to the Council machinery and to regard exceptions to that rule as temporary.

E. ORGANIZATION AND FUNCTIONS OF OTHER NATIONAL SECURITY COUNCIL UNITS

It has already been pointed out that one of President Eisenhower's major innovations in the machinery of the Council was the introduction of the position of Special Assistant to the President for National

Security Affairs. This official now plays a central role in the operation of the whole structure, excepting only the work of the Operations Coordinating Board. Mr. Gray himself has provided what is probably the most complete and yet succinct summary of the present duties and responsibilities of the Special Assistant:

Responsibility for agenda, and presentation of material for discussion at Council meetings; as necessary, briefing the President before Council meetings on agenda items; determining, in collaboration with the NSC Executive Secretary, the agenda and scheduling of work for Planning Board meetings; presiding at, and participating in, Planning Board meetings; supervising the work of the NSC staff through the Executive Secretary; attending and participating in meetings of the Operations Coordinating Board, the Council on Foreign Economic Policy and other relevant groups; attending as an observer at meetings of the Cabinet; and such other assignments related to national security affairs as the President may direct.

The general role and organization of the Planning Board have already been noted. Its membership is composed of representatives and observers from the departments and agencies represented on the Council, whether statutory or not. For example, at present a special assistant to the Secretary of the Treasury and an Assistant Director of the Bureau of the Budget sit on the Board. Also present is an officer representing the Joint Chiefs of Staff. It is clear that under present arrangements the Special Assistant for National Security Affairs plays a key role in the work of the group. Under both Mr. Truman and Mr. Eisenhower, there seems to have been the hope that the Senior Staff–Planning Board could be developed into a working team of high-level departmental officials who would devote a substantial portion of their time and efforts to its activities. In both cases, this hope has been disappointed. For those who represent their agencies on the Planning Board, this is but one among a number of very important and time-consuming responsibilities and, usually, just one among a number of very important meetings that must be regularly attended each week. Indeed, a standard complaint is that not infrequently these officials must miss Board meetings and are themselves represented by subordinates. Under Mr. Eisenhower, it has even been necessary to organize a body subsidiary to the Board to do some of its work for it—the Planning Board assistants. The meetings of the Board assistants are not regularly scheduled, but they average about five sessions a month.

Under Mr. Cutler, the Planning Board was meeting regularly on a three-times-a-week basis. Mr. Gray informs us that the Board now meets regularly twice a week, on Tuesday and Friday afternoons "from 2 o'clock till 5—or such further time as I may keep them in session." Apparently the latter comment is not a mere idle remark because Planning Board sessions have a reputation among those who attend them of lasting often far longer than the scheduled 3 hours.

The Operations Coordinating Board follows a somewhat different pattern. It convenes

at an informal luncheon meeting each Wednesday in the Department of State. The luncheon is attended by the designated members and the Executive Officer [i.e., of the Board staff]; other officials are invited as required for discussion of specific subjects. Thereafter the Board convenes in formal session for the transaction of business indicated in the advance agenda.

. . . A typical meeting includes the following principal items:

a. Reports indicating general effectiveness of assigned national security policies and future problems and difficulties in [their] implementation, for transmittal to the NSC.

b. Operations plans for specific countries or regions, as developed by OCB working groups or committees to facilitate effective interdepartmental coordination.

c. Special reports for either the Board or the Council by OCB working groups or committees, on their own initiative or by request, analyzing a specific problem and proposing action.

d. Oral reports to clarify issues or stimulate discussion.

In addition to the two Presidential special assistants and the other designated members noted earlier, the Under Secretary of the Treasury and the Chairman of the Atomic Energy Commission regularly attend the weekly meetings. The Board assistants, who do the "final staff work on subjects to be considered by the Board," meet regularly every Friday. The 50-odd working groups of the Board meet as frequently as is required by their work. They may meet as little as once a month; on the other hand, when they are in process of developing or reviewing an operations plan, they may be meeting on an almost daily basis and devoting a great deal of their time to the work of the interdepartmental working group.

❖❖❖❖

F. RELATED DEPARTMENTAL ARRANGEMENTS

Each agency participating in the National Security Council structure has developed some specialized staff arrangements and designated personnel to deal with the flow of documents and substantive problems emerging from its activities. The Vice President also has on his staff an aid responsible for National Security Council matters.

1. Department of State

Within the Department of State, the Policy Planning Staff is the unit designated to handle National Security Council and Planning Board matters. The Assistant Secretary who is director of the staff is also the Department's representative on the Planning Board. Within the staff, there are two officers who work full time on Council and Planning Board matters; one acts as alternate to the Assistant Secretary for the Planning Board and the other represents the Department on the Planning Board assistants group. Much of the actual drafting of policy papers for the Planning Board is done in the appropriate geographical or functional units of the Department, working closely with members of the Policy Planning Staff. Since members of the Council staff have reasonably good working relations with these units, as well as with the Department's intelligence bureau, the procedures involved in developing a draft document are presumably well developed and well established and should raise no special difficulties.

The Under Secretary of State has on his immediate staff an officer designated as special assistant for Operations Coordinating Board matters. He is the Department's representative on the Operations Coordinating Board assistants group and works with the Department's representatives on the various Board working groups, which are in fact usually chaired by the Department of State's representative.

2. Department of Defense

Although the Deputy Secretary of Defense is the formally designated representative of the Department of Defense on the Operations Coordinating Board, there was a recent period when the Assistant Secretary for International Security Affairs in actual fact represented the Department of Defense on both the Planning Board and the Operations Coordinating Board. He still acts as the Deputy Secretary's alternate on the Coordinating Board, and at times attends meetings of the Security Council itself with the Secretary of Defense. One of his three Deputy Assistant Secretaries is specifically designated as responsible for National Security Council affairs.

The participation of the Chairman of the Joint Chiefs of Staff in the Council is supported by a small staff within the Joint Staff, usually headed by a general or flag officer of two-star rank. This officer is the Joint Chiefs of Staff representative on the Planning Board. He also attends all the meetings of the Joint Chiefs so that he is presumably in a position to reflect their thinking in Planning Board discussions. The Joint Chiefs have no representation per se on the Operations Coordinating Board.

Under the Deputy Assistant Secretary charged with National Security Council affairs, there are specific offices, with quite small combined civilian-military staffs of several persons, dealing with National Security Council affairs and Operations Coordinating Board affairs. The Deputy Assistant Secretary is the Assistant Secretary's alternate for Planning Board meetings. The Director of the Office of National Security Council Affairs is the Department of Defense representative at the Planning Board Assistants meetings, while the Director of the Coordinating Board office sits as Defense Department member of that Board Assistants group.

The three services themselves have specifically designated units or officers responsible for National Security Council and Operations Coordinating Board matters. In the Army staff, under the Deputy Chief of Staff for Operations, and, more specifically, the Director for Plans, there is a Special Assistant for National Security Council Affairs—at present a full colonel—who is at the same time chief of the International and Policy Planning Division of the staff. Operations Coordinating Board matters are handled separately by a Special Assistant for Operations Coordinating Board Affairs in the Office of the Director for Operations. The International and Policy Planning Division is in effect the international security affairs staff for the Army Chief of Staff and has approximately 20 action officers, any of whom may work on Planning Board drafts depending upon the subject matter.

The Air Force has an International Affairs Division set up very much like the Army's under the Director of Plans, Deputy Chief of Staff, Plans and Programs. However, at present, the Air Force does have an officer specifically designated as Assistant for National Security Affairs who plays a coordinating role. Most of the work on drafts is done by action officers within the International Affairs Division.

The Navy is organized and operates somewhat differently in this field. All National Security Council and Operations Coordinating Board matters are handled by the Politico-Military Policy Division (Op-61), headed by a rear admiral, under the Deputy Chief of Naval Operations, Plans and Policy. Within this unit, there are different officers responsible for the Planning Board and the Operations Coordinating Board. Since the Navy does not use the action officer technique in this field, drafts are circulated to the relevant units within the overall Navy staff for comments, which are then pulled together by the responsible officers within Op-61.

3. Other agencies

While the Departments of State and Defense are the most important participating agencies in the structure and have the most substantial arrangements for supporting this participation, the general pattern is similar in other agencies. For example, the Under Secretary of the Treasury represents the Treasury Department on the Operations Coordinating Board and a special assistant to the Secretary of the Treasury sits on the Planning Board. Similar arrangements are found within the Bureau of the Budget.

G. DEVELOPMENT OF A NATIONAL SECURITY COUNCIL PAPER

The usual end product of the work and deliberations of the Planning Board and the Council is a National Security Council policy paper dealing with the particular problem, geographical area or functional question. Each paper, when finally approved by the President, has some specific numerical designation and is classified as top secret with only a relative handful of numbered copies in circulation. The routine format of these papers was described several years ago by Mr. Robert Cutler in the following terms: "the covering letter, the general considerations, the objectives, the courses of action to carry out the objectives, the financial appendixes, the supporting staff study; for they invariably appeared in this sequence in the final document." It is often the case that a national intelligence estimate on the particular situation or problem will be requested from the Central Intelligence Agency and thus become a part of the documentation.

Gordon Gray distinguishes three types of National Security Council paper: "fundamental policy; geographical policy, on a single foreign country or on a region; and functional papers not related to a specific geographical area." As an example of the continuing experimentation and the developing character of the Council structure, a rather recent innovation has been the "special discussion paper" which Mr. Gray describes in the following terms:

Additionally, on many occasions the Planning Board will present to the Council, without recommendations, a special discussion paper consisting of a series of seemingly feasible alternatives, with the pros and cons of each carefully set forth. The Council will discuss the alternatives and thereby provide guidance to the Planning Board as a basis for developing a draft policy statement.

The original impetus which leads to a new policy paper or the review and revision of a paper already in existence may come from a number of sources. The President himself, or some other member of the Council, may ask the Planning Board to look into a question and come up with a draft paper if this proves desirable. In the course of its periodic assessments of U.S. policies and programs, the Operations Coordinating Board may conclude that a review of existing policy in some particular area is in order and may so recommend to the Council. The President's Special Assistant for National Security Affairs may himself initiate consideration of some matter. The development may start within one of the participating departments, perhaps even rather far down in the organizational hierarchy. Most obviously, the process may be triggered by some compelling event on the international scene.

However the process is initiated, the request or suggestion is usually turned over to the Planning Board which in turn will ask one of the participating departments to prepare a first draft. Since most of the papers fall into the broad category of foreign policy, the Department of State normally prepares the original draft document. The Council does consider major military policy questions and in those cases, of course, the first draft is likely to be produced by the Military Establishment.

Within the State Department, as indicated above, the draft paper will probably be a joint product of members of the interested bureaus and offices and of the Policy Planning Staff. At times, there may be informal consultation even at this stage with opposite numbers in other departments, such as Defense and Treasury. When the draft has been completed, it will be circulated to the representatives of the other agencies, and then the matter will be placed on the agenda of the Planning Board, presumably allowing enough time for the other participating agencies to develop their views on the paper. However, a frequent complaint is that often there is not enough time available between receipt of the drafts and discussion in the Planning Board to prepare adequate papers on the particular problems.

Since the Military Establishment probably has the most elaborate machinery for developing views on Planning Board papers, it may be useful to trace the progress of one of these papers through the Pentagon. They travel through two separate channels, the Joint Chiefs of Staff organization and the Office of International Security Affairs in the Department of Defense. The responsible Deputy Assistant Secretary of Defense for International Security Affairs and the official under him who deals specifically with National Security Council and Planning Board matters meet weekly with the representatives of the three service staffs referred to earlier to brief them on upcoming Planning Board agenda items and the latest Board actions. These service representatives receive from the International Security Affairs officials the draft Planning Board documents, on which they are asked to comment. After they have developed their positions, their comments are sent to both the Deputy Assistant Secretary and to the two-star officer who is the Joint Chiefs of Staff representative on the Planning Board. While these two officials do consult on Planning Board matters and generally arrive at a common position, it does occasionally happen that there will be disagreement between them at the Planning Board level, the Council level, or both.

The draft policy paper will then be the subject of considerable discussion in the Planning Board. The Special Assistant, acting as chairman and with no departmental viewpoint to defend, is in a position to sharpen the discussion, clarifying areas of agreement and disagreement. The paper may be sent back to the originating department for redrafting, or other departments may contribute drafts of their own. After some discussion in the Board, it may be turned over to the Board assistants for further study and redrafting. Mr. Gray comments: "After the Planning Board has discussed a paper, it is usually turned over to the Board assistants to be redrafted. Normally the Board assistants meet 4 to 8 hours on a paper before sending a redraft back to the Planning Board." Gray describes the procedures of the Planning Board in the following terms:

Normally, consideration of a geographical policy starts off with a study of the latest national intelligence estimate on the country and a briefing by the CIA adviser on the most recent developments in the area. The Planning Board normally does not send a paper forward without meeting three or four times on it. However, in crisis situations the Planning Board may have to complete a paper in one meeting; and on occasion the NSC has had to take action without referring the matter to the Planning Board at all.

. . . no departmental representative is reticent in marshaling the arguments in support of any position he sees fit to take. Moreover, it is the established practice for Planning Board members to bring experts from their own staffs. For example, when a paper on a foreign country is being discussed, the State Department will bring the area people concerned and the Defense Department may bring the people who deal with the military assistance programs.

Mr. Cutler comments: "The number of times a particular subject comes before a Planning Board meeting depends upon its importance and complexity. A dozen meetings or more may be necessary before the final version of a particular statement is acceptable to the Board."

The draft policy paper prepared by the Planning Board is usually circulated to the members of the Council 10 days in advance of the time it will be discussed at the Council meeting. Among other things, this 10-day period gives the Joint Chiefs of Staff time to meet and discuss the paper and prepare written comments on it, which are then also circulated in advance to Council members. Usually, members of the Council are briefed on the various agenda items by their own agency representatives on the Planning Board sometime before the meeting.

Under present circumstances, according to Mr. Gray, the "President looks to the Special Assistant at Council meetings to present the items upon the agenda, to brief the Council on their background, to explain any 'splits' and to initiate discussion." With regard to "split papers," Mr. Gray states:

It is true that despite the best efforts of the Chairman of the Planning Board, policy papers go to the Council from time to time with split recommendations on minor issues. It is not true that major splits are not generally reflected in such papers. In fact, more than half the policy statements which are sent to the Council from the Planning Board contain split views largely on important issues on which one or more of the NSC agencies have indicated a strong divergence of opinion. A recent paper dealing with a fundamental policy contained 19 splits when it was sent to the Council from the Planning Board and required 5 successive Council meetings before final approval.

According to Messrs. Dillon Anderson, Cutler, and Gray—the three men who have served as Special Assistants for National Security Affairs under President Eisenhower—there is often vigorous discussion and exchange of views at the Council table, very much encouraged by the Chairman, the President. Some observers feel that the past two Secretaries of State. Dean Acheson and John Foster Dulles, combining great personal ability and intellectual force with extremely close relations with their Chief Executives, tended to dominate Council discussions.

Mr. Gray also reports:

It is seldom that arguments are made in the Council—except by the President or Vice President—which have not been previously discussed in the Planning Board; although I will say that Council members do not always fully espouse the position taken by their Planning Board representatives and are sometimes persuaded by their own wisdom or by the persuasiveness of others to a different view.

While items may occasionally stay on the Council agenda for several meetings, a decision is usually reached on a particular paper at the same meeting at which it has been presented and discussed. Presumably, after hearing the views of his departmental chiefs and top advisers, the President will reach his own decision, and in the process resolve such differences or splits as may have been present in the original paper. It seems reasonable to assume that the split papers are likely to be among those demanding more than one meeting and discussion. However, Mr. Cutler reports:

The statement of our basic national security policy, to which all our other security policies are subsidiary, is reviewed annually in the Council. Frequently this searching review will extend, as it did in the 1958 calendar year, over a period of several months. It may require a dozen Planning Board meetings and appear on the agenda of several meetings of the National Security Council.

No formal votes are taken at the Council meetings. After each meeting, a written record of action is prepared for each Presidential decision made and is then circulated in draft to "those who were present at the meeting for comment before" it is submitted "to the President for his consideration, change if necessary, and final approval."

EXECUTIVE AGREEMENTS AND THE TREATY POWER

DOCUMENT 24 DESTROYERS FOR BASES

Secretary of State John Hay's mordant observation that one-third of the Senate would vote against anything may or may not be the key to the recurrent difficulty of getting treaties approved (not "ratified" —the President ratifies a treaty after the Senate has approved it, and he may even at that stage refuse to put it into operation by withholding ratification). Nevertheless, for the past hundred years or more, efforts have been made to institute international arrangements without recourse to the formality of treaties. When it appeared impossible in 1844 to garner the support of two-thirds of the Senate for a treaty admitting Texas to the Union, President Tyler suggested the employment of a joint resolution, which required a simple majority in both houses. In January 1845 such a resolution passed the House (120 to 98), and in February it narrowly survived in the Senate (27 to 25). Texas was then annexed and the constitutional problem was left to lawyers and polemicists. Typically, those opposed to the annexation declared the action unconstitutional, while those who favored it (mostly Southerners) took a broad view of constitutional authority.

Under the Constitution, treaties are the "supreme law of the land" and are on the same level as acts of Congress. (If a treaty and a statute conflict, the most recent is binding.) Since the Supreme Court has held that executive agreements have the same constitutional standing as treaties, there has been a good deal of furor about the possibility of a President, unchecked by the Senate, betraying the national interest by means of executive agreements. The notion is politically absurd, but it has stimulated a good deal of right-wing rhetoric—in particular, since the "Destroyers for Bases" deal in 1940 in which President Roosevelt circumvented Congress to aid the British in their desperate resistance to Nazi Germany. There is reason to suspect

*that a majority in both houses of Congress would have supported the
President, but because of the strength of isolationist sentiment these
legislators were leery of a forthright commitment on the issue. The
President took them off the hook by acting on his own after obtaining
from his Attorney-General an ingenious justification of his action. The
isolationists were furious, but Congress shortly appropriated funds to
develop the bases and, despite frenetic isolationist urging, never challenged the President's decision.*

*Attorney-General Jackson, as he later noted, had the vexing task
of supplying the President with a constitutional rationale for the
transfer. He chose to explain it as a shrewd Yankee horse trade in
which the United States received valuable real estate for some decrepit
old junk—though in fact the destroyers were no more antique than
most of those then active in the Royal Navy, which similarly dated
from World War I. And in real power terms there was no likelihood
that the bases would fall into enemy hands. This document presents
Jackson's quite ingenious justification for the transaction.*

Aug. 27, 1940.

The President.
The White House.

My Dear Mr. President:

In accordance with your request I have considered your constitutional and statutory authority to proceed by Executive Agreement with
the British Government immediately to acquire for the United States
certain off-shore naval and air bases in the Atlantic Ocean without
awaiting the inevitable delays which would accompany the conclusion
of a formal treaty.

The essential characteristics of the proposal are:

a. The United States to acquire rights for immediate establishment
and use of naval and air bases in Newfoundland, Bermuda, the Baha-
mas, Jamaica, St. Lucia, Trinidad and British Guiana; such rights to
endure for a period of ninety-nine years and to include adequate provisions for access to, and defense of, such bases and appropriate provisions for their control.

b. In consideration it is proposed to transfer to Great Britain the
title and possession of certain over-age ships and obsolescent military
materials now the property of the United States, and certain other

FROM Opinion by Attorney-General Robert Jackson to President Franklin
D. Roosevelt, August 27, 1940, New York *Times,* September 4, 1940. Copyright by The New York Times. Reprinted by permission.

small patrol boats which, though nearly completed, are already obsolescent.

c. Upon such transfer all obligation of the United States is discharged. The acquisition consists only of rights, which the United States may exercise or not at its option, and if exercised may abandon without consent. The privilege of maintaining such bases is subject only to limitations necessary to reconcile United States use with the sovereignty retained by Great Britain. Our government assumes no responsibility for civil administration of any territory. It makes no promise to erect structures, or maintain forces at any point. It undertakes no defense of the possessions of any country. In short, it acquires optional bases which may be developed as Congress appropriates funds therefor, but the United States does not assume any continuing or future obligation, commitment or alliance.

QUESTIONS OF AUTHORITY

The questions of constitutional and statutory authority, with which alone I am concerned, seem to be these:

First. May such an acquisition be concluded by the President under an Executive Agreement or must it be negotiated as a Treaty subject to ratification by the Senate?

Second. Does authority exist in the President to alienate the title to such ships and obsolescent materials, and if so, on what condition?

Third. Do the statutes of the United States limit the right to deliver the so-called "mosquito boats" now under construction or the over-age destroyers by reason of the belligerent status of Great Britain?

There is, of course, no doubt concerning the authority of the President to negotiate with the British Government for the proposed exchange. The only questions that might be raised in connection therewith are (1) whether the arrangement must be put in the form of a treaty and await ratification by the Senate or (2) whether there must be additional legislation by the Congress.

Ordinarily (and assuming the absence of enabling legislation) the question whether such an agreement can be concluded under Presidential authority or whether it must await ratification by a two-thirds vote of the United States Senate involves consideration of two powers which the Constitution vests in the President.

POWER AS COMMANDER IN CHIEF

One of these is the power of the Commander in Chief of the Army and Navy of the United States, which is conferred upon the President by the Constitution but is not defined or limited. . . .

I do not find it necessary to rest upon that power alone to sustain the present proposal. But it will hardly be open to controversy that the vesting of such a function in the President also places upon him a responsibility to use all constitutional authority which he may possess to provide adequate bases and stations for the utilization of the naval and air weapons of the United States at their highest efficiency in our defense. It seems equally beyond doubt that present world conditions forbid him to risk any delay that is constitutionally avoidable.

The second power to be considered is that control of foreign relations which the Constitution vests in the President as a part of the Executive function. The nature and extent of this power has recently been explicitly and authoritatively defined by Mr. Justice Sutherland, writing for the Supreme Court. In 1936, in United States v. Curtiss-Wright Export Corp., et al., 299 U.S. 304, he said:

It is important to bear in mind that we are here dealing not alone with an authority vested in the President by an exertion of legislative power, but with such an authority plus the very delicate, plenary and exclusive power of the President as the sole organ of the Federal Government in the field of international relations—a power which does not require as a basis for its exercise an act of Congress, but which, of course, like every other governmental power, must be exercised in subordination to the applicable provisions of the Constitution.

It is quite apparent that if, in the maintenance of our international relations, embarrassment—perhaps serious embarrassment—is to be avoided and success for our aims achieved, Congressional legislation which is to be made effective through negotiation and inquiry within the international field must often accord to the President a degree of discretion and freedom from statutory restriction which would not be admissible were domestic affairs alone involved.

Moreover, he, not Congress, has the better opportunity of knowing the conditions which prevail in foreign countries, and especially is this true in time of war. He has his confidential sources of information. He has his agents in the form of diplomatic consular and other officials. Secrecy in respect of information gathered by them may be highly necessary, and the premature disclosure of it productive of harmful results.

POWER OVER FOREIGN RELATIONS

The President's power over foreign relations, while "delicate, plenary and exclusive," is not unlimited. Some negotiations involve commitments as to the future which would carry an obligation to exercise powers vested in the Congress.

Such Presidential arrangements are customarily submitted for ratification by a two-thirds vote of the Senate before the future legislative power of the country is committed. However, the acquisitions which you are proposing to accept are without express or implied promises on the part of the United States to be performed in the future.

The consideration, which we later discuss, is completed upon transfer of the specified items. The Executive Agreement obtains an opportunity to establish naval and air bases for the protection of our coastline, but it imposes no obligation upon the Congress to appropriate money to improve the opportunity. It is not necessary for the Senate to ratify an opportunity that entails no obligation.

The transaction now proposed represents only an exchange with no statutory requirement for the embodiment thereof in any treaty and involving no promises or undertakings by the United States that might raise the question of the propriety of incorporation in a treaty. I therefore advise that acquisition by Executive agreement of the rights proposed to be conveyed to the United States by Great Britain will not require ratification by the Senate.

PRESIDENTIAL DECLARATIONS OF FOREIGN POLICY

DOCUMENT 25 ## THE EISENHOWER DOCTRINE ON THE MIDDLE EAST

One of the lessons that historians have drawn from the history of Nazi Germany is that Hitler capitalized on the uncertainty and disarray of his enemies. It is sadly clear in retrospect that firm Franco-British resistance in 1936, when Hitler occupied the Rhineland, would have led to a German retreat and possibly a coup by the German Army against the Nazi leader. War broke out in Europe in 1939 because Hitler was convinced that under no circumstances would the French and British fight for Poland.

Influential American policy-makers such as Secretary of State Dean Acheson argued in the post-World War II period that the greatest risk of war with the Soviet Union arose from Russian uncertainty about American intentions. Indeed, Acheson was criticized after the outbreak of the Korean War for not having made it clear that South Korea lay within our defense perimeter; one high Yugoslav official later stated that Stalin would not have authorized the Korean invasion if the Soviets had been certain that the United States would intervene. It is not always easy, of course, to predict how the American people will react to a commitment of American troops: in 1954, the American people would have objected strenuously if President Eisenhower had tried to commit troops in Indochina—largely because of the bad reputation of French colonialism. But several years later, when President Kennedy sent troops to preserve the autonomy of South Vietnam, it caused hardly a ripple of public reaction. In short, American willingness to accept commitments abroad depends on factors other than geography.

Beginning in 1956, Nikita Khrushchev made a series of bellicose speeches threatening American allies in Europe and the Middle East

181

*with "a hail of rockets" if they engaged in "aggressive action." In
1957, with the political situation in the Middle East in flux as a consequence of the abortive Suez action by the French, British, and
Israelis, President Eisenhower undertook to define in precise terms
the extent of American commitment in that area so the Soviets would
not be under false illusions in formulating their policy. To buttress
the point, and for political reasons discussed earlier (see Document
17), he asked Congress to approve this "Eisenhower Doctrine," reproduced here. And, acting under its authority in July 1959, he dispatched the United States Marines to Lebanon to maintain the peace.*

To the Congress of the United States:

❋❋❋❋

The Middle East has abruptly reached a new and critical stage in
its long and important history. In past decades many of the countries
in that area were not fully self-governing. Other nations exercised
considerable authority in the area and the security of the region was
largely built around their power. But since the First World War there
has been a steady evolution toward self-government and independence.
This development the United States has welcomed and has encouraged.
Our country supports without reservation the full sovereignty and independence of each and every nation of the Middle East.

The evolution to independence has in the main been a peaceful
process. But the area has been often troubled. Persistent cross-currents
of distrust and fear with raids back and forth across national boundaries have brought about a high degree of instability in much of the
Mid East. Just recently there have been hostilities involving Western
European nations that once exercised much influence in the area.
Also the relatively large attack by Israel in October has intensified
the basic differences between that nation and its Arab neighbors. All
this instability has been heightened and, at times, manipulated by International Communism.

Russia's rulers have long sought to dominate the Middle East. That
was true of the Czars and it is true of the Bolsheviks. The reasons are
not hard to find. They do not affect Russia's security, for no one plans
to use the Middle East as a base for aggression against Russia. Never
for a moment has the United States entertained such a thought.

The Soviet Union has nothing whatsover to fear from the United

FROM Special Message to Congress on the Situation in the Middle East,
January 5, 1957, *Public Papers of the Presidents of the United States: Dwight
D. Eisenhower, 1957* (Washington, D.C., Government Printing Office, 1958),
pp. 6–16.

PRESIDENTIAL DECLARATIONS OF FOREIGN POLICY

States in the Middle East, or anywhere else in the world, so long as its rulers do not themselves first resort to aggression.

That statement I make solemnly and emphatically.

Neither does Russia's desire to dominate the Middle East spring from its own economic interest in the area. Russia does not appreciably use or depend upon the Suez Canal. In 1955 Soviet traffic through the Canal represented only about three fourths of 1% of the total. The Soviets have no need for, and could provide no market for, the petroleum resources which constitute the principal natural wealth of the area. Indeed, the Soviet Union is a substantial exporter of petroleum products.

The reason for Russia's interest in the Middle East is solely that of power politics. Considering her announced purpose of Communizing the world, it is easy to understand her hope of dominating the Middle East.

This region has always been the crossroads of the continents of the Eastern Hemisphere. The Suez Canal enables the nations of Asia and Europe to carry on the commerce that is essential if these countries are to maintain well-rounded and prosperous economies. The Middle East provides a gateway between Eurasia and Africa.

It contains about two thirds of the presently known oil deposits of the world and it normally supplies the petroleum needs of many nations of Europe, Asia and Africa. The nations of Europe are peculiarly dependent upon this supply, and this dependency relates to transportation as well as to production. This has been vividly demonstrated since the closing of the Suez Canal and some of the pipelines. Alternate ways of transportation and, indeed, alternate sources of power can, if necessary, be developed. But these cannot be considered as early prospects.

These things stress the immense importance of the Middle East. If the nations of that area should lose their independence, if they were dominated by alien forces hostile to freedom, that would be both a tragedy for the area and for many other free nations whose economic life would be subject to near strangulation. Western Europe would be endangered just as though there had been no Marshall Plan, no North Atlantic Treaty Organization. The free nations of Asia and Africa, too, would be placed in serious jeopardy. And the countries of the Middle East would lose the markets upon which their economies depend. All this would have the most adverse, if not disastrous, effect upon our own nation's economic life and political prospects.

Then there are other factors which transcend the material. The Middle East is the birthplace of three great religions—Moslem, Christian and Hebrew. Mecca and Jerusalem are more than places on the map. They symbolize religions which teach that the spirit has supremacy over matter and that the individual has a dignity and rights of which no despotic government can rightfully deprive him. It would be intolerable if the holy places of the Middle East should be subjected to a rule that glorifies atheistic materialism.

International Communism, of course, seeks to mask its purposes of domination by expressions of good will and by superficially attractive offers of political, economic and military aid. But any free nation, which is the subject of Soviet enticement, ought, in elementary wisdom, to look behind the mask.

Remember Estonia, Latvia and Lithuania!

❖❖❖❖

Thus, we have these simple and indisputable facts:

1. The Middle East, which has always been coveted by Russia, would today be prized more than ever by International Communism.

2. The Soviet rulers continue to show that they do not scruple to use any means to gain their ends.

3. The free nations of the Mid East need, and for the most part want, added strength to assure their continued independence.

Our thoughts naturally turn to the United Nations as a protector of small nations. Its charter gives it primary responsibility for the maintenance of international peace and security. Our country has given the United Nations its full support in relation to the hostilities in Hungary and in Egypt. The United Nations was able to bring about a cease-fire and withdrawal of hostile forces from Egypt because it was dealing with governments and peoples who had a decent respect for the opinions of mankind as reflected in the United Nations General Assembly. But in the case of Hungary, the situation was different. The Soviet Union vetoed action by the Security Council to require the withdrawal of Soviet armed forces from Hungary. And it has shown callous indifference to the recommendations, even the censure, of the General Assembly. The United Nations can always be helpful, but it cannot be a wholly dependable protector of freedom when the ambitions of the Soviet Union are involved.

Under all the circumstances I have laid before you, a greater responsibility now devolves upon the United States. We have shown, so that none can doubt, our dedication to the principle that force shall not be used internationally for any aggressive purpose and that the integrity and independence of the nations of the Middle East should be inviolate. Seldom in history has a nation's dedication to principle been tested as severely as ours during recent weeks.

There is general recognition in the Middle East, as elsewhere, that the United States does not seek either political or economic domination over any other people. Our desire is a world environment of freedom, not servitude. On the other hand many, if not all, of the nations of the Middle East are aware of the danger that stems from International Communism and welcome closer cooperation with the United

States to realize for themselves the United Nations goals of independence, economic well-being and spiritual growth.

If the Middle East is to continue its geographic role of uniting rather than separating East and West; if its vast economic resources are to serve the well-being of the peoples there, as well as that of others; and if its cultures and religions and their shrines are to be preserved for the uplifting of the spirits of the peoples, then the United States must make more evident its willingness to support the independence of the freedom-loving nations of the area.

Under these circumstances I deem it necessary to seek the cooperation of the Congress. Only with that cooperation can we give the reassurance needed to deter aggression, to give courage and confidence to those who are dedicated to freedom and thus prevent a chain of events which would gravely endanger all of the free world.

✳✳✳✳

The action which I propose would have the following features.

It would, first of all, authorize the United States to cooperate with and assist any nation or group of nations in the general area of the Middle East in the development of economic strength dedicated to the maintenance of national independence.

It would, in the second place, authorize the Executive to undertake in the same region programs of military assistance and cooperation with any nation or group of nations which desires such aid.

It would, in the third place, authorize such assistance and cooperation to include the employment of the armed forces of the United States to secure and protect the territorial integrity and political independence of such nations, requesting such aid, against overt armed aggression from any nation controlled by International Communism.

These measures would have to be consonant with the treaty obligations of the United States, including the Charter of the United Nations and with any action or recommendations of the United Nations. They would also, if armed attack occurs, be subject to the overriding authority of the United Nations Security Council in accordance with the Charter.

The present proposal would, in the fourth place, authorize the President to employ, for economic and defensive military purposes, sums available under the Mutual Security Act of 1954, as amended, without regard to existing limitations.

✳✳✳✳

The proposed legislation is primarily designed to deal with the possibility of Communist aggression, direct and indirect. There is imperative need that any lack of power in the area should be made good, not by external or alien force, but by the increased vigor and security of the independent nations of the area.

Experience shows that indirect aggression rarely if ever succeeds where there is reasonable security against direct aggression; where the government disposes of loyal security forces, and where economic conditions are such as not to make Communism seem an attractive alternative. The program I suggest deals with all three aspects of this matter and thus with the problem of indirect aggression.

❈❈❈❈

And as I have indicated, it will also be necessary for us to contribute economically to strengthen those countries, or groups of countries, which have governments manifestly dedicated to the preservation of independence and resistance to subversion. Such measures will provide the greatest insurance against Communist inroads. Words alone are not enough.

Let me refer again to the requested authority to employ the armed forces of the United States to assist to defend the territorial integrity and the political independence of any nation in the area against Communist armed aggression. Such authority would not be exercised except at the desire of the nation attacked. Beyond this it is my profound hope that this authority would never have to be exercised at all.

❈❈❈❈

In the situation now existing, the greatest risk, as is often the case, is that ambitious despots may miscalculate. If power-hungry Communists should either falsely or correctly estimate that the Middle East is inadequately defended, they might be tempted to use open measures of armed attack. If so, that would start a chain of circumstances which would almost surely involve the United States in military action. I am convinced that the best insurance against this dangerous contingency is to make clear now our readiness to cooperate fully and freely with our friends of the Middle East in ways consonant with the purposes and principles of the United Nations.

❈❈❈❈

The occasion has come for us to manifest again our national unity in support of freedom and to show our deep respect for the rights and independence of every nation—however great, however small. We seek not violence, but peace. To this purpose we must now devote our energies, our determination, ourselves.

DWIGHT D. EISENHOWER

DOCUMENT 26 THE ALLIANCE FOR PROGRESS

American policy toward Latin America has undergone a number of shifts in the past half-century. Until President Roosevelt inaugurated the "Good Neighbor Policy" in 1933, we treated the nations of South and Central America as virtual colonies and the Caribbean states as protectorates. The externals of American policy changed with Roosevelt, but the realities of American power—largely in the hands of private businesses—remained about the same from the vantage point of the Latinos. In essence, the United States so dominated the Latin-American economy by the end of World War II that a simple shift in American behavior (from regular to instant coffee, for example) could destroy the economic security of millions of people. Moreover, the internal structure of most Latin-American societies was inherently highly unstable: a small élite of landowners and businessmen, working in conjunction with the military, dominated a huge mass of illiterate and poverty-stricken peasants. As usual, it took a catastrophe—the transformation of Cuba into a Soviet satellite by the Castro dictatorship—to arouse the American people to the baleful condition of Latin America and the perils of inertia.

President Kennedy in this address formulated the American (Latin Americans would say the North American) response to the crisis south of the Rio Grande, the Alliance for Progress. Based on the assumption that only a healthy democratic society can adequately resist the virus of Fidelismo and provide stability, the President committed the United States to a long-range program of technical and economic aid to be coupled with far-reaching internal reforms (taxation, land reform, and so forth) within the Latin-American community. The burden of transformation was to be carried by the Latin Americans themselves with the United States supplying a minimum of $20 billion spread over a decade to stimulate and underpin the process.

In his statement, and in later addresses, the President worked to mobilize American support for this gigantic project. Congress later approved the program in principle and appropriated the initial funds, but the success or failure of the Alliance will hang on the skill and political effectiveness of its administrators, on their ability to give these objectives institutional meaning.

. . . One hundred and thirty-nine years ago this week the United States, stirred by the heroic struggle of its fellow Americans, urged the independence and recognition of the new Latin American Republics. It was then, at the dawn of freedom throughout this hemisphere, that Bolívar spoke of his desire to see the Americas fashioned into the greatest region in the world, "greatest," he said, "not so much by virtue of her area and her wealth, as by her freedom and her glory."

Never in the long history of our hemisphere has this dream been nearer to fulfillment, and never has it been in greater danger.

The genius of our scientists has given us the tools to bring abundance to our land, strength to our industry, and knowledge to our people. For the first time we have the capacity to strike off the remaining bonds of poverty and ignorance—to free our people for the spiritual and intellectual fulfillment which has always been the goal of our civilization.

Yet at this very moment of maximum opportunity, we confront the same forces which have imperiled America throughout its history—the alien forces which once again seek to impose the despotisms of the Old World on the people of the New.

I have asked you to come here today so that I might discuss these challenges and these dangers.

We meet together as firm and ancient friends, united by history and experience and by our determination to advance the values of American civilization. For this New World of ours is not a mere accident of geography. Our continents are bound together by a common history, the endless exploration of new frontiers. Our nations are the product of a common struggle, the revolt from colonial rule. And our people share a common heritage, the quest for the dignity and the freedom of man.

The revolutions which gave us birth ignited, in the words of Thomas Paine, "a spark never to be extinguished." And across vast, turbulent continents these American ideals still stir man's struggle for national independence and individual freedom. But as we welcome the spread of the American revolution to other lands, we must also remember that our own struggle—the revolution which began in Philadelphia in 1776, and in Caracas in 1811—is not yet finished. Our hemisphere's mission is not yet completed. For our unfulfilled task is to demonstrate to the entire world that man's unsatisfied aspiration for economic progress and social justice can best be achieved by free men working within a framework of democratic institutions. If we can do this in our own hemisphere, and for our own people, we may yet realize the

FROM Address at a White House Reception for Members of Congress and for the Diplomatic Corps of the Latin American Republics, March 13, 1961, *Public Papers of the Presidents of the United States: John F. Kennedy, 1961* (Washington, D.C., Government Printing Office, 1962), pp. 170–75.

prophecy of the great Mexican patriot, Benito Juarez, that "democracy is the destiny of future humanity."

As a citizen of the United States let me be the first to admit that we North Americans have not always grasped the significance of this common mission, just as it is also true that many in your own countries have not fully understood the urgency of the need to lift people from poverty and ignorance and despair. But we must turn from these mistakes—from the failures and the misunderstandings of the past to a future full of peril, but bright with hope.

Throughout Latin America, a continent rich in resources and in the spiritual and cultural achievements of its people, millions of men and women suffer the daily degradations of poverty and hunger. They lack decent shelter or protection from disease. Their children are deprived of the education or the jobs which are the gateway to a better life. And each day the problems grow more urgent. Population growth is outpacing economic growth—low living standards are further endangered—and discontent—the discontent of a people who know that abundance and the tools of progress are at last within their reach—that discontent is growing. In the words of José Figueres, "once dormant peoples are struggling upward toward the sun, toward a better life."

If we are to meet a problem so staggering in its dimensions, our approach must itself be equally bold—an approach consistent with the majestic concept of Operation Pan America. Therefore I have called on all people of the hemiphere to join in a new Alliance for Progress —*Alianza para Progreso*—a vast cooperative effort, unparalleled in magnitude and nobility of purpose, to satisfy the basic needs of the American people for homes, work and land, health and schools— *techo, trabajo y tierra, salud y escuela.*

First, I propose that the American Republics begin on a vast new Ten Year Plan for the Americas, a plan to transform the 1960's into a historic decade of democratic progress.

These 10 years will be the years of maximum progress–maximum effort, the years when the greatest obstacles must be overcome, the years when the need for assistance will be the greatest.

And if we are successful, if our effort is bold enough and determined enough, then the close of this decade will mark the beginning of a new era in the American experience. The living standards of every American family will be on the rise, basic education will be available to all, hunger will be a forgotten experience, the need for massive outside help will have passed, most nations will have entered a period of self-sustaining growth, and though there will be still much to do, every American Republic will be the master of its own revolution and its own hope and progress.

Let me stress that only the most determined efforts of the American nations themselves can bring success to this effort. They, and they alone, can mobilize their resources, enlist the energies of their people, and modify their social patterns so that all, and not just a privileged few, share in the fruits of growth. If this effort is made, then outside assistance will give vital impetus to progress; without it, no amount of help will advance the welfare of the people.

Thus if the countries of Latin America are ready to do their part, and I am sure they are, then I believe the United States, for its part, should help provide resources of a scope and magnitude sufficient to make this bold development plan a success—just as we helped to provide, against equal odds nearly, the resources adequate to help rebuild the economies of Western Europe. For only an effort of towering dimensions can ensure fulfillment of our plan for a decade of progress.

Secondly, I will shortly request a ministerial meeting of the Inter-American Economic and Social Council, a meeting at which we can begin the massive planning effort which will be at the heart of the Alliance for Progress.

For if our Alliance is to succeed, each Latin nation must formulate long-range plans for its own development, plans which establish targets and priorities, ensure monetary stability, establish the machinery for vital social change, stimulate private activity and initiative, and provide for a maximum national effort. These plans will be the foundation of our development effort, and the basis for the allocation of outside resources.

A greatly strengthened IA-ECOSOC, working with the Economic Commission for Latin America and the Inter-American Development Bank, can assemble the leading economists and experts of the hemisphere to help each country develop its own development plan—and provide a continuing review of economic progress in this hemisphere.

Third, I have this evening signed a request to the Congress for $500 million as a first step in fulfilling the Act of Bogotá. This is the first large-scale Inter-American effort, instituted by my predecessor President Eisenhower, to attack the social barriers which block economic progress. The money will be used to combat illiteracy, improve the productivity and use of their land, wipe out disease, attack archaic tax and land tenure structures, provide educational opportunities, and offer a broad range of projects designed to make the benefits of increasing abundance available to all. We will begin to commit these funds as soon as they are appropriated.

Fourth, we must support all economic integration which is a genuine step toward larger markets and greater competitive opportunity. The fragmentation of Latin American economies is a serious barrier to industrial growth. Projects such as the Central American common market and free trade areas in South America can help to remove these obstacles.

Fifth, the United States is ready to cooperate in serious, case-by-case examinations of commodity market problems. Frequent violent changes in commodity prices seriously injure the economies of many Latin American countries, draining their resources and stultifying their growth. Together we must find practical methods of bringing an end to this pattern.

Sixth, we will immediately step up our Food for Peace emergency program, help establish food reserves in areas of recurrent drought, help provide school lunches for children, and offer feed grains for use in rural development. For hungry men and women cannot wait for economic discussions or diplomatic meetings—their need is urgent—and their hunger rests heavily on the conscience of their fellow men.

Seventh, all the people of the hemisphere must be allowed to share in the expanding wonders of science—wonders which have captured man's imagination, challenged the powers of his mind, and given him the tools for rapid progress. I invite Latin American scientists to work with us in new projects in fields such as medicine and agriculture, physics and astronomy, and desalinization, to help plan for regional research laboratories in these and other fields, and to strengthen cooperation between American universities and laboratories.

We also intend to expand our science teacher training programs to include Latin American instructors, to assist in establishing such programs in other American countries, and translate and make available revolutionary new teaching materials in physics, chemistry, biology, and mathematics, so that the young of all nations may contribute their skills to the advance of science.

Eighth, we must rapidly expand the training of those needed to man the economies of rapidly developing countries. This means expanded technical training programs, for which the Peace Corps, for example, will be available when needed. It also means assistance to Latin American universities, graduate schools, and research institutes.

We welcome proposals in Central America for intimate cooperation in higher education—cooperation which can achieve a regional effort of increased effectiveness and excellence. We are ready to help fill the gap in trained manpower, realizing that our ultimate goal must be a basic education for all who wish to learn.

Ninth, we reaffirm our pledge to come to the defense of any American nation whose independence is endangered. As confidence in the collective security system of the OAS spreads, it will be possible to devote to constructive use a major share of those resources now spent on the instruments of war. Even now, as the government of Chile has said, the time has come to take the first steps toward sensible limitations of arms. And the new generation of military leaders has shown an increasing awareness that armies can not only defend their countries—they can, as we have learned through our own Corps of Engineers, . . . help to build them.

Tenth, we invite our friends in Latin America to contribute to the enrichment of life and culture in the United States. We need teachers of your literature and history and tradition, opportunities for our young people to study in your universities, access to your music, your art, and the thought of your great philosophers. For we know we have much to learn.

In this way you can help bring a fuller spiritual and intellectual life to the people of the United States—and contribute to understanding and mutual respect among the nations of the hemisphere.

With steps such as these, we propose to complete the revolution of the Americas, to build a hemisphere where all men can hope for a suitable standard of living, and all can live out their lives in dignity and in freedom.

To achieve this goal political freedom must accompany material progress. Our Alliance for Progress is an alliance of free governments, and it must work to eliminate tyranny from a hemisphere in which it has no rightful place. Therefore let us express our special friendship to the people of Cuba and the Dominican Republic—and the hope they will soon rejoin the society of free men, uniting with us in common effort.

This political freedom must be accompanied by social change. For unless necessary social reforms, including land and tax reform, are freely made—unless we broaden the opportunity for all of our people —unless the great mass of Americans share in increasing prosperity— then our alliance, our revolution, our dream, and our freedom will fail. But we call for social change by free men—change in the spirit of Washington and Jefferson, of Bolívar and San Martín and Martín— not change which seeks to impose on men tyrannies which we cast out a century and a half ago. Our motto is what it has always been— progress yes, tyranny no—*progreso sí, tiranía no!*

But our greatest challenge comes from within—the task of creating an American civilization where spiritual and cultural values are strengthened by an ever-broadening base of material advance—where, within the rich diversity of its own traditions, each nation is free to follow its own path towards progress.

The completion of our task will, of course, require the efforts of all governments of our hemisphere. But the efforts of governments alone will never be enough. In the end, the people must choose and the people must help themselves.

And so I say to the men and women of the Americas—to the *campesino* in the fields, to the *obrero* in the cities, to the *estudiante* in the schools—prepare your mind and heart for the task ahead—call forth your strength and let each devote his energies to the betterment of all, so that your children and our children in this hemisphere can find an ever richer and a freer life.

Let us once again transform the American continent into a vast crucible of revolutionary ideas and efforts—a tribute to the power of the creative energies of free men and women—an example to all the world that liberty and progress walk hand in hand. Let us once again awaken our American revolution until it guides the struggle of people everywhere—not with an imperialism of force or fear—but the rule of courage and freedom and hope for the future of man.

THE COMMANDER-IN-CHIEF AND THE CONDUCT OF FOREIGN POLICY

DOCUMENT 27 TRUMAN'S ARMED INTERVENTION IN KOREA

When on June 25, 1950, the North Koreans invaded South Korea, the United States called for an emergency meeting of the United Nations Security Council. That body (which the Russians were temporarily boycotting) immediately called upon the U.N. to help preserve the integrity of South Korea and authorized the United States to act for the world body. General Douglas MacArthur was appointed U.N. Commander, and President Truman ordered our Far Eastern forces to participate in the "police action." This selection presents the crisp message in which he informed Congress of his actions—he did not request a declaration of war or even legislative approval.

In Korea the Government forces, which were armed to prevent border raids and to preserve internal security, were attacked by invading forces from North Korea. The Security Council of the United Nations called upon the invading troops to cease hostilities and to withdraw to the thirty-eighth parallel. This they have not done, but on the contrary have pressed the attack. The Security Council called upon all members of the United Nations to render every assistance to the

FROM Statement by President Harry S. Truman, June 27, 1950, *Congressional Record*, Eighty-First Congress, second session (Washington, D.C., Government Printing Office, 1950), Vol. 96, p. 9265.

United Nations in the execution of this resolution. In these circumstances I have ordered United States air and sea forces to give the Korean Government troops cover and support.

The attack upon Korea makes it plain beyond all doubt that communism has passed beyond the use of subversion to conquer independent nations and will now use armed invasion and war. It has defied the orders of the Security Council of the United Nations issued to preserve international peace and security. In these circumstances the occupation of Formosa by Communist forces would be a direct threat to the security of the Pacific area and to United States forces performing their lawful and necessary functions in that area.

Accordingly I have ordered the seventh fleet to prevent any attack on Formosa. As a corollary of this action I am calling upon the Chinese Government on Formosa to cease all air and sea operations against the mainland. The seventh fleet will see that this is done. The determination of the future status of Formosa must await the restoration of security in the Pacific, a peace settlement with Japan, or consideration by the United Nations.

I have also directed that United States forces in the Philippines be strengthened and that military assistance to the Philippine Government be accelerated.

I have similarly directed acceleration in the furnishing of military assistance to the forces of France and the associated states in Indochina and the dispatch of a military mission to provide close working relations with those forces.

I know that all members of the United Nations will consider carefully the consequences of this latest aggression in Korea in defiance of the Charter of the United Nations. A return to the rule of force in international affairs would have far-reaching effects. The United Nations will continue to uphold the rule of law.

I have instructed Ambassador Austin, as the representative of the United States to the Security Council, to report these steps to the Council.

DOCUMENT 28 THE SENATE DEBATE
ON THE COMMANDER-
IN-CHIEF'S AUTHORITY

Following President Truman's decision to send American troops to defend South Korea in June 1950 (see Document 27), a resolution endorsing his action was introduced into both houses of Congress. It touched off a constitutional debate in the Senate where Senator

Robert A. Taft of Ohio—"Mr. Republican" to his generation—expressed grave doubts on the legality (though not the objectives) of the President's interpretation of his power as Commander-in-Chief. Several days later, Senator Paul Douglas of Illinois replied at some length on the constitutional question, indicating that in his view President Truman had followed a well-beaten path of precedents going back to the Administration of George Washington.

Since this debate, a new dimension has entered the situation: the threat of "fifteen-minute war" posed by intercontinental ballistic missiles with nuclear warheads. At a time when Congress, if in session, might have only fifteen minutes to declare war before the missiles hit (assuming it chose to spend its time in that fashion), the whole discussion of constitutional prerogatives has a slightly medieval quality. In another type of crisis, such as the Cuban confrontation of October 1962 (to be discussed in Document 30), where the threat of escalation demands a flexible and immediate response, Congress can hardly be consulted—and policy frozen until it reaches a conclusion—at a point where further application of force might lead to a nuclear response. To put it bluntly, the decisions of peace and war today rest in the hands of the President.

***

MR. TAFT: Mr. President, I have only a few words to say on the legal right of the President's act.

Although I should be willing to vote to approve the President's new policy as a policy, and give support to our forces in Korea, I think it is proper and essential that we discuss at this time the right and power of the President to do what he has done. I hope others will discuss it, because I have not thoroughly investigated the question of the right and the power of the President to do what he has done.

TRUMAN'S His action unquestionably has brought about a de facto war with the Government of northern Korea. He has brought that war about without consulting Congress and without congressional approval. We have a situation in which in a far distant part of the world one nation has attacked another, and if the President can intervene in Korea without congressional approval, he can go to war in Malaya or Indonesia or Iran or South America. Presidents have at times intervened with American forces to protect American lives or interests, but I do not think it has been claimed that, apart from the United Nations Charter or other treaty obligations, the President has any right to precipitate any open warfare.

FROM Speeches of Senators Robert A. Taft and Paul R. Douglas, June 28 and July 5, 1950, *Congressional Record,* Eighty-First Congress, second session (Washington, D.C., Government Printing Office, 1950), Vol. 96, pp. 9322–23, 9647–49.

It is claimed that the Korean situation is changed by the obligations into which we have entered under the Charter of the United Nations. I think this is true, but I do not think it justifies the President's present action without approval by Congress. I stated when we were discussing the bill to implement the United Nations Charter that I felt that once the American representative on the Security Council voted in favor of using armed forces then the President was entitled to go ahead and use those forces without further action by Congress. I objected to the bill because it gave the President unlimited power to tell our representative on the Security Council how he must vote so that he could commit the country to the use of armed forces without congressional authority. I felt that giving the President the right to tell our representative on the Security Council how he should or should not vote, in effect gave him the right to put the United States into war, provided the other sections of the bill were complied with.

Section 6, however, dealt particularly with the time in which armed forces may be used to support the United Nations. What it says is this:

The President is authorized to negotiate a special agreement or agreements with the Security Council which shall be subject to the approval of the Congress by appropriate act or joint resolution, providing for the numbers and types of armed forces, their degree of readiness and general location, and the nature of facilities and assistance, including rights of passage, to be made available to the Security Council on its call for the purpose of maintaining international peace and security in accordance with article 43 of said Charter. The President shall not be deemed to require the authorization of the Congress to make available to the Security Council on its call in order to take action under article 42 of said Charter and pursuant to such special agreement or agreements the armed forces, facilities, or assistance provided for therein: *Provided,* That nothing herein contained shall be construed as an authorization to the President by the Congress to make available to the Security Council for such purpose armed forces, facilities, or assistance in addition to the forces, facilities, and assistance provided for in such special agreement or agreements.

So, we have enacted the circumstances under which the President may use armed forces in support of a resolution of the Security Council of the United Nations. The first requisite is that we negotiate an agreement to determine what forces shall be used, and in what quantity, and that the agreement be approved by Congress. No agreement has ever been negotiated, of course, and no agreement has ever been presented to Congress. So far as I can see, and so far as I have studied the matter, I would say that there is no authority to use armed forces in support of the United Nations in the absence of some previous action by Congress dealing with the subject and outlining the general circumstances and the amount of the forces that can be used.

Other questions arise out of the United Nations Charter which I think should be explored. At least, they should be debated by this body.

Article 27 provides that decisions of the Security Council on all matters shall be made by an affirmative vote of seven members, including the concurring votes of the permanent members. The word "veto" was never used in the United Nations Charter. It simply provides that there must be the concurring votes of the five permanent members. In this case Soviet Russia has not voted. They never even appeared at the meeting. It is suggested, I understand, that gradually, under the practice adopted, a veto must be expressed by a negative vote; even though that seems directly contrary to the language of article 27. I am not a student of that subject. I merely suggest that the question, and the fact that Korea is not a member of the United Nations, ought to be explored and debated very fully by the Senate. I do not think there is any immediate rush about it. I merely do not like to have this action go by with the approval of the Senate, if it is what it seems to me, namely a complete usurpation by the President of authority to use the Armed Forces of this country. If the incident is permitted to go by without protest, at least from this body, we would have finally terminated for all time the right of Congress to declare war, which is granted to Congress alone by the Constitution of the United States.

****

MR. DOUGLAS: Mr. President, I should like to ask the indulgence of the Senate to speak for a few minutes on what I believe to be the constitutional and legal basis for the action of the President in authorizing the use of our Armed Forces to repel the invasion of southern Korea.

While the action of the President in sending our Armed Forces to the aid of southern Korea has been overwhelmingly approved by the people of this country, there have been voices of criticism raised from divergent quarters. The most common charge has been that the President's action was unconstitutional. It is alleged that since the Constitution in article I, section 8, gives solely to the Congress the power to declare war, the use of armed force by the President without congressional assent is consequently an abrogation of these powers and therefore a violation of the Constitution. At the root of this argument is, therefore, the contention that for us to use armed force against the persons or forces of other countries is in effect a declaration of war and hence should only be authorized by act of Congress.

This issue has been repeatedly debated throughout our history and in all likelihood it will continue to be discussed for a long time to come. If we can judge the future by the past, it will probably be raised in the future about President Truman's present action. In order to produce greater clarity of thought in the present and to decrease possible future bitter controversy, I believe it may be worth while to analyze this contention in a dispassionate manner.

I. THE LEGISLATIVE INTENT OF THE CONSTITUTIONAL CONVENTION OF 1787 AS REGARDS THE USE OF ARMED FORCES

The true meaning of the provision will be made much clearer if we trace the legislative history inside the Constitutional Convention of 1787 of the phrase, "to declare war," and arrive at the legislative intent behind that phrase. We can do this from the very full and accurate notes of the debates which were taken by the leading figure in the convention, James Madison, and which were published after his death in, I believe, 1840.

If we turn to this chronicle, we find that when the drafting committee, or the committee on detail, as it was called, submitted its draft on August 6, 1787, it gave to Congress not the right to declare war, but instead the broader right to make war . . . .

It was not until August 17 that this clause was debated. Mr. Pinckney of South Carolina opened the discussion by saying that he opposed "vesting this power in the legislature." "Its proceedings," he declared, "were too slow." After further discussion by Mr. Butler of South Carolina, James Madison, and Elbridge Gerry, of Massachusetts, both moved to strike out the verb "make" and to substitute the verb "declare." I should like to call the attention of the Senate to the fact that this was for the purpose, as Madison wrote in his notes, of "leaving to the Executive the power to repel sudden attacks."

This amendment was shortly thereafter accepted on this same date of August 17, 1787, by a vote of 7 States to 2, with one State, Massachusetts, being recorded as absent, although one of its delegates, Mr. Gerry, had previously moved the amendment, and Three States being absent entirely from the convention. . . .

From this discussion and vote it is clear that the convention did not want to tie our country's hands by requiring congressional assent for all employment of armed force. It is obvious, instead, that, as Madison said, they wanted to leave to the President the power to use force "to repel sudden attacks," even though not authorized to do so by Congress. This, as the founding fathers were careful to distinguish, was not equivalent to a declaration of war.

I know it will be objected that this use of legislative intent to justify present action is faulty. It will be argued that it was the difficulty and slowness in stagecoach days of assembling Congress which caused the constitutional fathers to give to the President the interim powers of using force to repel attacks. It will be contended that the need for this has passed in these days of the airplane when Congress can be called into session on a day's notice.

But this tremendous increase in the speed of assembling Congress has been accompanied by an equal and, indeed, even greater increase in the rapidity of delivering deadly attacks. War in the days of the founding fathers was even more leisurely an institution than the stagecoach itself. It was speeded up in the nineteenth century by the tactics of Napoleon and the German general staff. But now with tanks, airplanes, and the atom bomb, war can become instantaneous and disaster can occur while Congress is assembling and debating. For death and destruction can now come to whole cities and possibly to nations in a matter of seconds. For these reasons, therefore, it would be unwise to insist that the President cannot use armed force in advance of formal congressional approval.

But there is one further point which should be faced. Congress was already in session when President Truman on June 26 ordered our naval and air forces to repulse the Communist attacks on South Korea. Why, then, it may be asked, should not the issue in the present instance have been submitted to Congress, which was then in session?

The answer is, I think, a double one. In the first place, in all such military operations success or failure may depend on a matter of hours and even the slightest delay may prove fatal. Secondly, our own congressional procedures are themselves subject to some delay. As events have shown, Congress has overwhelmingly approved of this action once it was taken. This is shown by the unanimous votes in favor of both the extension of the draft and of military aid. But there might well have been some minority opposition to the Korean policy had it been submitted to Congress in advance. In the House, it is true, debate could have been restricted within reasonable limits by action of the Rules Committee, but formal approval could still have been withheld if insisted upon by one Member until the actual engrossing of the bill a day later. This parliamentary device has been used in the past in the House to delay action and without mentioning any one person, it is very probable that it would have been used in the present case.

In the Senate, the right of unlimited debate might well have permitted one or two Senators to slow us up. It should be remembered, moreover, that when cloture is proposed, it cannot be voted upon for 2 days after the petition asking for it has been signed and submitted and that, thereafter each dissenter will be permitted to speak for an hour. In short, even though the recommendation of the Executive were later to be supported by an overwhelming vote of both Houses, so much valuable time might be lost in the interval that the military action authorized might come much too late to be effective.

III. SOME LEADING INSTANCES OF PRESIDENTIAL USE OF ARMED FORCE WITHOUT CONGRESSIONAL DECLARATION OF WAR AND THE REASONS THEREFOR

My colleague, the senior Senator from Illinois [Mr. Lucas] has already mentioned the fact that our Armed Forces have been used by Executive direction—and I include in that the decisions of the military as well as at the direction of the President—against the forces and persons of other countries in over a hundred instances without any declaration of war. I shall merely mention a few of these incidents. . . .

First. Naval hostilities with France, 1793.
Second. Jefferson's expedition against the Barbary pirates, 1804.
Third. The Seminole War, 1817.
Fourth. Polk's occupation of disputed Texas-Mexican border territory, 1846.
Fifth. Intervention in Samoa, 1840–41, 1888, 1899.
Sixth. Use of naval forces in Chile, 1891.
Seventh. Boxer Rebellion in China, 1900.
Eighth. Theodore Roosevelt's intervention in Panama, 1903.
Ninth. Santo Domingo, 1904.
Tenth. Nicaragua, 1895, 1910, 1912, 1926.
Eleventh. Haiti, 1914.
Twelfth. Wilson's intervention at Vera Cruz, 1914.
Thirteenth. Santo Domingo, 1916.
Fourteenth. The pursuit of Pancho Villa, 1916.
Fifteenth. Intervention in Russia—Archangel and Siberia, 1919.

These and a host of other instances indicate that Presidents have frequently used their power to use the Armed Forces of the United States against other countries without a prior declaration of war by Congress. In a few cases, the exercise of this power was probably unwise. In most cases, however, it was distinctly wise, benefiting both this country and the world as a whole.

There is indeed a good reason, besides the need for speed, why the President should have been permitted to use force in these cases without a formal declaration of war by Congress. That is because international situations frequently call for the retail use of force in localized situations which are not sufficiently serious to justify the wholesale and widespread use of force which a formal declaration of war would require.

In other words, it may be desirable to create a situation which is half-way between complete peace, or the absence of all forces, and outright war marked by the exercise of tremendous force on a wholesale scale. This is most notably the case when big powers deal with small countries, and in situations where only a relatively temporary application of force is needed to restore order and to remove the threat of aggression. It would be below the dignity of the United States to declare war on a pigmy state, but it might be necessary to apply force in such a case in order to prevent attacks on American lives and property.

Such an intermediate method is also particularly useful when dealing with satellite or puppet states of another big power. Force can be used against a satellite without necessarily stirring up the opposing big power, as would almost certainly occur were war formally to be declared. It is made easier, therefore, for the other big power lurking in the background to save its face by pretending not to notice what is happening to its satellite, and therefore in effect to disavow it.

This is peculiarly appropriate to the present situation, since northern Korea is really under the direction of Communist Russia. This need for the use of force without the launching of war has been recognized in international law by the peculiar status given to the employment of naval forces, for the use of naval force is not regarded as an act of war in itself. It is this fact which accounts in part—and, of course, only in part—for the maintenance and use of the Marine Corps in times past in so-called minor incidents. As part of the Navy, they were in a sense State Department troops.

IV. WAS OUR SECURITY THREATENED?

But there is one step more which is required to make the argument conclusive. Up to the invasion of Korea, the use of armed force had been almost invariably ordered by our Presidents as a protection against immediate and direct attacks or threats to American lives and property. The vast majority of these cases could, therefore, be regarded as direct acts of defense to repulse direct attacks or as retaliatory measures for such aggression.

Our present intervention to check the provocatory invasion of South Korea by the North Korean Communists under almost certain Russian direction is of a somewhat different kind. The damage to American mission schools and churches and American business houses, while real, was not in any sense the primary reason for our intervention. That should be recognized.

The basic reason for our intervention was the recognition by the President, and, I believe, by the Nation, of the fact that, if the Communists were successful in taking over southern Korea without our imposing any effective opposition, they could be depended upon to make similar invasions of other areas. This would notably be true of Burma, Indochina, Persia, Jugoslavia, Greece, Berlin, and west Germany. Let us make no mistake about it; our own ultimate safety would then have been threatened, for both the will to conquer of the Russian police state would have been whetted and many of our actual and potential allies, seeing others abandoned, would have begun to make terms with the Communists.

The disastrous experience of the 1930's in the efforts by the western democracies to appease Hitler by allowing him to take over, by aggression, country after country, and the bad record made by the Russians, particularly since 1945, are convincing proof that if we permit an aggressor to take over another country by force, we do not avert danger for ourselves, but, instead, bring it even closer. It means, instead, that if we adopt such a course, ultimately we must either yield our liberties or, if we defend them—as I hope and believe we would—that we would have to do so on terms far more disadvantageous to us than would originally have been the case. Peace is indivisible—as Mr. Litvinov once remarked, and as the Russians are now trying to forget.

The ultimate security of the United States depends upon convincing the Communist aggressors that we will resist aggression and will check it in its earliest stages. Vigorous and effective action when aggression begins prevents it from coming closer and rallies potential friends to one's cause. The best time to put out a fire is immediately after it starts, and before it can gain headway.

The decision of the President to aid South Korea was, therefore, both in the best interests of the United States and in no sense violated constitutional theory or practice. It was, instead, a sound measure to guard against an ultimate and indirect threat to the security of the United States, building upon the precedents previously established for dealing with immediate and direct threats.

V. USE OF OUR ARMED FORCES ALSO A POLICE ACTION UNDER THE UNITED NATIONS

Let us also realize that once the United Nations called upon its members to lend military aid, first to the United Nations—as in its proclamation of June 24—and then to Korea itself, in its resolution of June 26, in forcing the invaders back to the boundary line at the thirty-eighth parallel, any use of armed force by us was not an act of war, but, instead, merely the exercise of police power under international sanction. For war is the anarchic use of force by one nation against another for the purpose of imposing its own will, and in the absence of an international authorization. What we are really doing in Korea is to serve as a police force to carry out the decision of the United Nations that its member nations should help to repel the invasion of South Korea. We are, therefore, serving as agents of an international authority designed to protect the peace of the world, and not as anarchic or self-appointed users of force.

This is, indeed, probably the only manner in which an international police force could as a practical matter be created. An international police force would not be born in a vacuum. We can only hope that when the present emergency has been ended the free nations will learn this lesson and will establish a permanent international police force which can be used in just such situations as that which has arisen without throwing the main burden upon any one country.

Our actions are therefore as much in harmony with international law as were the President's in harmony with our own internal constitutional law.

VI. DANGERS OF FUTURE PRESIDENTIAL ACTION AND POSSIBLE RESTRAINTS

There are, of course, grave dangers which are created in thus giving to the President in his role as Commander in Chief discretionary powers to use our Armed Forces in advance of a declaration of war by Congress. A reckless and a militaristic President—which President Truman is not—could commit us to a program of aggression. Once embarked upon such a course of action, it would admittedly be difficult for Congress to order a withdrawal, since not only national pride and prestige would be involved, but also actual national safety as well.

What protection is there against such possible future abuses? As I see it, there are two: first, the sobering and terrible responsibilities of the office of President itself; and second, the fact that if such an act were to be grossly at variance with the national interest and against the public will, the President would render himself liable to impeachment at the hands of Congress. This is certainly something of a deterring influence.

I submit, moreover, that we of the Congress could make it easier for the President to consult us in the event of such a national emergency, and to share any attendant responsibility, by so revising our rules that congressional action in such matters can be speeded up. The House, for example, might waive for this range of subjects the formal engrossing of a bill, and the Senate could for such issues permit the vote on cloture to come more quickly after the submission of the petition. These are reforms which in my judgment we should effect, if in the future we are legitimately to claim more joint powers in such matters.

VII. SUMMARY

Summing up, Mr. President, I hope that this brief review of the issues will be convincing proof that the acts of the President in helping to protect southern Korea from Communist aggression were in thorough harmony with the legislative intent of the framers of the Constitution, in line with sound historical precedent, in conformity with international law and the rules of the United Nations, and in the best interests of our own ultimate security and the peace of the world.

****

DOCUMENT 29 THE DEFENSE OF QUEMOY AND MATSU

In the fall of 1958, the Chinese Communists began an intensive bombardment of Quemoy and Matsu, two small islands a few miles from the mainland of China, held by the Nationalists. When it appeared as though an invasion might be imminent, a strong faction within the Republican leadership urged a United States commitment to defend the islands. Presidents Truman and Eisenhower had both made flat pledges to defend Taiwan (Formosa) from Communist invasion, but unlike Quemoy and Matsu, this Nationalist bastion lies a hundred-odd miles off the Chinese mainland, so that the U.S. Seventh Fleet and the planes of the Far Eastern Air Force can more readily shield it from attack. Many responsible political figures argued that it would be no more than a quixotic gesture to attempt the impractical defense of the two small "rocks," and they further asserted that these islands had no role in the defense of Taiwan. The debate became rather complex: it was noted on one side, for example, that a withdrawal from Quemoy and Matsu would undermine our reputation in Asia and discourage anti-Communist regimes. Opponents, however, indicated that, on our advice, the Chinese Nationalists had evacuated some other islands with no noticeable impact on Asian morale or on the strategic position of Taiwan. Our European allies took a dim view of a confrontation with the Chinese Reds, sharing the sentiments expressed in General Omar Bradley's statement when he was chairman of the Joint Chiefs of Staff that this would be the "wrong war, in the wrong place, with the wrong enemy, at the wrong time."

While the bombardment and the debate continued, the American Navy began to convoy supplies to the beleaguered Nationalist garrisons. Conflict appeared inevitable. At this point Senator Green, chairman of the Senate Foreign Relations Committee (actually acting as spokesman for a broad pressure group both in and out of the Congress) sent the President a letter (which was leaked to the press) indicating his great concern with the apparent course of American policy. President Eisenhower took a high line in his reply, but in the course of his letter made it clear that the United States would not become involved in war solely to protect the islands. This exchange is a good example of the role of Senatorial pressure in the conduct of foreign affairs.

SENATOR GREEN TO PRESIDENT EISENHOWER

September 29, 1958

Dear Mr. President:

There are many indications of a real danger that the United States may become involved in military hostilities in defense of Quemoy and Matsu. These indications comprise newspaper reports from the Far East, communications which I have received from very many Americans, dispatches from friendly nations throughout the world, as well as concern expressed publicly by many prominent Americans well informed in the field of foreign policy, and your own statements to the American people.

Recently I have expressed my own views stating that "it does not appear to me that Quemoy is vital to the defense of either Formosa or the United States." I have suggested that military action in the area should not be ordered unless you, Mr. President, are sure beyond any reasonable doubt that the security of Formosa itself is in fact directly threatened. Subsequent to your address of September 11, I proposed that if there is danger of military involvement in this area—a danger

FROM Letter by Senator Theodore Francis Green to President Dwight D. Eisenhower, September 29, 1958, *Department of State Bulletin,* October 20, 1958, pp. 604–05, and from Letter to Senator Theodore Francis Green Concerning the Situation in the Far East, October 5, 1958, *Public Papers of the Presidents of the United States: Dwight D. Eisenhower, 1958* (Washington, D.C., Government Printing Office, 1959), pp. 723–25.

which you indicated existed—Congress should be called immediately into session.

The purpose of this letter, Mr. President, is to bring to your attention my deep concern that the course of events in the Far East may result in military involvement at the wrong time, in the wrong place, and on issues not of vital concern to our own security, and all this without allies either in fact or in heart. Furthermore, it is my impression, confirmed by the press and by my own mail, that United States military involvement in defense of Quemoy would not command that support of the American people essential to successful military action.

My decision to send this letter to you has involved a great deal of soul-searching on my part. At one point, I seriously contemplated calling the Committee on Foreign Relations back to Washington so that it might meet with cabinet members to learn fully the nature of our possible involvement. That course was rejected for the present because I felt such a public act might interfere with the conduct of negotiations in which your representatives are now engaged. I also contemplated the advisability of seeking in advance of this letter the consensus of views of the members of the Committee so that our joint views might be brought to your attention. But that action was rejected because it would be time consuming and because of the possibility that such action might be construed as a political maneuver.

It is not my intention to make this letter to you public at this time. I am sending copies of it, however, to each member of the Committee on Foreign Relations with the thought that he may wish to provide you independently with his views, particularly with reference to those I have set forth in this letter. I am sending a copy also to Senator Lyndon Johnson.

With respect and deep concern, I remain

Sincerely yours,
THEODORE FRANCIS GREEN
Chairman
Committee on Foreign Relations

PRESIDENT EISENHOWER TO SENATOR GREEN

Dear Senator Green:

I acknowledge your letter of September twenty-ninth with reference to the situation in the Far East. I note that you are concerned that the United States might become involved in hostilities in defense of Quemoy and Matsu; that it does not appear to you that Quemoy is vital to the defense of Formosa or the United States; that in such hostilities we would be without allies, and, finally, that military involvement in the defense of Quemoy would not command that support of the American people essential to successful military action.

Let me take up these points in order:

1. Neither you nor any other American need feel that the United States will be involved in military hostilities merely in defense of Quemoy or Matsu. I am quite aware of the fact that the Joint Resolution of Congress (January 29, 1955), which authorized the President to employ the armed forces of the United States in the Formosa area, authorized the securing and protection of such positions as Quemoy and Matsu only if the President judges that to be required or appropriate in assuring the defense of Formosa and the Pescadores.

I shall scrupulously observe that limitation contained in the Congressional authority granted me.

2. The Congressional Resolution had, of course, not merely negative but positive implications. I shall also observe these. I note that it does not appear to you that Quemoy is vital to the defense of Formosa or the United States. But the test which the Congress established was whether or not the defense of these positions was judged by the President to be required or appropriate in assuring the defense of Formosa. The Congressional Resolution conferring that responsibility on the President was adopted by almost unanimous vote of both Houses of the Congress. Since then the people of the United States reelected me to be that President. I shall, as President and Commander-in-Chief of the Armed Forces of the United States, exercise my lawful authority and judgment in discharging the responsibility thus laid upon me.

I welcome the opinions and counsel of others. But in the last analysis such opinions cannot legally replace my own.

The Chinese and Soviet Communist leaders assert, and have reason to believe, that if they can take Quemoy and Matsu by armed assault that will open the way for them to take Formosa and the Pescadores and, as they put it, "expel" the United States from the West Pacific and cause its Fleet to leave international waters and "go home."

I cannot dismiss these boastings as mere bluff. Certainly there is always the possibility that it may in certain contingencies, after taking account of all relevant facts, become necessary or appropriate for the defense of Formosa and the Pescadores also to take measures to secure and protect the related positions of Quemoy and Matsu.

I am striving to the best of my ability to avoid hostilities; to achieve a cease-fire, and a reasonable adjustment of the situation. You, I think, know my deep dedication to peace. It is second only to my dedication to the safety of the United States and its honorable discharge of obligations to its allies and to world order which have been assumed by constitutional process. We must not forget that the whole Formosa Straits situation is intimately connected with the security of the United States and the free world.

3. You say than in the event of hostilities we would be without allies "in fact or in heart." Of course, no nation other than the Republic of China has a treaty alliance with us in relation to the Formosa area. That is a well known fact—known to the Congress when it adopted

the Formosa Joint Resolution and known to the Senate when it approved of our Treaty of Mutual Security with the Republic of China. But if you mean that the United States action in standing firm against armed Communist assault would not have the approval of our allies, then I believe that you are misinformed. Not only do I believe that our friends and allies would support the United States if hostilities should tragically, and against our will, be forced upon us, I believe that most of them would be appalled if the United States were spinelessly to retreat before the threat of Sino-Soviet armed aggression.

4. Finally, you state that even if the United States should become engaged in hostilities, there would not be "that support of the American people essential to successful military action."

With respect to those islands, I have often pointed out that the only way the United States could become involved in hostilities would be because of its firm stand against Communist attempts to gain their declared aims by force. I have also often said that firmness in supporting principle makes war less, rather than more, likely of occurrence.

I feel certain, beyond the shadow of a doubt, that if the United States became engaged in hostilities on account of the evil and aggressive assaults of the forces of Communism, the American people would unite as one to assure the success and triumph of our effort.

I deeply deplore the effect upon hostile forces of a statement that if we became engaged in battle, the United States would be defeated because of disunity at home. If that were believed, it would embolden our enemies and make almost inevitable the conflict which, I am sure, we both seek to avoid provided it can be avoided consistently with the honor and security of our country.

Though in this letter I have explained the facts and the principles that guide the government in dealing with the critical Formosa Straits situation, I cannot close without saying that our whole effort is now, and has always been, the preservation of a peace with honor and with justice. After all, this is the basic aspiration of all Americans, indeed of all peoples.

Inasmuch as there have been public reports on the essence of your letter, I feel I should make this reply public.

With great respect and best wishes,

Sincerely,
DWIGHT D. EISENHOWER

DOCUMENT 30 KENNEDY QUARANTINES CUBA

In October 1962 the President of the United States, discovering that the Russians had been slipping intermediate-range ballistic missiles into Cuba, suddenly called for a showdown with the U.S.S.R. In a solemn statement to the American people, President Kennedy announced the Soviet action (which violated earlier Soviet promises not to equip their Cuban ally with "offensive" weapons) and informed the nation of his intention to eliminate this missile base by all means at his disposal, beginning with a quarantine of ships carrying military equipment to Cuba. President Kennedy received almost unanimous support from the American public and from Congress— the consensus was that action to remove the missiles had to be taken even at the risk of war.

For almost a week, the world lived on the brink while the President and his advisors awaited an acceptable Soviet reply and gradually increased the pressure by alerting the Strategic Air Command and mobilizing troops in Florida for a possible invasion. The Administration was later accused of also managing the news in such a way as to create additional pressure on Khrushchev—of leaking rumors of new decisions, movements of landing craft to Florida, and the like, which allegedly misled American newspapermen and the Soviets alike. (It is more heinous to mislead a newspaperman than to murder a bishop— at least in the view of American editors.)

The whole operation was brilliantly controlled from the White House; there were no loud bellicose speeches, displays of chauvinism, or other manifestations of an earlier age when war was greeted with cheers. The President soberly and with restraint made his point and always left the Soviet leadership ample room for retreat from their untenable position. All in all, it was a striking demonstration of responsible Presidential leadership in the nuclear age. This selection includes the President's speech to the nation on October 22 and the proclamation of the Cuban blockade on October 23.

MESSAGE TO THE NATION

Good evening, my fellow citizens:

This Government, as promised, has maintained the closest surveillance of the Soviet military build-up on the island of Cuba.

Within the past week, unmistakable evidence has established the fact that a series of offensive missile sites is now in preparation on that imprisoned island.

The purpose of these bases can be none other than to provide a nuclear strike capability against the Western Hemisphere.

Upon receiving the first preliminary hard information of this nature last Tuesday morning at 9 A.M., I directed that our surveillance be stepped up. And having now confirmed and completed our evaluation of the evidence and our decision on a course of action, this Government feels obliged to report this new crisis to you in full detail.

TWO TYPES OF MISSILE SITES

The characteristics of these new missile sites indicate two distinct types of installations. Several of them include medium range ballistic missiles, capable of carrying a nuclear warhead for a distance of more than 1,000 [nautical] miles. Each of these missiles, in short, is capable of striking Washington, D.C., the Panama Canal, Cape Canaveral, Mexico City, or any other city in the southeastern part of the United States, in Central America or in the Caribbean area.

Additional sites not yet completed appear to be designed for intermediate range ballistic missiles—capable of traveling more than twice as far—and thus capable of striking most of the major cities in the western hemisphere, ranging as far north as Hudson Bay, Canada, and as far south as Lima, Peru. In addition, jet bombers, capable of carrying nuclear weapons, are now being uncrated and assembled on Cuba, while the necessary air bases are being prepared.

This urgent transformation of Cuba into an important strategic base —by the presence of these large, long-range and clearly offensive weapons of sudden mass destruction—constitutes an explicit threat to the peace and security of all the Americas, in flagrant and deliberate defiance of the Rio pact of 1947, the traditions of this nation and hemisphere, the joint resolution of the 87th Congress, the Charter of the United Nations, and my own public warnings to the Soviets on Sept. 4 and 13.

FROM Message to the Nation by President John F. Kennedy, October 22, 1962, New York *Times,* October 23, 1962, and Blockade Proclamation by President John F. Kennedy, October 23, 1962, New York *Times,* October 24, 1962. Copyright by The New York Times. Reprinted by permission.

This action also contradicts the repeated assurances of Soviet spokesmen, both publicly and privately delivered, that the arms build-up in Cuba would retain its original defensive character, and that the Soviet Union had no need or desire to station strategic missiles on the territory of any other nation.

HE SEES ADVANCE PLAN

The size of this undertaking makes clear that it had been planned some months ago. Yet only last month, after I had made clear the distinction between any introduction of ground-to-ground missiles and the existence of defensive antiaircraft missiles, the Soviet Government publicly stated on Sept. 11 that "the armaments and military equipment sent to Cuba are designed exclusively for defensive purposes," that "there is no need for the Soviet Union to shift its weapons . . . for a retaliatory blow to any other country, for instance Cuba," and that "the Soviet Union has so powerful rockets to carry these nuclear warheads that there is no need to search for sites for them beyond the boundaries of the Soviet Union."

That statement was false.

Only last Thursday, as evidence of this rapid offensive build-up was already in my hand, Soviet Foreign Minister Gromyko told me in my office that he was instructed to make it clear once again, as he said his Government had already done, the Soviet assistance to Cuba "pursued solely the purpose of contributing to the defense capabilities of Cuba," that "training by Soviet specialists of Cuban nationals in handling defensive armaments was by no means offensive," and that "if it were otherwise, the Soviet Government would never become involved in rendering such assistance."

That statement also was false.

DECEPTION CITED

Neither the United States of America nor the world Community of nations can tolerate deliberate deception and offensive threats on the part of any nation, large or small.

We no longer live in a world where only the actual firing of weapons represents a sufficient challenge to a nation's security to constitute a maximum peril.

Nuclear weapons are so destructive, and ballistic missiles are so swift, that any substantially increased possibility of their use or any sudden change in their development may well be regarded as a definite threat to the peace.

For many years, both the Soviet Union and the United States— recognizing this fact—have deployed strategic nuclear weapons with great care, never upsetting the precarious status quo which ensured that these weapons would not be used in the absence of some vital challenge.

Our own strategic missiles have never been transferred to the territory of any other nation under a cloak of secrecy and deception; and our history—unlike that of the Soviets since World War II—demonstrates that we have no desire to dominate or conquer any other nation or impose our system upon its people.

Nevertheless, American citizens have become adjusted to living daily on the bull's eye of Soviet missiles located inside the U.S.S.R. or in submarines.

In that sense, missiles in Cuba add to an already clear and present danger—although, it should be noted, the nations of Latin America have never previously been subjected to a potential nuclear threat.

CHANGE IN STATUS QUO

But this secret, swift and extraordinary build-up of Communist missiles—in an area well-known to have a special and historical relationship to the United States and the nations of the Western Hemisphere, in violation of Soviet assurances, and in defiance of American and hemispheric policy—this sudden, clandestine decision to station strategic weapons for the first time outside of Soviet soil—is a deliberately provocative and unjustified change in the status quo which cannot be accepted by this country, if our courage and our commitments are ever to be trusted again by either friend or foe.

The 1930's taught us a clear lesson: Aggressive conduct, if allowed to grow unchecked and unchallenged, ultimately leads to war. This nation is opposed to war. We are also true to our word.

Our unswerving objective, therefore, must be to prevent the use of these missiles against this or any other country, and to secure their withdrawal or elimination from the Western Hemisphere.

Our policy has been one of patience and restraint, as befits a peaceful and powerful nation, which leads a world-wide alliance. We have been determined not to be diverted from our central concerns by mere irritants and fanatics.

HE OUTLINES STEPS

But now further action is required—and it is under way; and these actions may only be the beginning. We will not prematurely or unnecessarily risk the costs of worldwide nuclear war in which even the fruits of victory would be ashes in our mouth—but neither will we shrink from that risk at any time it must be faced.

Acting, therefore, in the defense of our own security and that of the entire Western Hemisphere, and under the authority entrusted to me by the Constitution as endorsed by the resolution of the Congress,

I have directed that the following initial steps be taken immediately:

First: To halt this offensive build-up, a strict quarantine on all offensive military equipment under shipment to Cuba is being initiated. All ships of any kind bound for Cuba, from whatever nation or port, will, if found to contain cargoes of offensive weapons, be turned back. This quarantine will be extended, if needed, to other types of cargo and carriers. We are not at this time, however, denying the necessities of life as the Soviet attempted to do in their Berlin blockade of 1948.

Second: I have directed the continued and increased surveillance of Cuba and its military build-up. The Foreign Ministers of the OAS in their communiqué of Oct. 6 rejected secrecy on such matters in this hemisphere. Should these offensive military preparations continue, thus increasing the threat to the hemisphere, further action will be justified. I have directed the armed forces to prepare for any eventualities; and I trust that, in the interest of both the Cuban people and the Soviet technicians at these sites, the hazards to all concerned of continuing this threat will be recognized.

Third: It shall be the policy of this nation to regard any nuclear missile launched from Cuba against any nation in the Western Hemisphere as an attack by the Soviet Union on the United States requiring a full retaliatory response upon the Soviet Union.

Fourth: As a necessary military precaution, I have reinforced our base at Guantanamo, evacuated today the dependents of our personnel there and ordered additional military units to stand by on an alert basis.

Fifth: We are calling tonight for an immediate meeting of the organs of consultation under the Organization of American States, to consider this threat to hemispheric security and to invoke Articles 6 and 8 of the Rio treaty in support of all necessary action. The United Nations Charter allows for regional security arrangements—and the nations of this hemisphere decided long ago against the military presence of outside powers. Our other allies around the world have also been alerted.

Sixth: Under the Charter of the United Nations, we are asking tonight that an emergency meeting of the Security council be convoked without delay to take action against this latest Soviet threat to world peace. Our resolution will call for the prompt dismantling and withdrawal of all offensive weapons in Cuba, under the supervision of UN observers, before the quarantine can be lifted.

Seventh and finally: I call upon Chairman Khrushchev to halt and eliminate this clandestine, reckless and provocative threat to world peace and to stable relations between our two nations. I call upon him further to abandon this course of world domination, and to join in an historic effort to end the perilous arms race and transform the history of man.

He has an opportunity now to move the world back from the abyss of destruction—by returning to his Government's own words that it had no need to station missiles outside its own territory, and withdrawing these weapons from Cuba—by refraining from any action which will widen or deepen the present crisis—and then by participating in a search for peaceful and permanent solutions.

This nation is prepared to present its case against this Soviet threat to peace, and our own proposals for a peaceful world, at any time and in any forum—in the O.A.S., in the United Nations, or in any other meeting that could be useful—without limiting our freedom of action.

We have in the past made strenuous efforts to limit the spread of nuclear weapons. We have proposed the elimination of all arms and military bases in a fair and effective disarmament treaty. We are prepared to discuss new proposals for the removal of tensions on both sides—including the possibilities of a genuinely independent Cuba, free to determine its own destiny. We have no wish to war with the Soviet Union—for we are a peaceful people who desire to live in peace with all other peoples.

DIFFICULT WITH INTIMIDATION

But it is difficult to settle or even discuss these problems in an atmosphere of intimidation. That is why this latest Soviet threat—or any other threat which is made either independently or in response to our actions this week—must and will be met with determination. Any hostile move anywhere in the world against the safety of freedom of peoples to whom we are committed—including in particular the brave people of West Berlin—will be met by whatever action is needed.

Finally, I want to say a few words to the captive people of Cuba, to whom this speech is being directly carried by special radio facilities. I speak to you as a friend, as one who knows of your deep attachment to your fatherlands, as one who shares your aspirations for liberty and justice for all. And I have watched with sorrow how your nationalist revolution was betrayed—and how your fatherland fell under foreign domination.

Now your leaders are no longer Cuban leaders inspired by Cuban ideals. They are puppets and agents of an international conspiracy which has turned Cuba against your friends and neighbors in the Americas—and turned it into the first Latin-American country to become a target for nuclear war—the first Latin-American country to have these weapons on its soil.

These new weapons are not in your interest. They can only undermine it. But this country has no wish to cause you to suffer or to impose any system upon you. We know your lives and land are being used as pawns by those who deny you freedom.

Many times in the past, the Cuban people have risen to throw out 'tyrants who destroyed their liberty, and I have no doubt that most Cubans today look forward to the time when they will be truly free —free from foreign domination. Free to choose their own leaders. Free to select their own system. Free to own their own land. Free to speak and write and worship without fear or degradation. And then shall Cuba be welcomed back to the society of free nations and to the associations of this hemisphere.

My fellow citizens: Let no one doubt that this is a difficult and dangerous effort on which we have set out. No one can foresee precisely what course it will take or what costs or casualties will be incurred. Many months of sacrifice and self-discipline lie ahead—months in which both our will and our patience will be tested—months in which many threats and denunciations will keep us aware of our danger. But the greatest danger of all would be to do nothing.

The path we have chosen for the present is full of hazards, as all paths are—but it is the one most consistent with our character and courage as a nation and our commitments around the world. The cost of freedom is always high—but Americans have always paid it. And one path we shall never choose is the path of surrender or submission.

Our goal is not the victory of might but the vindication of right—not peace at the expense of freedom, but both peace and freedom, here in this hemisphere, and, we hope, around the world. God willing, that goal will be achieved.

BLOCKADE PROCLAMATION

Whereas the peace of the world and the security of the United States and of all American states are endangered by reason of the establishment by the Sino-Soviet powers of an offensive military capability in Cuba, including bases for ballistic missiles with a potential range covering most of North and South America; and

Whereas by a joint resolution passed by the Congress of the United States and approved on Oct. 3, 1962, it was declared that the United States is determined to prevent by whatever means may be necessary, including the use of arms, the Marxist-Leninist regime in Cuba from extending, by force or the threat of force, its aggressive or subversive activities to any part of this hemisphere, and to prevent in Cuba the creation or use of an externally supported military capability endangering the security of the United States; and

Whereas the Organ of Consultation of the American republics meeting in Washington on Oct. 23, 1962, recommended that the member states, in accordance with Articles 6 and 8 of the Inter-American Treaty of Reciprocal Assistance, take all measures, individually and collectively, including the use of armed force, which they may deem necessary to insure that the Government of Cuba cannot continue to receive from the Sino-Soviet powers military materiel and related supplies which may threaten the peace and security of the continent and to prevent the missiles in Cuba with offensive capability from ever becoming an active threat to the peace and security of the continent:

EFFECTIVE DATE GIVEN

Now, therefore, I, John F. Kennedy, President of the United States of America, acting under and by virtue of the authority conferred upon me by the Constitution and statutes of the United States, in accordance with the aforementioned resolutions of the United States Congress and of the Organ of Consultation of the American Republics, and to defend the security of the United States, do hereby proclaim that the forces under my command are ordered, beginning at 2 P.M. Greenwich time, Oct. 24, 1962, to interdict, subject to the instructions herein contained, the delivery of offensive weapons and associated materiel to Cuba.

For the purposes of this proclamation, the following are declared to be prohibited materiel:

Surface-to-surface missiles; bomber aircraft; bombs, air-to-surface rockets and guided missiles; warheads for any of the above weapons; mechanical or electronic equipment to support or operate the above items; and any other classes of materiel hereafter designated by the Secretary of Defense for the purpose of effectuating this proclamation.

To enforce this order, the Secretary of Defense shall take appropriate measures to prevent the delivery of prohibited materiel to Cuba, employing the land, sea and air forces of the United States in cooperation with any forces that may be made available by other American states.

The Secretary of Defense may make such regulations and issue such directives as he deems necessary to insure the effectiveness of this order, including the designation, within a reasonable distance of Cuba, of prohibited or restricted zones and of prescribed routes.

Any vessel or craft which may be proceeding toward Cuba may be intercepted and may be directed to identify itself, its cargo, equipment and stores and its ports of call, to stop, to lie to, to submit to visit and search, or to proceed as directed. Any vessel or craft which fails or refuses to respond to or comply with directions shall be subject to being taken into custody.

VESSELS MAY BE REROUTED

Any vessel or craft which it is believed is en route to Cuba and may be carrying prohibited materiel or may itself constitute such materiel shall, wherever possible, be directed to proceed to another destination of its own choice and shall be taken into custody if it fails or refuses to obey such directions. All vessels or craft taken into custody shall be sent into a port of the United States for appropriate disposition.

In carrying out this order, force shall not be used except in case of failure or refusal to comply with directions, or with regulations or directives of the Secretary of Defense issued hereunder, after reasonable efforts have been made to communicate them to the vessel or craft, or in case of self-defense. In any case, force shall be used only to the extent necessary.

In witness whereof, I have hereunto set my hand and caused the seal of the United [States of America to be] affixed.

Done in the City of Washington this 23d day of October in the year of Our Lord, 1962 and of the independence of the United States of America the 187th.

JOHN F. KENNEDY

STUDY QUESTIONS

1. I declined to adopt the view that what was imperatively necessary for the Nation could not be done by the President unless he could find some specific authorization to do it. My belief was that it was not only his right but his duty to do anything that the needs of the Nation demanded unless such action was forbidden by the Constitution or by the law.

Trace the high points in the historical development of this conception of the President's role, as enunciated by Teddy Roosevelt. Discuss its political and constitutional implications; illustrate with examples from this volume.

2. The American President, unlike the British Prime Minister or the French Premier, lacks institutional links with Congress. What factors are responsible for this lack? What informal substitutes have Presidents devised to fill the gap? What additional links might be set up?

3. "Policy disagreements between the President and Congress, particularly in the domestic sphere, are often due to the fact that each serves a different master." Discuss. Are there additional factors also causing conflict? Describe and evaluate the tactics the President can use to counteract Congressional recalcitrance.

4. "Congress," a critic has observed, "has a vested interest in an inefficient executive branch and a number of techniques for achieving this goal." Evaluate this observation and discuss the extent to which the doctrine of separation of powers is in political terms fictitious.

5. Critics have complained that the executive branch lacks adequate mechanisms for acting in areas traditionally reserved to the private economy, such as pricing or labor-management policies. Using examples from this volume, evaluate and explain the success or failure of Presidential interventions in these areas. What sources of support did the Presidents try to mobilize? What price did they pay even when successful?

6. Evaluate the effectiveness of Presidential machinery for initiating and implementing civil-rights measures. How is this a function of the federal system? In what ways is vigorous action in this area a political liability to a President? In what ways is it an asset?

7. In political terms, what differences in circumstances made Lin-

coln's and Roosevelt's use of emergency powers successful where Truman failed? How did the difference between Roosevelt's and Truman's tactics contribute to the differing results?

8. As seen from examples in this volume, in what respects has judicial interpretation of the President's role enhanced his powers? How has it limited them?

9. What factors—political, institutional, technological, etc.—account for the President's relative weakness in domestic affairs as contrasted with his strength in foreign affairs? Why is it easier for the President to set up long-range policies in the foreign sphere than in the domestic arena?

10. "The President has been called 'the sole organ of the nation in its external relations.' However, Congress imposes very real limitations on his power to *implement* his foreign policies." How does Congress do so? What tactics can the President use to minimize this role of Congress? What post-World War II developments have contributed to the President's growing dominance over Congress in foreign affairs?

11. Evaluate the strengths and weaknesses of the executive apparatus charged with implementing Presidential foreign policies. What conflicts arise between the military and diplomatic arms of this machinery?

12. As Samuel P. Huntington has said, certain Presidents have used the Commander-in-Chief clause "to justify an extraordinarily broad range of non-military Presidential actions largely legislative in nature." Using examples from this volume, analyze the powers of the President as Commander-in-Chief, discussing how his foreign-policy and military roles enhance each other. What conflicts arise from this dual role?

SELECTED
BIBLIOGRAPHY

BINKLEY, Wilfred E., *The President and Congress*, 3rd ed. (New York, Knopf, 1962).

BLUM, John Morton, *The Republican Roosevelt* (New York, Atheneum, 1962).

————, *Woodrow Wilson and the Politics of Morality* (Boston, Little, Brown, 1956).

BROWNLOW, Louis, *The President and the Presidency* (Chicago, Public Administration Service, 1949).

BURNS, James MacGregor, *The Deadlock of Democracy: Four-Party Politics in America* (Englewood Cliffs, N.J., Prentice-Hall, 1963).

————, *Roosevelt: The Lion and the Fox* (New York, Harcourt, Brace & World, 1956).

CHEEVER, Daniel S., and Henry Field Haviland, Jr., *American Foreign Policy and the Separation of Powers* (Cambridge, Harvard U. Press, 1952).

CORWIN, Edward S., *The Presidency: Office and Powers*, 4th ed. (New York, New York U. Press, 1957).

————, and Louis W. Koenig, *The Presidency Today* (New York, New York U. Press, 1956).

DONOVAN, Robert J., *Eisenhower: The Inside Story* (New York, Harper, 1956).

EISENHOWER, Dwight D., *Mandate for Change: The White House Years* (New York, Doubleday, 1963).

FENNO, Richard F., Jr., *The President's Cabinet* (Cambridge, Harvard U. Press, 1959).

FINER, Herman, *The Presidency: Crisis and Regeneration* (Chicago, U. of Chicago Press, 1960).

HAVILAND, Henry Field, Jr., *et al.*, *The Formulation and Administration of United States Foreign Policy* (Washington, D.C., Brookings, 1960).

HELLER, Francis, *The Presidency* (New York, Random House, 1960).

HENRY, Laurin L., *Presidential Transitions* (Washington, D.C., Brookings, 1960).

HERRING, E. Pendleton, *Presidential Leadership* (New York, Farrar & Rinehart, 1940).

HOFSTADTER, Richard, *The American Political Tradition: And the Men Who Made It* (New York, Knopf, 1948).

HUGHES, Emmet J., *The Ordeal of Power* (New York, Atheneum, 1963).

HUNTINGTON, Samuel P., *The Common Defense: Strategic Programs in National Politics* (New York, Columbia U. Press, 1961).

HYMAN, Sidney, *The American President* (New York, Harper, 1954).

LONGAKER, Richard P., *The Presidency and Individual Liberties* (Ithaca, Cornell U. Press, 1961).

MAY, Ernest R., *The Ultimate Decision* (New York, Braziller, 1960).

MILTON, G. F., *The Use of Presidential Power, 1789–1943* (Boston, Little, Brown, 1944).

MOWRY, George E., *Theodore Roosevelt and the Progressive Movement* (New York, Hill & Wang, 1960).

NEUSTADT, Richard E., *Presidential Power: The Politics of Leadership* (New York, Wiley, 1960).

Public Papers of the Presidents of the United States (Washington, D.C., Government Printing Office).

RANDALL, J. G., *Lincoln the President*, 4 vols. (New York, Dodd, Mead, 1945–55).

RANKIN, Robert S., *et al.*, *The Presidency in Transition* (Gainesville, Fla., Kallman, 1949).

ROCHE, John P., and Leonard W. Levy, *Parties and Pressure Groups* (New York, Harcourt, Brace & World, 1964).

ROOSEVELT, Theodore, *Theodore Roosevelt: An Autobiography* (New York, Scribner, 1920).

ROSSITER, Clinton, *The American Presidency*, rev. ed. (New York, Harcourt, Brace & World, 1960).

SCHLESINGER, Arthur M., Jr., *The Age of Jackson* (Boston, Little, Brown, 1945).

———, *The Age of Roosevelt*, 3 vols. (Boston, Houghton Mifflin, 1957–60).

SORENSEN, Theodore C., *Decision-Making in the White House: The Olive Branch or the Arrows* (New York, Columbia U. Press, 1963).

STEIN, Harold, ed., *American Civil-Military Decisions* (University, U. of Alabama Press, in prep.).

TAFT, William Howard, *Our Chief Magistrate and His Powers* (New York, Columbia U. Press, 1916).

TRUMAN, Harry S, *Memoirs*, 2 vols. (New York, Doubleday, 1958).

TUGWELL, Rexford G., *The Democratic Roosevelt* (New York, Doubleday, 1957).

———, *Enlargement of the Presidency* (New York, Doubleday, 1960).

WHITE, Theodore H., *The Making of the President, 1960* (New York, Atheneum, 1961).

WILSON, Woodrow, *Congressional Government* (Boston, Smith, Peter, 1958).

4
5
6
7
8
9
0
1
2
3